R

MW01534893

Poems, stories, and creative nonfiction from the Summer 2015, Fall 2015, Winter 2016, and Spring 2016 online issues
baltimorereview.org

Founding and Senior Editor
Barbara Westwood Diehl

Editorial Staff

Brandon Arveson
Taylor Daynes
Dan Ferrara
Amanda Fiore
David Fishman
Jean Free
Benjamin Goldberg
Jonathan Green
Julia Heney
Colleen Hollister
Hilary Jacqmin
Gail Johnson
Mallory Jones

Lisa Lance
Jennifer Lee
Amanda Hart Miller
Holly Morse-Ellington
Bobbi Nicotera
Lalita Noronha
KL Parr
Shannon Robinson
Michael Salcman
Seth Sawyers
Dean Bartoli Smith
Holly Sneeringer
Lucas Southworth
Lynn Stansbury

Webmaster: Matt Diehl

Cover art: Carrie Guss

ISSN 1092-5716

Editor's Note

The Baltimore Review is now, with much gratitude and no small amount of pride, celebrating 20 years of publishing. We celebrate all the writers in the U.S. and beyond who have been a part of the journal over the years, as well as the members of the local literary community—all volunteer—who have kept us going since we first put out a call for submissions in 1996 and received seed money from the Maryland State Arts Council. And, of course, we celebrate our readers. Thank you!

We are pleased to present the poems, stories, and creative nonfiction of contributors to the following online issues: Summer 2015, Fall 2015, Winter 2016, and Spring 2016.

We encourage you to visit our website to listen to contributors read and comment on their work.

About *The Baltimore Review*: The journal was founded by Barbara Westwood Diehl in 1996 as a publication of the Baltimore Writers' Alliance, publishing poems and short stories. The journal later became an independent nonprofit organization in 2004. Susan Muaddi Darraj led the journal from 2003 to 2010, expanding contributions to include creative nonfiction and interviews. In 2011, Barbara Westwood Diehl resumed leadership of the journal and now serves as Senior Editor.

In 1996, we began with a mission to showcase the best writing from the Baltimore area and beyond. Our mission remains just that. In our online format, we can now bring that fine writing to a wider audience, and more frequently. We can also explore new ways to bring you the world of writing, writers, and the writing life.

To our contributors, our editors, the Baltimore literary community, and the network of writers throughout the world—thank you for your vision.

Visit us on Facebook. Follow us on Twitter.
Contact us at editor@baltimorereview.org

Contents

Fall 2015 Issue

Poems

Stories

Creative Nonfiction

Winter 2016 Issue

Poems

Stories

Creative Nonfiction

Contest

Spring 2016 Issue

Poems

Stories

Creative Nonfiction

Contributors

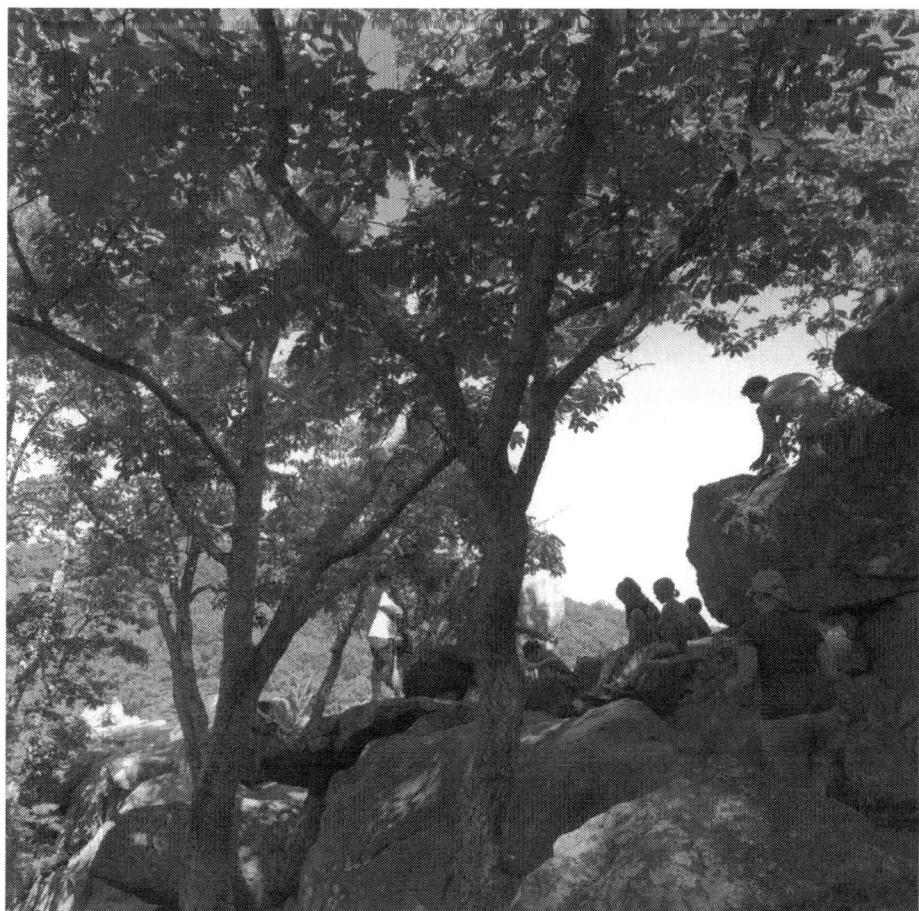

Summer 2015

The Surveyor

Gary Hawkins

Who says the eye loves level,
loves plumb, loves the stiff weeks
in spring when the tractors
cirrus the grey hills,
dragging under the grey sun,
loves the dashes terraced into slopes,
the stooped women back of houses
staking their rows, and their cellars
where lidless jars align the shelves,
loves the split rail and the culvert,
loves the section line running out to the county seat,
loves the thin border of macadam and weeds
that a collie runs a full mile
defining his property from me—I who love
to wander the river trails,
to meander and bend,
to slow in the mud of red clay,
to cut off the sky deep in the hackberry and the low mesquite,
to lose my way.

Nothing Howls

John Walser

Nothing howls
in the before daybreak meadow.

Nothing thrashes.

The moon, a temple orange
low large on the horizon
rough skinned
waits sour for morning.

Powerlines filament buzz
like walls honeycombed over decades
plaster stained by sweetness.

New frogs hesitate
when I shoulder scuff gravel
close to the long grass dew:
spring peepers
stop their throated bell trills.

I dreamed last night after an April storm
rain sweeps pushing from all directions

the scarlet tanager that broods five eggs
outside my office window.

I dreamed weather reports about anvil clouds
thunders' hyperbole, red and green radar buds
tornadoes that knock down towns with names

like wildflowers
like cupboard essentials
like pioneer stock.

I dreamed the freckles of a woman's chest.

And when I woke lizard smooth
and no three in the morning could cure that

I walked:

tables of fields
moon silvered furrows
shades of grove tree blindness.

But now
the marsh ditch water is shallow with blue algae.

The green leaves, the air, the unmarked pathway
outlined with cardinal feathers.

Just before sunrise birds
sound like chlorophyll smudges on my shoes
like dragonfly wings (wax paper, olive oil, water, sunlight)
like shriveling blackberries.

And nothing breaks from the brush.

Nothing takes flight over my head.
No rooks, no pheasants scatter
at this slight intrusion,
no chimes of wings, no burst of confusion.

Nocturne with Orders to Yokosuka

Jehanne Dubrow

The night before you leave,
        our bed is a port city bristling
with an arsenal of ships.

        The dog swims through the covers,
creating currents in her dreams.
        How lucky, this peace of hers,

while I'm the reactor
        whose waters will not cool,
fuel made molten, the quick

        contamination of all life
along the coast. I turn away
        from this, your departure, real

as a story I watch on the news,
        by which I mean debris
in the sea and metal-sting

                in the mouth—
days after the tidal wave,
        the crew was told to stop drinking

from the tap, stop showering,
        all tests returning negative,
though how to explain the pain,

fingers puffed up
like poisonous fish—fear a thing,
    which cannot be measured.

When you're away I'll say tsunami.
    I'll say certain uncertain threat,
my words potassium iodide

    against whatever tide or wind,
whatever catastrophe is rushing
    undersurface toward the land.

Moon Among Mammals

———————

Caitlin Scarano

The moon is not always female,
human. Moon can be a man
missing teeth or an animal

with an oar-shaped tongue,
who watched me sleepwalk
through the snakes of my half-life.

When I woke to a gunshot
it was only a bird's
skull on the antique window

glass in my mother's belly. A collie
digging up pecans in the backyard
that was as wide as a country

but shrunk to a wink
when my sisters and I aged
to white eyeshadow and Camels

behind the rotting playhouse.
When I visited my father last
winter, he was dying

of liver cancer. I once saw that dog,
the collie, kill a hen with her eyes
open. I once saw my father

climb a tree so tall he disappeared
into the moon's laughing
milk-white mouth.

Intruder

————————

Jen DeGregorio

As soon as I opened the apartment door
I knew. Kitchen chairs askew and so
close to the edge of the table
that a passing train's rattle might've
tipped it, a blue bowl
from which the scent of milk
soured the air.

The living room shelves
had a rifled-through look
with mail stuffed between books
spilled onto the floor. Had my bank accounts
been breached? Checks seized? But the letters
were all sealed, dusty in the window's weak light
under which one plant—brittle, yellow—
wanted water.

What did the intruder want
if not the accounts? Something quick
to pawn? Yet nothing of value
was gone: flatscreen, laptop
unplugged on the couch. In the bedroom
rumpled sheets, pillow blackened with what seemed to be
mascara. Mine

or the intruder's? Strange
to think of her like that. As someone
with a face. As a woman
who wept at night, feeling
alone in a stranger's apartment.

Cartel Sadness

Robert Evory

The cartel needs my sadness so it walks into the crossfire
They say they just want to talk
My sadness is unreported income
My sadness is in a fistfight with itself
The cartel flies a dust cropper in to pick up the winner
The cartel wants my sadness to cook
The cartel is poisoning itself from the inside
The cartel is struggling for position
The cartel has a hospital in the desert where its rival can't find them
The cartel split my sadness among the henchmen
The rival planted a bomb and my sadness smelled it out
Sadness wears a bulletproof vest
Sadness will never have a chalk outline
Sadness sent rival a message
A rocking chair and a string of chicken wire
Sadness can't be dusted for prints
The cartel needs a triggerman
Sadness pasted a letter from words in a magazine
Sent it to the Gestapo called grief
Yakuza called fear
Sadness put a husband and wife back to back to save a bullet
Sadness is in the green revolution, purple revolution
Velvet, orange, and blue revolutions
Sadness is bankrupting the world
Sadness is wanted for espionage
And extradition to Singapore
Sadness holds the man named trust for ransom
Sadness says "I love you" on the battlefield
Sadness is dug out from under your home

Sadness and freedom tremble together
Sadness calls the Moon by her real name
Opens her door naked to the world
Sadness is the dough that didn't rise
The wine turned to vinegar
Sadness is a motorcycle stunt driver for expectations
Sadness is freeing chicks from their nest
Pulls up the vein of an addict
Sadness shoots up between the toes
Sadness is in a diner at dawn with a broken wrist eating meatloaf
Sadness is sucking the tit of depression
Kissing indifference on the mouth
Tonguing between the thighs of hope
Sadness is night living in the mind that doesn't rise
Sadness is a bead of truth we all have to stroke

Spell for the End of Grief

Amie Whittemore

No incantations, no rosemary and statice,
no keening women in grim dresses.
No cauldrons, no candles, no hickory wands.
No honey and chocolate, no sticky buns.
No peonies and carnations, no handkerchiefs.
No dark and lusty liaisons.

Only you and me to see it out.
Sweet self, let me wash your toes,
brush your hair, let me rock you gently.
Together we'll change the sheets
and I'll pull you to me, little spoon.
You be the marrow, I'll be the bone.

Rattlesnake Master

Amie Whittemore

I knew this ellipsis among coneflowers wouldn't cure me.
Though I collected its green-white doorknobs,
though it nodded enthusiastically about light,

if I sucked its taproot after a bite, I'd still unclot
and cool like those tuberculosis patients
who once sought the "healing air" of Mammoth Cave.
Paraffin, spotty coughs, soft footsteps punctuating the dark—

beneath every prairie is another prairie.
Parsed of color, roots like nesting vipers,
it threads through fungi a pale network,
whose velvet and dew crumbles in my fingers.

Loam whets the air. A borer moth clamps
a Rattlesnake Master's stalk, shooting alerts
through root-webs; poison rises in spines.
I imagine a braid through the dark—

those TB patients holding hands—last becoming first
as he wades toward—they are certain—that mouth
                              where daylight lolls like a tongue.

The Culvert

Curtis Smith

The boy's father woke him after midnight. The old man's smell in the dark. Cigarettes. The foundry's gray dust. The boy had been dreaming. A field where the grass broke like ice beneath his steps, a sun as frigid as it was bright. The boy lost between worlds. His father's hand on his shoulder.

"Come with me."

The boy in his underwear. The angling of hallway light. The doorway a frame for his father's silhouette. Rain on the roof—soft, steady—and through the window screen, a coolness rare this hot summer. He shuffled behind his father. The hallway, the stairs. Sleep still in his joints. His eyes blinking but unable to focus. The dining room. The kitchen sink cluttered with the dishes the boy had promised to wash. They stood on the stoop. The porch light stretched across the parched lawn. The rain steadier than the boy had imagined. At the light's fringe, his older brother. His soaked T-shirt clinging to his shoulders. His shaved head upon the picnic table.

The grass was wet beneath the boy's bare feet. The rain on his neck. They sat the brother up. The boy cradled his brother's head and wiped the drops from his brow. They swung the brother into a sitting position, the boy and his father each taking a side, and with the count of three, they lifted him to his feet. His brother's head pitched forward, his legs useless. His brother the football star. The Marine. A torso thick with muscle. Scabs across his knuckles. The boy a head shorter and eighty pounds lighter. He blinked the rain from his eyes and fought the push of dead weight. His feet kicked through empty beer cans. They took the porch steps one at a time. Pain in the boy's shoulders. The brother mumbled. Names the boy didn't know. A village in the sand half a world away.

The boy faltered inside the kitchen door. His knees struck the linoleum, his brother on top of him, a tangling of bodies until his father managed to roll the brother aside. Gasping, their hair matted and dripping, they looked upon the brother, his skin sickly in the yellow light. His father peeled off the brother's wet clothes and slipped a couch pillow beneath his head. The boy draped him with the afghan their mother had knitted. Blood tucked deep in the knots, the needle in her trembling fingers. Those final, wasting months.

"Go back to sleep" his father said.

From his bedroom window, the boy watched his father load their deer rifles and shotguns into his car's trunk. His retreating taillights glistened red on the wet macadam. The boy went downstairs and stretched out on the couch. He wished he could rejoin his dream, but he knew he couldn't. Instead, he listened to the rain in the gutter. His brother's raspy breath.

~

The boy raced after the thief who'd stolen his bike. The drumbeat built in the boy's chest. The bike plucked from his dandelioned lawn, its front wheel still spinning, the thief making his bid before the boy could open the porch door. The thief black. In three blocks, he'd be home free, the boy risking a beating if he crossed the boundary the older boys marked with fistfights and worse. The thief in a bathing suit, a towel draped around his neck. Long legs and bony kneecaps. His bare feet slipped from the pedals, and the bike's rusted chain caught and spit. The boy a strong runner, the winner of his school's field-day races. His sneakers barely kissing the pavement. The bike's lock in his hand, a length of cable sheathed in plastic, a metal clasp. Another wilting afternoon, and amid the laziness and heat, their chase elevated into spectacle. The porch sitters lowered their newspapers. One of the corner thugs hurled a rock that struck the thief's arm. Next came a bottle, the glass shattering, a spray of sun-glistening glass. The thief veered down a narrow street. A wrong turn, a dead end into the old tool mill. His towel fell into the road.

"Get the little nigger!" a corner boy yelled. Another: "Make your brother proud!"

Honeysuckle choked the lot's sagging fence. The gate long gone. The macadam cratered, rocks and potholes, and all around, the smother of vegetation. Saplings and brown grass rose from cracked concrete. Ivy twined the glassless windows. The mill a shell of crumbling brick. The stories from inside—the dog fights and soiled mattresses. The needles and

15

vials. The boy moving faster. Beneath him, stretches of scarred earth. His lungs filled like sails.

The thief hit a pothole. The tremor rose into the handlebars, a wobbling moment before the bike bucked sideways. Thief and bike went down, a clatter of metal, a meaty thud.

The boy thirty yards away. Twenty. Ten. A transformer high on a utility pole hissed, and in the boy, another type of electricity, the white light of clarity, of rightness. The thief stood. Blood on his elbow and knee. His side scraped raw. His eyes wide. He ran, an escape kinked by pain, strides undercut by stones and broken glass.

The boy adjusted his gait and set an arm's length between them. Close enough to hear the thief's gasps. Close enough to see the outline of his bony shoulders, the nubs of his spine. Close enough to smell the pool's chlorine on his skin.

The boy swung the lock above his head, a helicopter's orbit. The clasp whispered through the honeysuckled air. Everything clear. Everything bright. The thief's hair cropped close; the boy's eyes fixed on the back of his skull.

~

Crickets thrummed in the creek-bank weeds. A black sky, no moon, no stars. The heaviness of rain but not a drop. The boy peeled off his socks and tucked them into his sneakers. He slipped into his flip flops. The water cool. The creek narrow and shallow. He drifted to the middle. The sluggish current around his shins. The overgrown banks rose on either side, an erasing of the things he knew. The boy feeling as if he were lost within a scar.

His flip flops caught on hidden rocks, so he moved slowly. He turned on his flashlight and cast a halo over the water's ugliness. An overturned shopping cart. A bald tire. A shattered sink. Oily rainbows curled around the rocks. Foam along the weedy banks. The last generation's minnows and frogs long gone. The boy thought of his brother in their backyard, silent, home yet lost. He thought of his father fading a shift at a time in the foundry upstream. He thought of his mother.

He paused before the yawning culvert. A metal pipe he could walk through, his head unbowed, a thirty-yard passage beneath a cross street and the foundry's rail line. He aimed his flashlight into the opening. A spider web pulsed with a moth's struggle. Further, the dull glow of close set eyes. The boy threw a rock. The rats clambered upon themselves, wet fur and long tails. The culvert echoed with their scrape and splash.

He knew the girl—her name, her face. At recess, she'd huddled with her friends in their winter coats, a breathy haze knitted above their heads. On Christmas Eve he'd walked behind her and her father in the communion line. Her blond hair shimmered in the candlelight; a tinsel strand on her father's gray suit. Last spring, the police found her in the culvert. Naked, the rats upon her. In the woods beyond the culvert's other end, her father hung from a tree.

The boy turned off the flashlight. One step, then another. The culvert's far end waiting, an unblinking eye. A new sound, a seashell's whisper of breeze and water. The smell of rust. Spider webs broke over him. His hands outstretched but touching nothing.

Cain

Lina Ferreira

Before the invention of murder there were Cain and Abel, and they were both brothers, and they were both black.

There wasn't a lot of record keeping back then, but it's not hard to fill in the details.

Abel was better than Cain. Maybe he never forgot to visit his mother on Sundays, and never turned down a good roast. Maybe Cain was a vegetarian, maybe. Details. What is certain is the color of their skin. Black. Black like their mother, black like their father. Black like toucan wings and *ollas de barro*, and black like the God that made them.

Cain was a little older, maybe. But maybe they were twins. It's possible. Or maybe Abel was one of those slow-to-come siblings who waits seven years, or twenty five, before stitching up a body inside their mother Eve. And maybe he was easy to kill.

It's possible they were both only children when it happened. Or when it started. When Cain began drinking and yelling at girls who passed by their house to lift their skirts and show the goods. By age eleven, likely, he had a bottle in his hand and loaded dice in his pocket. While his brother, their parents' favorite, never missed mass or broke a promise. Which maybe at first didn't bother Cain. But maybe by the age of eleven or twelve Cain was fed up with it, so he invented murder.

There are reports of a jaw being used, but this is a mistake. That's another story. But as first things go, they are usually messy, and clumsy, and hardly ever go as planned. So it's very likely the matter was too grisly to discuss, so maybe no one talked about it. Likely no one could, anyhow. "Murder," was Cain's contribution to the dictionary, a brand new fangled thing, stumbling on stilt and still wet with afterbirth. And people must have run around for days trying to cobble incongruous words together to make sense to figure out what to call it, and make sense of it, and pin it down with a word like a pin through a beetle's back. But because God is omnilexical, down He came looking for Cain the minute he'd heard what Cain had done.

Down from a cloud, down from a tree, down from the top of a red brick house to speak to Cain with a voice made of gravel and dirt and broken glass and knotted rope. And Cain trembled. From his toes, through his knees. Up his spine, like smoke, like vines, as if weevils were chewing holes through his bones. Cain trembled.

His organs came loose and rattled inside him like stones in a tin can. His eyes shrunk inside his sockets and he shuddered as if he had his brother wrapped around his throat.

Not maybe. Certainly. Cain heard God's voice and he must have heard his brother somewhere in there too because it shook him from skin to core, and back again, and it shook the black right off Cain's face, and down his arms, and belly and back. And it soaked into his shirt, and socks, and Cain became as white as the underbelly of a pupa, became translucent as hatched snakes. White like madness and blindness, became another brand new thing too.

Diorama

_____

Gregory Wolos

He's proud of the diorama concealed in the back of his tractor trailer. Is it art? Maybe. It's got to be something more than the stolen contents of a brother's apartment.

He's stuck in traffic now, stopped dead between Boston and Springfield in an eastbound lane of the Mass Pike. People are getting out of their cars and trucks, peering over vehicles lined up as far as the eye can see. And across the median the westbound lanes are empty enough for touch football or a picnic: Whatever happened ahead is bad enough to have stopped the flow of traffic in both directions.

Next to him on the passenger seat sits Puck, the little poodle mix he took from the apartment along with the furniture. The dog's giving him the eye, and he slaps his knee, though he knows Puck's too old and timid to make the leap over the gear shift box. He picks up the dog, leashes it, tucks it under his arm, and swings out of his truck's door onto pavement rubbed shiny by millions of tires—but his boots are probably the first to touch this exact spot. The smells of asphalt and exhaust rise through the cool March air. Puck tugs like a fish too small to keep, making for the dirty snow on the highway's shoulder. A girl with a blond ponytail pokes her crimped face out of the driver's side window of the car they're behind.

"Hey," she calls, "you know what's wrong?"

He shakes his head, unprepared to speak. The dog scrapes at the pavement, eager for the snow. "Nope," he says. "Nothing on the radio. Got an iPhone?"

"It's out of power, and I don't have a car-charger," the girl whines, like a kid who has yet to learn about real trouble. She yanks her head back into her car without another word. He notices the college sticker, "Framingham State University," on her rear window and guesses that she's late for class, then squints up and down the highway at the sun-glared roofs and windshields. Everybody is missing something. He follows Puck to a crust of snow and watches the dog squat. If the young woman were to join him at the rear of the truck, her face would uncrimp when he revealed the diorama. She'd forget about missing whatever she's missing and lift a hand to her open mouth. She'd insist that he invite the multitudes stranded on the highway to behold the display.

Puck finishes, and he leads the dog to the back of the trailer where he stands and stares at the roll-down door as if he's penetrating it with X-ray vision. He reads the phone number printed after the question, "How's My Driving?" He knows the number has been disconnected because he's tried it.

The diorama replicates the brother's apartment as seen for the last time before it was emptied. He considers the contents repossessed, since most of it originally belonged to his parents. It's furniture he grew up with. He's never seen the old dioramas from the natural history museums, but he's heard about them—how they're full of dead animals shot long ago in Africa—antelopes and rhinos and wild dogs. He's heard that behind the panes of dusty glass you can see hundred-year-old bullet holes in some of the stuffed carcasses. There aren't any bullet holes in any of the furniture laid out in the back of this truck, but would it be so surprising if there were? Puck is sitting on the asphalt, showing a pink tongue the size of a postage stamp. If dioramas included living things, maybe the dog should be in it, curled up on the rug his mother spent decades braiding out of clothes her kids had outgrown.

There's a tall bookcase in the diorama, its shelves jammed with familiar paperbacks. Beside the bookcase is a formica-topped kitchen table he and the brother had sat at for thousands of childhood breakfasts. On the table are a few liquor bottles and shot glasses, super-glued into place so they won't roll off when the truck turns corners or bounces through potholes. One of the bottles is filled with water to look like vodka, another with tea to look like whiskey. Also on the table is a yellow legal pad, its wrinkled pages covered with writing.

He'd considered hanging framed apology-letters on the inner walls of the truck behind the furniture, but that would have been inauthentic: a diorama should represent a creature's natural habitat, and an abuser attempting recovery would have mailed his apology letters out, not displayed them. Then he'd had the idea of filling a legal pad with rough drafts of apology letters that he could leave on the table as part of the display. He'd used a template:

Dear {Recipient},

I am writing to you today because I am making amends to people I have harmed as a result of my addiction to {substance}. Specifically, I know that I harmed you by {state action}. For this, I am deeply sorry.

I know that sometimes apologies are more of a burden than a blessing, but I would like the chance to apologize to you in person. This will allow us to discuss how I harmed you and what I can do to make things right. If you do not feel that you wish to forgive me, or you do not wish to have any contact with me, I understand. However, please know that I am deeply sorry for what I have done to you and would like to do whatever I can to repair our relationship.

If you would find it acceptable for me to make amends in person, please contact me at {phone/email}. Otherwise, rest assured that this letter will be my only attempt to contact you, because I do not wish to impose on your life.

Sincerely,

{Sender}

As he copied the template letter, inserting "alcohol and drugs" for "*substance*" and "irresponsible behavior" for "*action*," he didn't try to imitate the brother's handwriting. He addressed the first letter in the pad to himself. Hadn't he been the biggest victim? The next two letters went to "Mom" and to "Dad," separate letters that could have been sent in a single envelope. Three letters didn't seem like enough, so he'd kept going. He composed the next for his own ex-wife, and then one to his daughter, who must be old enough to read by now. They'd been victims, too. These two letters would never have been sent, since the brother wouldn't have had any more idea of the address than he did.

At the last moment, to fill the pad, he'd added one final letter—an apology to the dog. It must have been unsettling to have been snatched out of the apartment by someone you weren't sure you could trust, even if his scent was familiar. He'd signed this last letter with his own name, and only now, standing at the back of his closed truck, leash in hand, does he wonder whose signature he'd used to close all the other apologies.

~

He's dozing behind the wheel—traffic hasn't budged for an hour—and wakes to find the dog gazing at him with eyes like chocolate chips. He's been dreaming of the family furniture fallen into disrepair under the brother's care: the table supporting the bottles and legal pad full of apologies is scarred and warped; the sofa he and the brother had shared for Saturday morning cartoons now leaks stuffing and smells of kitchen grease. He's absorbed that smell, having slept on the sofa for countless nights since he's begun transporting the diorama.

He dreamt of the photograph of his uniformed uncle, his mother's brother, hanging now in the diorama behind the sofa. He'd never known the young soldier, who'd barely been out of his teens when he'd died "on foreign soil." His mother said she saw him in her children. "God gave me back the brother he took when he gave me you," she told them. "A brother means everything."

But in his dream on the Mass Pike, he's seen something else on the wall of the diorama, dwarfing the photo of the dead uncle: his own tattooed flesh, stripped off his body in a single piece and hung like an animal hide. The sight of his stretched skin lingers—he feels a hot knife pierce his ribcage, sees himself peeled from himself like wet linen. What if the brother on some lonely evening had woken from troubled sleep to find that skin stretched out on the wall, its tattoos as purple as bruises and as indecipherable as hieroglyphics? What if the brother pulled the skin from the wall and wrapped himself in it?

He winces from the bright sunlight, and, hoisting Puck to his lap, laces his fingers like a collar around the dog's neck. There are tattoos of musical notes on his knuckles, but he's unable to remember why he chose them—he doesn't play an instrument and can't read music. Maybe they're the sound of a punch. Maybe they begin a melody for the diorama.

He releases Puck's throat, cups a palm over the dog's head, and shifts his attention to the car in front of him. "Framingham State University," he reads aloud. Someday his daughter will be as old as the young woman with the drained cellphone, and maybe she'll go to college. By then she'll have made up a history that explains her absent father. If he finds her and her mother, he'll show them the diorama he travels with. He'll give them as much time as they need to study it. On the beat up table, between the liquor bottles and pad full of apologies, there is a stale, pink-iced donut. He'll tell his daughter to take it, not for eating, but because it's pretty and once was something. "This is yours," he'll say, as if to remind her of an event she's forgotten.

When traffic moves—when traffic moves again, he'll continue on to the towns south of Boston. He'll look for the cemetery where his parents rest and back his truck up to the stones engraved with their names and dates. He'll raise the door with the "How's My Driving" number and show them the diorama that displays their son's history. "Come and see your boy," he'll shout at the monuments. "Read the letters on the pad. Look at the bottles on the table and the flesh hanging on the wall." Then he'll hold up his fist and turn it slowly like a globe and listen for its music, hoping it will tell him where to take the brother's story next.

Shueyville

_____

Kate Folk

Rob and Terry and I stand ski-masked in the Sorensons' kitchen. Rob idly snaps the cuff of his purple latex glove and says, "Jesus. Looks like somebody's already robbed the place."

He's right; the house is a mess, which surprises me, because Sue Sorenson looked so neatly stitched together in her Facebook photos. In the kitchen sink sit three white bowls, the bottoms congealed with milk-bloated bran flakes. Cupboard doors are flung open. The hall closet is open too, scarves and hats thrown to the floor, as if someone had clawed through in the last panicked minutes. Their flight to Denver left ungodly early, Sue had complained on her Facebook wall.

Terry starts sorting through cabinets in the living room. He pulls out a ball of cords, the tangled umbilicals of electronics the Sorensons have lost interest in. Rob heads to the basement, where a surprising number of the Midwestern rich keep their most precious heirlooms and antiques in unlabeled cardboard boxes.

I go upstairs to the master bedroom, seeking jewelry. The men favor a quick and brutal style of searching, inspired by those movies where FBI agents come into a drug dealer's house and rip it apart looking for the stash. I can't bring myself to do that. I find it touching, the order people impose on their valuables. In the top left drawer of Sue's heavy oak bureau, velvet boxes and silk-lined pouches nestle together. Among my finds are a rose pearl necklace that should fetch us five hundred; four white gold bangles inlaid with diamonds, two hundred each; a golden cat pendant with rubies for eyes, seven hundred at least. I put these things in a striped pillowcase I brought from home. I spare a pair of earrings that dangle with smoky glass teardrops—a worthless family keepsake.

I wander down the hall opening doors, seeing what bonuses I can pick up. A bathroom; a guest room admirably free of clutter, the closet hung with a single flowered dress. Finally I reach the room at the end of the hall. Its door is ajar. I nudge it wide.

I'm confronted with the broad back of the Sorensons' only child, Alex, a chubby sixteen-year-old whose Facebook profile is locked down by advanced privacy settings. He's wearing Bose headphones and playing *Call of Duty* on two enormous monitors that angle in toward each other like department store mirrors. Below the padded seat of his swivel chair, one socked foot taps the carpet. His other leg is sheathed in a red cast reaching up to his knee. A pair of crutches leans against his closet door. The room is filthy. Empty bottles of Mountain Dew line the windowsill. The white carpet is barely visible under a flotsam of clothing. The bed is unmade, the wastebasket overflowing with tissues. A pizza box yawns at the foot of the bed, cheese forming a crusty wheel in its center.

I run downstairs. Terry's on his knees in the living room, swaddling the plasma TV in bubble wrap.

"The kid's upstairs," I say. "Broke his foot or something. Can't ski."

With his mask on, Terry's all lips and blue eyes. He didn't want me to join them in the first place. Rob, who I've known since high school, convinced him they could use me for my jewelry-appraising skills.

"Get Rob," Terry says. "Time to go."

We load our haul into the rental truck. Terry and Rob are carrying the plasma screen toward the front door when Alex wobbles into the foyer.

"What are you doing in my house?" he says. His tone is curious and gently scolding, as if we are children he's discovered marking a wall with crayons.

It happens in a sulfurous burst, before I can stop it. Terry drops his end of the TV and puts Alex in a chokehold. The crutches clatter to the floor. Alex screams from the pressure on his injured foot. It's a horrible sound. Quickly, as if I've always known how to do such things, I grab a knit cap from the floor in front of the hall closet and stuff it deep into Alex's mouth.

~

Rob and Terry are coworkers at the Bennigan's in the sprawling mall north of town. Rob's a server; Terry's a line cook. I thought Rob was joking, two years ago, when he told me they'd been burglarizing rich people's homes. We were a little drunk, smoking cigarettes in the alley behind The Lark's Head. I was miserable, still living with my dad and working part-time at Hobby Lobby. At that point I had never stolen anything, not even a pack of gum

I met Terry that weekend, at Rob's place. He was a tall man in his forties, wearing an oatmeal-colored thermal and faded black jeans. The three of us stood in the kitchen and Terry asked blunt questions about my childhood. The interaction seemed to bore him. While I talked he scraped a peeled orange with his thumbnail, building a soft mound of pith on the counter.

I allowed myself to be convinced. The people we steal from are rich and insured. Families come home from their ski and beach vacations and are a little deflated by the loss of their valuables, but what do they expect? This is the consequence of having things others don't.

Alex has altered the terms of this equation. It's late afternoon, the low sun cloaked in marrowy haze, as we drive away from the Sorensons' house. Terry turns on the radio to cover the moans from the back of the box truck. We're just outside Shueyville, twenty miles from home, but Terry mentioned earlier that he knows the area because his uncle used to own a dairy farm here.

I start to speak, and Terry shushes me. "I'll take care of this," he whispers.

We stop at an abandoned farmhouse. I hold the front door open while Terry and Rob carry Alex inside. The house has been gutted. The wood floor is stained in black patches, the shadows of fires set by squatters. Sallow daylight filters through newspapered windows. I watch from the porch while the men tie Alex to a chair.

Back in the truck, Rob says, "Why couldn't we have just tied him up in his own house?"

"He'll freeze in there," I add.

"Oh, boo hoo," Terry says. "I didn't tie the ropes tight. He'll be home in a few hours. Anyway, he's got lots of blubber to keep him warm."

I watch the snow-blanketed fields clip by, hills undulating like the backs of partly-submerged animals. I think about Alex's swollen foot, how Rob and Terry had to support his weight up the steps of the farmhouse. They carried him roughly, but with a certain tenderness, as if he were their injured teammate.

Terry drops me off at my apartment. I drive straight to my dad's house to make him dinner and clean whatever he'll allow me to. I push the front door against the weight of boxes piled in the foyer. When I was a kid, my dad owned a consignment shop, which was where I learned to gauge the value of jewelry at a glance. The store never turned much of a profit, even before my dad started bringing things home with him. He now claims he's going to start an eBay store.

My dad's sitting in his La-Z-Boy in the living room, polishing silver candlesticks with a cloth.

"Hey," he says. "What's new?"

I pick my way through the boxes, lean down to kiss his cheek.

"Not much, Daddo," I say.

I wedge into the narrow space beside his chair. Whenever I'm back in this house, I feel like I can't breathe. Since my mom left, it has only gotten worse.

When I was sixteen, my mom's hair started falling out. Honey-brown strands tinseled the carpet, coiled their way into our food and formed delicate nests on the cushions. My mom claimed the hair loss was her body's declaration that she couldn't spend another day in this house, where the evidence of my dad's failure choked every room and hallway. It was the justification she needed to move back in with her parents, in Houston. I still think she pulled the hairs out herself.

It was supposed to be a temporary thing, but soon after she moved home, my mom attended a church BBQ, where she met a silver-haired plastic surgeon named Chuck. She divorced my dad, married Chuck and moved into his suburban mansion. Whenever I visited, I was obliged to babysit my stepbrothers, twin blonde boys whose grasping fingers were always busy with handheld gadgets. My mom's hair grew back, and she began dying it platinum blonde.

I lean against the side of my dad's chair. We watch the six o'clock news. I know it's too soon for there to be coverage of the Sorenson burglary and Alex's disappearance, but a part of me coils, waiting for it. I imagine Alex slowly working his limbs from the rope's grip. I imagine him crawling along the road's icy margin, his palms and knees bloodied by gravel.

When *Wheel of Fortune* starts, I go to the kitchen to make spaghetti. There's no counter space, and the stovetop is covered with Mason jars, so I cut tomatoes in the sink. My hands are still pale and pinched from the latex gloves. My upper lip itches; the ski mask always leaves a tingling rash.

I hand my dad his plate and he digs in, his eyes still on the TV.

"Where'd you get the Mason jars, Dad?"

"Picked those up at Goodwill for a nickel apiece," he says, without a trace of embarrassment.

"What will you do with them?" I say robotically. I've fought him on this a thousand times.

"Oh, you never know when they'll come in handy," he says.

We finish our spaghetti in silence, watching Vanna tap the rectangles of correctly-guessed letters. I lost interest in this show when they switched from turning letters to this touch-screen bullshit.

I wash our dishes and spread them to dry on the last open patch of kitchen floor.

~

In my apartment on Burlington, the walls are bare, the drawers more empty than full. I own a twin bed, a bookshelf with exactly fifty books, a narrow dresser, a lamp, a table, two straight-backed chairs, one set of silverware, one bowl, one coffee mug. I hold onto nothing. I allow objects to pass through me as if I'm made of water.

The air in my apartment feels curdled, a heat that catches in my throat. I put on sweatpants and a black t-shirt, make myself a cup of tea, then lie in bed with my laptop and scour the Shueyville news sites.

I call Rob. "I'm feeling weird," I say.

"Should I come over?" Rob says. His voice is timid, but hope swells the edges. We used to sleep together, on and off, sometimes in sprees of three or four nights. I haven't wanted to since we started robbing houses. It would feel tacky, like I'd imbued our criminal act with an aura of doomed romance. Like the whole thing turned me on.

"I just wanted to talk about what happened today," I say. "I can't stop thinking about that kid."

"Don't sweat it," Rob says. "Terry knows what he's doing."

Rob is anxious to get off the phone once he knows I'm not interested in sex. After we hang up, I lie awake for a long time. I remember how the wind had rattled the bones of the house. I remember the hoarse pitch of Alex's voice as he begged us not to leave him. A thread of saliva stretched from his mouth to the front of his thin white t-shirt. The last thing I saw before Terry eased the door shut was Alex's uninjured foot, stiff in its grimy sock, soundlessly thumping the floorboards.

~

Terry comes over in the morning and hands me an envelope. I part the flap and glance at the slim stack of twenties inside. It can't be more than three hundred dollars--utterly insufficient, considering what it required.

"Coffee?" I say. It's a perfunctory offer, and I'm surprised when he says yes. Terry sits at the table, his chair inches from the end of my bed. I feel him staring at my back while I remove last night's teabag from the mug, wash the mug, heat water for his coffee.

I set the coffee in front of him without bothering to ask if he wants milk. I sit and say, "What do you think happened to Alex?"

"The fat kid? I'm sure he's home by now."

"It hasn't been in the news."

"Well, it wouldn't be in the news around here, would it?"

"I've been checking the Shueyville sites."

"He's fine. Forget him."

My gaze drifts toward the window and Terry says, "Hey. Did you hear what I said? Don't do anything stupid."

I look at Terry's big, smooth hands, the furrows of his veins.

"I won't," I say. "What's done is done."

"Good," Terry says. He leaves without touching his coffee.

Around three, a mix of freezing rain and snow begins to sluice down. I get in my car and drive north on 380.

It's a half hour to Shueyville, then another twenty minutes of aimless driving on minimum maintenance roads. I'm forced to drive slowly through a screen of wet, heavy snow. By the time I find the farmhouse, the sky is black. The house leers before me, a white hull on a bare hump of earth. I pause with my hand on the knob. I fear seeing the corpse of Alex stiffened in the chair, his lips tinged blue. I'd stalled all day, cleaning bathroom grout and reorganizing my bookshelf by color

But the chair stands empty, ropes slack around it like a shed skin. I exhale slowly and fill my lungs with air.

I drive back toward the highway. Ahead, a figure limps along the shoulder. I slow and try to pass him, but when he hears the crunch of gravel under my tires he walks into the center of the road, waving his arms like a castaway signaling a plane.

Alex wrenches the passenger door open. The car heaves under his sudden weight. His breaths come loud and ragged, his dumpling-pale skin blotched red by the cold.

"What happened to you?" I say, doing my best to hit the right notes.

Alex tells me the story I already know. His body vibrates, his teeth chattering; I turn the heat to full blast, and we have to yell to be heard.

"I'll take you to the hospital," I say. "You're going to be fine." I glance down at his foot. The skin of his toes is a necrotic purple, the flesh swelling inside the cast like a wet loaf of bread. The big toenail is black as a hoof.

"Those fucking animals," Alex says. "I said I wouldn't tell anyone, and I wouldn't have."

I'm annoyed by his whiny tone. I think of my stepbrothers, the twins. They had regarded me with pale-eyed contempt, until one weekend my mom and Chuck went out of town and I allowed them to starve. I wrapped the refrigerator in chains, bungeed the cabinet doors. I sat guard in the kitchen, reading my mom's romance novels and Chuck's *Promise Keepers* book. At midnight, after they'd given up on whining and lain quiet for several hours on the living room floor, I called the twins over like dogs and allowed them to take Ritz crackers, one at a time, from the flat of my hand.

"You're lucky they didn't kill you," I say.

Alex is quiet. Then he says, "Why were you driving out here, anyway?"

"I live up the road," I say.

I feel Alex really looking at me for the first time. I imagine he's replaying the scene. Three people kidnapped him, and one was a woman. The heater roars, and neither of us speaks. Then Alex spasms with pain. He moans; his foot must be thawing, the nerves flickering back on.

"Please hurry," he says. "It feels like there's knives of fire in there."

31

I turn left at the highway, toward Shueyville. The blurry snow wads have hardened to sleet, needling my car's thin roof. Up ahead, I spot the yellow-orange square of a Shell station sign.

"I'm gonna get us some hot chocolate," I say. "Then we'll go straight to the hospital."

"Are you fucking kidding me?" Alex says. "Do you see my foot?"

"Your foot can wait," I say. "It's gone this long."

"Dumb bitch," Alex murmurs. I ignore him, pull into the station and park in the rear. I bring the keys with me. I stand among the shelves of energy bars, chips, bags of trail mix. I take out my phone and scroll to Terry's number. My fingertip hovers over the letters of his name.

"It's me," I say when he answers. "I've made a mistake."

It's from here that my life will ravel: in the bright shelter of a gas station, the icy sky sloughing off pieces of itself, waiting for what Terry will tell me to do.

Black and White

Geoff Wyss

The doorbell, a knock: two police officers in the morning sun.

Gary Wellman? the one in front asked, looking doubtfully at her clipboard.

Yes, ma'am, I said. The *ma'am* felt off; she was twenty years younger than me, her face as lineless as a baby's.

Mr. Wellman, my name is Officer Norris, Community Policing and Outreach. This is Officer Slattery. May we have a few moments of your time?

Absolutely, I said, trying to hide my eagerness. I hadn't been getting anything written and was thankful to escape the hum of the computer.

The gorgeous lawfulness I felt as they stepped in—I was a person who had so ordered his life that he could throw open the door to the authorities, I was really spotlessly good—was exactly equal to my embarrassment over the filth of my house: its drifts of dusty books, weeks-old junk mail, strewn Kleenexes, other inexplicable jetsam Slattery had to navigate on his way to squint at a photograph of my cats on the wall.

Norris placed half her butt on my couch.

Mr. Wellman, have you heard of predictive analytics?

I have, I said brightly, recalling a *Harper's* article.

The New Orleans Police Department, she recited with semi-memorized formality, has instituted a pilot program with the aid of federal monies. The mission of this program is to diagnose and prevent violent crime through the use of data. Algorithms are being utilized to locate citizens most in danger of homicide, either as perpetrator or victim.

I was by now in love with Norris for her tidy hands, for the youth that allowed her to believe what she was saying. She smelled several kinds of clean. Then this:

We would like to talk to you about your activities and any difficulties you may experience in the neighborhood. We also want to inform you about our job-training and mentoring programs. Mentoring is a key component of the program.

Wait. *I'm* on the list?

Are you Gary Wellman of 7901 Cohn Street? She liked her clipboard, and it pained her to distrust it.

I am, I said, though it felt like a lie—I'm always jarred outside myself when I hear my name aloud. How many names are on that list?

I could tell the question was unusual. But I was a middle-aged white man with a wall full of books. Slattery finally couldn't resist a peek over his shoulder.

Five hundred, she said.

I savored that idea for a second, that I was one of the five hundred most dangerous people in New Orleans. Then I said, trying to keep the regret out of my voice, Well, that's got to be a mistake.

Computer's infallible, Slattery said to the shelf of literary criticism.

Do you own a gun, Mr. Wellman? Norris asked.

My wife does. But it was a gift. It's never been out of its case.

I felt conflicted: I wanted to be good for Norris, but I wanted Slattery to see me as someone who needed to be handled with more than irony.

I have violent thoughts, I offered.

Any gang affiliations? Norris asked.

I'm a high school teacher! I exclaimed.

Slattery thumbed his belt and made for the door.

I petted my porch cat as she walked circles around the plants. Slattery leaned against the cruiser, his red scrape of hair aimed at a cell phone. Norris sat inside typing on a laptop.

This analytics stuff is bullshit, isn't it, I asked Slattery.

Don't sell yourself short, he said, eyes playing it as straight as his voice. You might be a killer.

~

There were so many stories in the world that all stories felt fake. My writing had withered under the panic of narratives on television, online, at the movies, in literary magazines, on tablets and phones. I would start a story with a more or less promising sentence—*I bought a drone*—and then lose faith that anyone was listening, that my little drone could share the air

34

with Flight 370 and Walter White, Katniss Everdeen, ISIS and Jay-Z. Those were stories for morons, yes, for people who thought *story* meant *things happening*; but plot is like an arms race; when everyone else is firing rounds in the air, the only way to be heard is to grab a gun.

I bought a drone, kitty cats, I said. They had come out of the bedroom to smell the air now that visitors had gone. I bought a drone. Then what?

I could never resume writing once the real world had intruded. I shut down the computer and called my wife.

Need anyone knocked off?

My boss.

Looks like I'm your man.

I told her about Norris and Slattery.

That's got to be Nate, she said.

Oh. I bet you're right.

Nate was my cousin and the sweetest guy in the world underneath his addictions and the things he did to maintain them. He had stolen both of our bikes and, the last time we let him in the house, my wife's credit card. The only time I had ever been arrested was with Nate. We were on our way to a Pelicans game, and he said he wanted to *stop and talk to a friend*. I knew roughly what that meant, but I liked the sensation of being whisked along into Nate's gray life. Even when ATF agents came through two doors at once, it didn't completely ruin my fascination at having watched humps of cocaine weighed on a scale—it wasn't my drug deal, I reasoned stupidly. By the time I got clear of the charges, it had cost me fifteen thousand dollars, and my fascination had turned to shame. I hadn't seen Nate in two years; some drug-idea had put him in a car and taken him to Houston.

But how fucked up are those analytics? I said. There's got to be five hundred people between here and Dante Street more likely to kill someone than I am.

They said kill or be killed.

Wait now.

I'm just saying.

My conception of myself raised its arms in protest as if to say, Who would want to kill me? Me, whom everybody loves so?

Are you going to the store today? she said.

I can.

Bananas. Pita chips. Apples.

My wife has an ill-named piece of furniture called a hope chest; that's where I found her gun, removed it from its case, and carried it to my car wrapped in a reusable net grocery bag. I didn't bother with the bullets; I just needed something to wave around in traffic if it came to that.

Contemporary narration is the account of the manufacturing of the work, not the actual work. I agreed with David Shields about that, but I had this drone and needed something for it to do. I let it follow me to the store, as good a place as any to fantasize about whom to kill. We fictionalize to kill. All characters move toward death. This woman blocking the bin of tomatoes with her cart; the couple with matching ponytails tonging salad-bar items: Everyone in range entered my sights and prepared to die. My drone captured my thoughtcrimes frame by frame. Fire is black in black and white.

In the example sentences I use to teach ninth-grade grammar, people are often *going to the store* because, I realized as I backtracked for pita chips, I so often go to the store; it's one of the changeless circles my life walks in; but today the circle had opened to a spiral because of my gun and drone. A gun in a story is an aesthetic idiocy. A gun in life is a cheat. But a gun in imagination—brandished to create a path down aisle ten—gives your mind an equal chance against the ugliness you subject it to. I laid the gun on the conveyor with my groceries. When the checker looked at me and laid her hand on it, the air between us turned to sex.

In the car I took out Norris's card and dialed.

I think I might take that mentor, I said.

We're looking you back up. This wasn't you who did these robberies, was it?

I just walked out of a grocery store where I fantasized about killing everyone, I said. And I felt absolutely no remorse.

That's not good.

I agree.

The dash clock read 10:40. It seemed like an ominous time for it to be. The world was revealed as a ticking machine.

The mentors are for helping people enroll in community college and so forth. Why aren't you at work today?

This question was gratifying—that Norris would expend her powers of detection on me.

We get the whole week after Mardi Gras.

Oh, she said, losing interest. Before she rang off, I said, Look up my parking tickets if you want a shock.

The mentor I imagined for myself was a black minister, Southern Baptist or A.M.E.—no postmodern mega-church types for me. He would study me with his heavy brow and re-pack my contents into their original box. The word *person* would mean something definite to him. I could follow the arrow of his voice toward the future.

I would prefer, I had almost told Norris, *if literally almost everyone were dead*. That was a heavy thought, so I drove it around for a while. There was almost no one whose death would bother me. *Bother* is the word, I thought as I went through the photo-enforced stoplight at Carrollton and Earhardt, exactly right for its lightness and smallness. Except for my wife—whom I excepted because she agreed with me, because if everyone died we would sit on the couch and comment on the justice of it—there was no one whose erasure would disconcert me more than, say, spilling coffee in the kitchen or misplacing a set of student quizzes. The only death I could not survive was my own. The only death from which I could not stand up and walk away unaffected, I wrote on the notepad I keep in the car, imitating Thomas Bernhard, was my own. It is in fact one of my most cherished beliefs that people deserve to die, and I have no intention of relinquishing it. I might have once said, I wrote, that I regret being someone who holds human life at so low a value, but I have stopped exhausting myself with *good intentions*.

At home I put a book in my lap. I turned on the TV. A half hour of "Caught Red-Handed," shoplifters swiping booze and batteries and getting tackled in parking lots. Then I asked the world for a Katy Perry video and turned to VH1 to watch a Katy Perry video. The book in my lap—Colum McCann's *Let the Great World Spin*—could not hope to say as much about the world as Katy Perry. Katy Perry's artificiality asks more questions about the real—is therefore more real—than the most seamless realist novel.

37

McCann's frantic assertions of verisimilitude were a thousand times more fake than Katy Perry, every sentence collapsing under the weight of its need to be believed. Colum McCann is that dead thing called *art*; Katy Perry contains art, the way discourse contains museums.

But you can't put that in a story, *my drone watched me watch TV*, so I got the bullets from the hope chest and loaded the gun for a walk around my neighborhood. I didn't want to shoot myself in the nuts from a pocket, so I put the gun in a fanny pack with the barrel pointing outward through the zipper and set off down my block. Though really, since I lived on a corner, either of two directions was my block, and I realized that I had been thinking of this one as mine because the people on it were white. So the gun was already teaching me things. . . . I disliked white people for their whiteness, but now that I could shoot them, they looked silly instead of evil. The man across the street with four fishing boats in his yard: It was a petty kingship he practiced behind his fence, a pageant he staged at the cost of his life. The woman two doors down with leather wrist cuffs and a bull ring in her nose: jailing herself so she could hold the keys. A sixty-year-old man named Kip. It was their ridiculousness more than their whiteness that made me one of them.

A left turn: a black block. The gun awoke and engaged. My drone flew support. This was the block where kids wouldn't move when I drove down it, moved only after they had slowed me to a crawl. The disturbing part wasn't being slowed—I never had anywhere to go—but that they would not look at me even as my fender brushed their legs, that there was no way to appeal to them about the pointlessness of the game we played. But the gun would give me language. When, in moments, I reached the trio of men blocking the sidewalk with the sails of their white T-shirts, the gun would be the preamble of an overdue dialogue. *I teach The Autobiography of Malcolm X, yo. Like Albert Murray I believe that black people are the omni-Americans. I can do all three verses of "Tha Shiznit."*

But when I got to them, they were busy discussing how somebody was a *motherfucking bitch*. The tape shows Whitey stepping into the grass around them and continuing on his way.

A left turn: a white block. I bought a drone. I sent the drone aloft from the command center of the family couch. But each *thing* I thought of for my drone to do felt false. I sent my drone away, but it kept coming back; I was the person of interest. The line my drone flew through the story would be the plot, but plot kills story. First we apply the "hook"—a barb through the lip of the story—then we drag it to its death dressed, as Virginia Woolf says, in the costume of "reality": well-appointed villas, railway carriages, coat buttons, door bells. Solidity, probability. It had taken a hundred years, but American fiction had chased itself back to the moment before the Armory show: locked inside the obedient known, matter and physics intact, fiction about danger that presents no danger to the reader. *A series of gig lamps symmetrically arranged.*

A final turn onto Fern Street: a block of sigh-sunk houses whose insult was the reminder that your life was contingent. A drive-by shooting had happened here, an apocalypse of blue lights and bullet cones that I had introduced casually into conversation for the next month. I could see this block from my front door, but I knew none of the people on it, even by sight, it was as darkly unknown to me as the Belgian Congo, heads on stakes and a currency of brass wire, bodies wasting under a tree . . .

Something ran at my legs, and I reached for the gun: It was Noopy, the neighbor's cat. Noopy is a poly, halfsize calico with dirty feet who looks you in the face during conversation. She felled a hindquarter against my leg and waited for her spanking. When it didn't come, she looked over her shoulder and called for my attention.

Mr. Gary can't pet you right now, Noopy.

Meow.

I know, but see Mr. Gary's fanny pack?

Meow.

That's Mr. Gary's deadly force.

Meow.

Oh, I see a cat belly. I see a very silly belly.

I stood there in the sun of a finally warm day. Noopy's tiny paws made me think everything was going to be OK.

For ten days during Mardi Gras, you know what comes next. There's a schedule, but it's a schedule of whimsy: sequence without consequence, time turned into a toy. Not that it's easy—there's a costume to assemble, parades every night and the drinking and shivering you do at them, and then, the next morning, dragging yourself to work with a sore throat and fuzzed eyes—but the labor you put into Mardi Gras is a parody of work that holds real work at bay. On Mardi Gras Day, I had drunk until I couldn't see the numbers on my money, and the release of that, of looking up at my friends from a puddle I had fallen into, was so complete that the only fitting second act was the iron-gray stillness of Lent. I had given up alcohol, but since I didn't believe in anything, I was the devil to my own resolutions, so here I was making a drink to fill the hour before my wife got home. Gin was my personal Jesus. I raised the glass to check its mystery against the light.

Everything I read when I drink is about reading. Words shed the dirt of their mishandling and once more, cleanly, mean. A few pages of Werner Herzog's *Conquest of the Useless*, the pleasure so intense I had to put it aside in favor of a *Harper's* essay about the self-diagnosis of medical conditions; then the chapter of *A Fan's Notes* where Exley meets Frank Gifford in a diner; then a few pieces of the earnest, useless advice about writing in Glimmer Train's *Writers Ask*; and then I pulled the brick of Harold Brodkey's *Stories in an Almost Classical Mode* from the shelf. These are the fragments my brain has been turned into by being forty-six in a world that is nineteen. Gin doesn't solve this problem, but it does dull the anxiety by turning the fragments into aphorisms. The hum of my drone in powersave mode could not be heard above the central hum of self.

At five my wife struggled in with her ballast of gym bags and book bags, and I grimaced up from the Brodkey as if I were engaged in a painstaking task so she would be less likely to hold my pleasure against me. There was a very fat, very lonely woman in my wife's office who had been meeting men online and then in cars and hotels to do desperate, dangerous things, and I heard the latest details of that—a portrait painter's dick sucked, his failure to return her calls, her plaints to the support group she had started online to collect sympathy for her amorous misfires.

You've heard about this strangers-kissing thing? my wife said.

I raised my eyebrows and waited; I resented being made into the chorus of these reports.

It's this thing where people walk up to strangers in public, she said, and kiss them without warning. Except not really because it's an ad for some clothing company. But Tara is so dumb, she thinks it's real. She quote *can't stop thinking about it and wants to go out and try it.*

From the drone, hovering now, my head-shake of disbelief looked more or less convincing. The co-worker did in fact sound noisy and awful, a language criminal, a broken carnival ride waiting to injure someone. But she had lit her lights and was spinning, and however we made fun of her, we could not stop watching. She represented nothing less than the most absorbing interest in my wife's life.

He made her do it through the zipper.

What?

He didn't want her to see his body.

The phone rang. I ignored it. A man too embarrassed to expose his body in the dusty light of a studio where paintings of Clint Eastwood lay stacked against the wall: This was life in its everyday brilliance overwhelming the bounds of what art could hold. The scene filled in for me as the caller hung up on the machine: Tara tugging the painter's belt and the wrestle of their hands. The business casual she knelt in, knees paired below a skirt. The echo of the studio as the world went by outside: these details made pathos on paper, but in life they made humanity, made the people real to me.

Clint Eastwood, you said?

Clint Eastwood, Katy Perry, that kind of shit. He sells them to tourists.

The phone rang again.

Come on, I complained. It's the dinner hour.

Mr. Wellman?

Hey, Officer Norris. Sorry, we screen. We're the last people in the world without caller I.D.

I was being talky, but I wanted her to know this me: yes, the guy who wanted everyone in the grocery store dead, but also the guy who halfway through a drink remembered that the way people deserved life was by being alive.

Mr. Wellman, we have reviewed your case.

Before you say anything: You know what I did today? Walked around the block with a gun.

That isn't wise.

That's what I'm saying.

I'm calling to inform you that an error was committed in dispatch. There is another individual possessing your same name.

That's the quantum me. That's stuff I did in the multiverse.

We're sorry to have disturbed you. Have a nice day.

I lowered the phone and crossed my arms.

You were a killer for a day, sweetie, my wife said in fake consolation.

I got the White Pages and splashed them into my lap.

The black you doesn't have a landline, she said. He's got a prepaid cell phone. And an actual gun.

She turned on the "Colbert" re-run—Neil DeGrasse Tyson, who had known he wanted to be an astrophysicist since he was a child. I tossed the White Pages and was trying to beat Tyson, through the gin, to the things I knew about Giordano Bruno when the air cracked open at a knock from the front door.

My wife muted the TV. My glass held halfway to my mouth. We were giving the knock a chance to go away. We both hated the outside world and imagined it out of existence as soon as we closed our door in the evening. But the knock repeated: urgent blows with the side of a fist.

U.P.S.? I whispered. But when I edged the curtain to peek out, it was Nate. Nate, and with him someone I had never seen before, a tall man with feathered hair and athlete's thighs in tight jeans, three steps behind on the sidewalk. High-top sneakers snug and clean.

It's Nate, I mouthed. But then I wasn't sure. I flew my drone out to confirm what I'd seen and found darker hair than I remembered, a flatter, emptier face. Instead of a genial squint ready for the next laugh, his eyes were rocks seeking a target.

Let us in, he said at conversational volume. He knew I was listening through my single-pane window. We heard the TV. We know you're in there.

Who am I? I said.

Don't play games, cuz.

I'm calling the police, my wife yelled through the door.

Tell them not to do that, the man on the sidewalk said in a voice so exaggeratedly gruff it had to be fake.

When my drone circled around this time, Nate was a light-skinned black man, his hair sharpened to corners at the temple, one hand edging toward his crotch.

I've got a gun, I said and pulled it from the table by the door.

What the fuck? my wife whispered.

We ain't got to do all that, Nate said.

We just want to talk to them, the man on the sidewalk said.

We just want to talk, cuz.

My drone was gathering an ecstasy of information. It dived in to note the brand name on the tall man's jeans—Jordache—and traced tight orbits around not-Nate's head. It was panting above the sidewalk, waiting for the next bit of fun, when the door flew open and I followed my gun into the street.

Five Handy Men

Daniel Uncapher

1. Rabbit

Rabbit lived at the foot of the hill in a tenement, last of its kind, a three-story overcrowded brick box with shanty tents propped outside the crumbling walls like a little Hoovertown. He was lucky enough to sleep inside the walls on the third floor where the most resourceful locals cooked crystal meth, the production of which garnered the modest valley considerable regional acclaim for its affordability, consistency, and availability.

One hazy September evening as the city school bus ferried half-asleep children by, a stovetop fire in a kitchen-manufactory broke out on the third floor, setting off a column of smoke in the middle of Main Street as black and broad as the pine knot and tar bonfires they burned to fight the miasma of Yellow Fever. The victims gathered on the sidewalk outside and watched their lives incinerate. Somebody called the police, who called the fire chief who called the mayor, a chicken-dealing Baptist who disliked the tenement complex as much as the next white man and told the fire chief to let the whole place burn down—make a show of saving her, but let her burn. Along the way, someone collected some insurance money, but it wasn't anyone standing on the sidewalk that day covered in ash and soot.

Rabbit got along as usual, moving into a trailer with a girl of his on the far side of the valley past yonder bend at Town Creek where the warehouses are, a far piece to walk, but he walked it every single morning to come work on my house just as he'd done since the day I moved in; he marched up the street, introduced himself as "Rabbit, because I'm lucky," and reckoned with me privately that an old house like mine needed to be scraped and painted just about all the way around, and that he just happened to be in the business of scraping and painting old houses.

Being in no business to employ fellow human beings and provide for the mouths of other families at that time, I offered $300 to drive him away, but in a great twist to my naiveté, he showed up the next day with a scraper and paintbrush and went right to work. Every day or two he'd ask for some money in advance, enough for a bottle, a can of tuna and a moon pie or two. He never counted the money I gave him, just took it and said thanks, just like he never used the telephone and he never signed checks; the old man was both numerically and alphabetically illiterate and, as far as I could tell, genuinely didn't realize I was ripping him off. I tried to teach him the alphabet for a few days like a player in some colonialist play until I decided just to pay him better and leave him alone, and he went back to painting and whistling in peace (handy people make excellent whistlers, and it comes all the more natural to Southerners—they can snap their fingers and hand bone, too, like their limbs are made out of wooden clappers and strings).

Rabbit managed to scrape three quarters of my house and paint half of it drippy, glistening eggshell white by the time his luck finally ran out. One balmy spring night in a corrugated warehouse near his girl's place on the riverbed, a gambling friend stabbed Rabbit in the back over twenty bucks and a bad hand. When the police arrived they found a hundred dollar bill folded up in the heel of his left shoe, and no one had anything to say about Rabbit again.

2. Matt

Matt did good work well, better than the insulting wages I'd become accustomed to paying by the precedent of a numerically illiterate cardplayer. On the first day he lugged his own mower and weed whacker all the way up the hill, set the tools of his trade down on the sidewalk in front of my house and politely alerted me to the state of the lawn. I agreed with his concerned assessment and turned him down. On the second day he returned while I was away and my roommate hired him for $15. When he stuck me with the bill my lawn looked better than it had in years, and I gave him a full twenty-dollar bill in a fit of pure generosity. Matt even had the good nature to pretend I was being generous.

He was a short man with a deeply furrowed brow like a Bodhisattva both stoic and skeptic. He wore rimless glasses when speaking with me and

45

I felt like he listened to me when I spoke, a not insignificant feat for the locals who find themselves dealing with we otherwise insufferable carpetbaggers.

I hired him to finish what Rabbit started, just to keep him around. I took long breaks from my writing to sit with him and talk. We talked about travel. I mentioned the continent, and he said he once went to Mexico; I shared my envy over Mexico and said he should go back. He mentioned something about passports. I clapped him on his paint-splattered back and assured him it was easy to get a passport; "It's never too late," I said. "I'll even take the picture for you."

There is a hollow over the ravine below a ridge on the far side of the hill under the shade of the kudzu called Possum Holler where Matt lived with his girlfriend and children. After a few months' work, he moved his family into a small white ranch home on Central Street right by Rascal's gas station downtown and directly next door to the local tax assessor, an excruciatingly fair-minded woman who photographed her new neighbor dealing dime bags from his porch with a telescopic lens one night and submitted her portfolio of work for inspection by the local police, who obliged the good publican by breaking down Matt's front door midweek at midnight and rousing his family out of bed at gunpoint, including their youngest son, autistic and hard of hearing, who screamed in terror at the home invasion. They confiscated half a pound of weed, a $12 digital scale, and all the money in the house including the children's' savings before finally hauling their father a few blocks up Main Street to jail.

When his wife bailed him out the next morning, he came to me for help. The police took the money that I had paid him just that week and claimed it for drug money. I typed up a letter on Matt's behalf formally stating that I paid him every cent of the cash the police confiscated, but it did him no good; on a rosy-fingered dawn several weeks later, he shot a man at the local Sonic Drive-In restaurant over an incident with some drinks, of which Sonic is a most famous and capable purveyor.

For that he was sent down to Parchman.

3. Earl

Earl ran a company called Rebel Electric and came highly recommended by every old boy you asked. Old houses like mine can be tricky, but Earl did what had to be done, he said, and that is true, although not always quite all the way, as the South itself, as a rule, is never quite all the way done.

He spoke softly, carried a big clipboard, and drove a humble white Ranger with a fading rebel flag decal stuck to the side. Like Matt, he wore half-moon glasses while he worked that looked rather fatherly and gave me advice on wiring up on some antiquated machinery I needn't bother wiring up, for which he befriended me on Facebook to share some eBay listings for the necessary power converters, which I never bought.

His Facebook posts dominated my feed thereafter, entertaining works of speculative fiction that made a few things about Earl's character quite apparent from the intimate content of his late-night compositions. He liked to relax after work with a drink or two, and when he drank to let loose, his mind ran even looser, dreaming up things he felt he should say—like calling out the Muslim president for being too friendly with the towelheads. When a friend and customer rebuked him for making such tasteless comments in public and threatened to withdraw her business, he threatened to withdraw his business right back and doubled-down on the rhetoric of the so-called "sand niggers," a troublesome construct of people better off transformed into glass—glass the whole desert, he said.

One winter he began fooling around with a younger girl, the 45-year-old fiancée of a construction worker from the nearby drive-by community of Mount Olivet who drove to Earl's house and beat the shit out of him over the affair. Earl got in his truck and chased the jilted lover up Cotton Road over the Yocona at Dallas Jones' crossing to the old railroad split called Grinder's Switch, halfway between Olivet and Taylor. They pulled onto the roadside gravel and Earl got out of his Rebel Electric Ranger with his 1911, firing 18 rounds into the back of the cuckold's new F-150. One bullet pierced the corner of the driver's seat and embedded itself in his shoulder, turning Earl's crime into, among a number of other things, attempted manslaughter.

They took him on down to Parchman to sort it all out.

4. Wade

Wade worked his way door-to-door up the street, introducing himself in a clear, flat voice in his attempt to draw the homeowner and potential employer's attention away from the dual teardrops tattooed under his right eye, one unfilled (which means, so I've heard, his friend was killed) and one filled (which means, or so I've heard, he killed his friend's killer). I have also heard that teardrops just mean you were somebody's bitch in prison, but then the distinction between filled and unfilled only complicates the riddle.

When he came to my door, I turned him away because I was both tight on cash and a little bit jaded from handymen. He lived around the block in the old kudzu-addled mobile home (long abandoned since its career as a meth lab of inconvenient proportions) with his girlfriend and three kids and told me I could find him there if I changed my mind. After he left, my neighbor came over and inquired on the nature of the young black man that came to her door; I told her not to worry, that he was a family man looking for work.

I hired him the next week to dig a brick walkway. He worked well enough to recommend him to my parents across town whose house needed more work than mine. They felt so bad for him that they moved him into one of their small rentals across the valley, offering to take rent in the form of services rendered. They lent him their truck and my mother sprained her back helping him move some of their old furniture in.

Over the next three months, he spent most of the day between my house and my parents' doing this or that or watching television or emptying the nickels and dimes from the change bowl by the front door. Then he began writing checks to himself from my parents' various checking accounts and cashing them at the local Piggly Wiggly, a self-service grocer that makes good money selling pig lard and bagged apples and cashing bad checks, like Wade's.

He stole $1200 over several weeks and upon confrontation admitted immediately that it was to pay for his weed addiction and he would pay the money back. We reported the theft to the police who deferred the matter to the banks affected, who deliberated on pressing charges. Wade promised to leave town if his family could stay in their new house, his girlfriend paying rent between her dual income of secretary at a local manufactory and a disability recipient, but the next weekend Wade stole a ladder off a neighbor's porch to cut it down and sell for scrap. The neighbor watched it happening and called the police on him, who arrested him for home invasion and sent him to Parchman over $20 of scrap aluminum.

His wife and children stayed in the house and continued to work at the manufactory and receive disability and make a go of it for the children, who grew up.

5. For Hire

Looking for a reliable handyman to do general scraping, painting, and landscaping at affordable rates. Come to the front porch of the Cedars at the top of the big hill across from the drug store for an interview. No references necessary.

Geography Lessons

Jaclyn Dwyer

When the man lets go of my arm and slips into a cracked door at the end of the alley, I don't run.

~

I was never good at geography. My husband and I play Wii Jeopardy and curse at Katie, the computer avatar with bad highlights, who sweeps the category from us both.

~

I keep walking, jostle through the streets of Morocco draped in my roommate's gear for the day, his camera tucked into an army green messenger bag. I militarize myself, dial in and charge toward the pink lights three blocks ahead. My brown map-print purse raps my hip with each step. The antique fabric warns HERE THERE BE MONSTERS in a tea-stained swath of sea that doesn't help me here.

~

When I was six, my godmother bought me a desk and topographic globe. Every country was a different color. I ran my finger over the mountain ranges, lingering over the soft bubbles where the land rose up like a keloid scar. After, she sent my mother postcards from Mississippi, Missouri, but I never saw her again.

~

"I'm meeting someone," I say to the man, "Someone is waiting for me." It's not a lie. I'd dropped my roommate at the Turkish bath and planned to reconvene at the coffee shop after his sweat and scrub. I lug all our gear for the day, alone in a crowd of strangers who do nothing when the man hooks his arm in mine.

~

In seventh grade, I won the class Geography Bee because the boy behind me whispered all the answers in my ear. Sherwood Forest.

Boomerang. I moved on to compete against the school and lost. No one was there to help me.

~

For half a block the man holds on in broad daylight, our elbows deadlocked against each other as I try to outpace him. The moment our feet leave curb for cobblestone, he tugs and tows me from the crowd. My bags hula hoop my hips in the alley where a door is propped open. Four fingers and a foot are waiting.

~

My sister and I used to rest our finger on the equator and spin. Wherever our fingers landed, that was where we were supposed to live. She landed on Moldova. Djibouti. I always seemed to end up in the middle of the ocean, my finger adrift in a flat span of blue.

~

When my roommate asks, "Who wants to go to Morocco for break?" I volunteer because it sounds romantic. My sister jokes, "Don't let him trade you for a camel." I laugh and look up Morocco on the map. My finger scans three continents to find it.

~

Early cartographers were explorers trying to make sense of the world. They gave shapes to the surface of things to document a navigable path, a dangerous route. I can't even be sure of which city this happened in.

~

The cities are steeped in deep blues and reds and greens. The hues of earth and water. The guidebook is color coded. My roommate carries the book. He buys a fistful of saffron and carries the bag the color of clay from Fes to Meknes. If you touch it, the saffron stains everything like rust that won't rub off.

~

In Marrakech I enter the medina squinting. My blue-tint lenses fail to filter the sun. I don't notice the snakes until someone shouts when I almost step on a spool of black scales. Triplet cobras, their bodies scrolled on red earth and a charmer in white, three upturned baskets by his side. But this is some other city. This is not Marrakech.

~

I make it back to the coffee house where I drown in pink lights and svelte Coke bottles I save and, ten years later, display on the same bookshelf as my wedding photos. My instinct is to persevere through preservation.

~

The world is divided into snakes and charmers. It is often difficult to tell what is before you until it is too late.

~

Now that I'm a mother, there are stories of my life I'm not supposed to tell, parts of the world I am supposed to shade over as if they aren't there. This is one of them. Still, I want to map out all the alleys where worlds close behind doors, where someone else is waiting, not just for the man who disappeared, but for me too.

The Winding

Kate Washington

"Where did you get that watch?" a stranger asked my mother. It was 1979, and I was seven, and we were in New Zealand, two seasons and 24 hours of travel removed from our California home. My mother was enduring her first major depressive episode; years later, she would tell me that on our flight home she had hoped the plane would crash over the wide Pacific, to end her misery. The stranger went on: "It wasn't in Seattle, by any chance? I lost one just like it there, and I've never seen another like it since. I'm almost sure I lost it downtown, at the Nordstrom. I went back to the lost and found, but it never turned up."

It's no surprise the stranger would recognize the watch instantly, would seek it on a stranger's wrist. I've never seen another like it either: a Seiko, gold tone, delicate yet mod, an artifact of the 1960s. The gold has worn away on the clasp and at the edges. Around the face, a tiny ring of beveled, silver-toned metal has a deceptive shine, like precious stones. My mother was trained by her mother to be a well-turned-out sorority girl, in a time when girls and women were expected to match gold jewelry with gold, silver with silver. By those rules, that silvery circlet kept the watch from clashing with her platinum engagement and wedding set.

Turn the watch over, and the plate on the back notes that the top is made of base metal, the back of stainless steel. The bracelet-style band is a chain of tiny, blocky striated chunks, pierced through with tiny parallel openings. Each link resembles a tiny version of the abstract sculptures that might hulk outside libraries or city halls of towns that were prosperous and consciously forward-thinking a half a century ago, the public art of places caught up in the midcentury boom in which my mother came of age. Every day since, my mother wound the watch, so faithfully that the gilt on its mechanism had slowly worn away on the knob.

I don't know where, or when, my mother got that watch, though I imagine it was at her college graduation, when that platinum engagement ring was already on her fourth finger. The details of the story of the stranger are a little fuzzy as well, but I cannot ask her to clarify. Some thirty years after that New Zealand trip, she completed the suicide she once longed for, overdosing on a cocktail of blood-pressure medicine and an antidepressant. I don't know when she last wound the watch, before her death, or exactly when it wound down after. For years after her death, I kept it in a drawer. Something superstitious in me shied away from its quiet, even ticks. I convinced myself that it couldn't possibly keep good time, that my cell phone was more reliable, that a watch on my wrist was just a distraction and a bother as I typed.

Years after that New Zealand trip, the story as I remember it goes, another stranger approached my mother. "Where did you get that watch?" my mother was once again asked. "I have the same one and I've never seen another like it," she continued. This woman had not bought her Seiko. For years, she confided, it had lain, unwound, neglected, in the lost and found at her workplace, the flagship Nordstrom in downtown Seattle, until some unknown deadline ran out and she was allowed to take it.

There was no way for my mother to connect the watch-seeker of years before to the watch-finder. I'm not sure if she even told the second woman about the first one. What would have been the point? Some circles do not close, and some losses can never be rectified; they can only be worn smooth as the years tick by.

We all have our talismans, those things we are seeking at every lost and found. Some eye a gold-toned watch on a stranger's wrist; some search for time itself, and some, like my mother, relief from time's painful march. My mother's watch, as odd and beautiful as she was, winds down as quietly as she did, after long and equally quiet persistence. It hangs on my wrist now, a wrist slowly thinning to be as knobby as hers. It keeps perfect time.

It's Clean

Jane Rose Porter

The knot of gold slipped from Lucy's fingers to the parquet floor when the phone rang. "Shit!" she called into the empty room and pressed the phone to her cheek, crawling along the floor of her studio apartment. She ran her fingers between the uneven grooves of the old floorboards in search of the gold chain and its elephant charm.

"What is it?" she said, groping along the slats of wood. Her father was calling. He always wanted to talk at the most inopportune moments, but she felt an obligation to answer when his name appeared on her phone. The last time she'd ignored his calls, her grandmother had suffered a heart attack and nearly died.

"Why such a rush? You've got someone over there waiting for you?" he said.

"Mind your business," she said.

"You know where I was today?" he went on. "You're not going to believe where I was today." Every phone call with him, like a bad standup routine.

"Hurry up, Dad. I'm late." She pressed her free cheek to the floor and peered under the sofa, thick with dust and hair.

"You know who called me?" he tried instead, as if this might go over better with the crowd. "The police! They told me, 'Come to the station.' She put twenty packets of yeast and a pound of flour in her purse and walked out without paying. They took her away in a cop car."

"Jesus," Lucy said, sitting upright on the floor.

Lucy's grandmother was eighty-one. That year, she'd started talking to the pictures on the walls. She slept most of the day, her face hollow with age, the loose flesh reminding Lucy of an old paper bag left out in the rain.

But that was not the image of her Lucy had in mind as she leaned against the frame of the couch. She saw a younger version of her grandmother now—plump and rosy-cheeked, lips painted metallic pink, dressed up for a weekend outing to the department store. The contrast between such elegance and this startled her in a way her father could not comprehend. He'd never shared those afternoons with them, browsing the aisles of clothes in their hunt for exquisite things.

He was yelling for her grandmother to turn the TV down.

"Are you talking to me or what?" Lucy said. Clothing was heaped on her bed and all around her on the floor—discarded outfits she'd considered for her date. Trying on clothes alone was never satisfying. It was nothing like the excitement of going with her grandmother into that big, bright department store. She thought of it now—how long ago it had been, how much had changed, how time took the people you loved away from you piecemeal, leaving just enough to make you to wish them back the way they once had been, back when you'd barely bothered seeing them.

It was the very first time she remembered now—when her grandmother took her into the women's department—a proud day for Lucy, who had been twelve years old. That was nearly twenty years ago. Shopping in the ladies section was a symbolic step into womanhood, just as the tiny triangles she'd dutifully strapped to her nearly concave chest had been a nod to the fact that she was, if not yet, then, very soon, to be a woman.

On that first day in the ladies department, Lucy had managed to find a few items that fit her—camisoles and spandex and a silvery silk skirt in the evening wear department, size 00. In the fitting room, her grandmother perched on the corner stool, Lucy stepped into that skirt—a shiny fabric, slippery and light, tiny silver beads stitched into its hem. The skirt fit perfectly and when she spun, its shimmer filled the trifold mirror.

"Beautiful," her grandmother had said. "Like it was sewn for you. How much?"

Lucy lifted the tag—two-hundred-fifty-dollars—and her face dropped.

"Ridiculous," her grandmother said, disgusted. "Take it off."

She pulled the skirt from Lucy's hands, flipped the fabric inside out, studying it a moment, silent.

"It's clean," she finally said. But Lucy did not yet understand.

Her father grumbled into the phone. "I don't know what to do with her," he said.

It had become their secret all those years ago, Lucy's closet filling with slinky rich treasures. Not even her father knew, too clueless about a thing like clothes to tell the difference between what was expensive and what was not. It was better this way, kept only between the two of them, as though what they did existed only in the fitting rooms they occupied, the walls hung in clean clothes. The closest thing to witnesses: their reflections in the glass.

"Clean?" Lucy said that afternoon in the fitting room.

"No security," her grandmother said in Russian and shook the flimsy skirt in her hands.

"You tell this to no one," she said. "Understand?"

Lucy knew only that she wanted this beautiful skirt in her closet, swishing against her hips, transforming her into a grown woman. Her grandmother forced a loud cough as she yanked the tag from the silver waistband of the skirt, clearing her throat dramatically. The plastic strip made a snapping sound so loud that Lucy worried the sales woman outside had heard, even above the cough. Her grandmother stuffed the tag into the pocket of a blazer hanging there, folded the skirt up small as a hanky, wrapped it in a napkin, and nestled it deep in her bag beneath her bulging beige wallet.

"All set," she said and gave Lucy a knowing look.

As they left the store, she walked ahead of her grandmother, her mind so dizzy with fear that she wasn't sure she would make it to her father's car at the curb.

"Buy anything good?" he asked when they got in and because she was unable to speak, her grandmother had answered for her—"I got some ideas for her birthday gift," she said and winked at Lucy in the mirror.

Who could suspect a little old lady and her granddaughter of such a thing?

They went every weekend, sometimes both days. Lucy browsed only in the women's department from then on, navigating the large sizes, searching the fancy, boxy, shoulder-padded clothes for things that might fit her. She tried on only clean clothes—items without the plastic security tags on them that had been returned or simply forgotten in the tagging process—things that could be bundled neatly and shoved to the bottom of a handbag. Lucy scanned the racks for those tags, dodging the sales ladies who mulled about and asked if she wanted to start a fitting room. "No thank you," she would say, sweating, and smile. "I need to find my grandma first."

There was no thrill in it for her, not in the act at least, the way she'd heard there was for some who stole. Only the shame. It was a terrifying, seductive, ugly thing. Later, the closest she would come to feeling it again was sex with men she did not know. But that revulsion lasted only a moment. She would be overcome with a desire for those elegant expensive things. After she'd try on an item that she liked, her grandmother on the stool beside her, they would say nothing, a silence thick between them. Always, after that first time with the silver skirt, Lucy knew to turn her back to her grandmother, the way one might during the gruesome moments in a film, unable to look without wincing, but staying until the end, nonetheless. She would wait for the cough, that *snap,* her grandmother clearing her throat, pleasantly chattering behind her back in Russian about what they would have for dinner, as the roaring tore through Lucy's head like traffic on a turnpike. "All set," her grandmother would say, and by then the item would have disappeared deep into her handbag.

Only weeks later, sometimes months, would she receive whatever treasures they'd acquired, wrapped in tissue paper. She would gasp and smile and try on her new gift, acting as though she was surprised. Every time, the two of them pretended like this, each one for the other's sake.

Her grandmother stole only for her, always those fancy grown-up clothes, filling Lucy's closet with so many thousands of dollars of stuff that Lucy could not begin to calculate how much. Yet they were never caught.

Over the years, she would manage to entirely forget those fitting room episodes until she'd come across something—a store alarm, a surveillance camera, a security tag left on a pair of jeans she'd bought, and now, her father calling with this news.

"What am I going to do with her?" he said.

"Why do you let her go shopping alone?"

"Why don't *you* come home and try to take her shopping?" he said. "When was the last time you did that with her, eh?"

It had not been since high school. Only after Lucy left home for college did she get a sense of the larger world and her tastes changed. She lost her desire for those shiny expensive clothes and stopped going shopping with her grandmother.

On holidays or visits home, Lucy and her grandmother would play dominos instead, watch *Wheel of Fortune,* boil compote. Occasionally Lucy would come home for a visit to find a delicate pair of cashmere gloves or a silk scarf waiting on her bed and the gnawing in her chest would return.

"On sale," her grandmother would lie and smile. Her gifts never had tags on them, not a single one.

Lucy did not respond to her father, could think only of those days years ago, those secret moments in the fitting room full of clean clothes, that dirty thing between her and her grandmother—their closest intimacy. When she thought of it now, there was a pain as though her ribs had been stretched apart—a bottle forgotten, frozen, burst inside of her. What they'd been careful to keep secret all those years was made ugly now by her grandmother's shoplifting, as though it had meant nothing then.

"I don't think there's any way to change her," she said.

"Just a minute Mama," her father called away from the receiver again. Then lowering his voice—"I got the pamphlets for that place," he said to her.

Lucy knew that the temptation was there—the desire, if only for a little while, for her father to do the same: to turn away. Still, sending your elders off was not a thing a Russian family did. You cared for them with the same painstaking martyrdom they'd raised you with—feeding, wiping, washing at any expense—living for them to live another day. It was the least you could do.

Lucy stretched her legs out against the floor and something small and sharp bit into the back of her thigh. It was the gold Ganesh charm, an elephant with its legs tucked beneath it and its arms outstretched, badly tangled in its chain. Her grandmother had given her the charm when she turned twenty-one. "So that you never forget," her grandmother had said, though she didn't know who Ganesh was, and at the time, neither did Lucy. "Like an elephant," her grandmother used to say. "I never forget."

But she had forgotten all the tact of stealth these days. Lucy's grandmother was most elephant-like now not in her memory, but in her right ankle, its thick seam where the vein was lifted years ago, swollen with fluid, her left leg more like a pigeon's—the clotted veins depleting her foot of blood. So many ways the body chose to break—one single body—rotting, sagging, peeling, drowning, splintering like wood. On her last visit home, Lucy had found her grandmother's lipstick in the butter compartment beside the enema jar in the refrigerator. "What's this doing here?" she had asked and her grandmother snatched the lipstick from her. "Your father. He's always stealing my stuff and hiding it," she'd said, but it didn't matter. Her mouth was pale and dry now anyhow, hardly any lips left to paint.

When Lucy's grandmother gave her that necklace, she felt the same swelling cracking shame. It came in the snapping jewelry box she reused each time she gave Lucy a gift. "How did you get this?" Lucy said to her. College had filled her full of virtuous ideals. She knew the answer and it disgusted her.

"What do you mean, how did I get it? At the store," her grandmother said. Then more softly—"I only want the best for you. You're the only one who matters in the world to me." More than the law, more than civil obedience, more than dignity. It was maddening to Lucy, how blind that woman's love could be. And yet Lucy had worn that necklace often, wore it still now. It was the last thing her grandmother had stolen for her.

"I don't know," her father said, sighing again. "In the brochure it says they play Bingo and go for walks. They say it's less lonely over there."

It was only recently, in the past few months that her grandmother had started lifting trifles—hairnets and spools of thread, boxes of raisins and denture cream. She dropped them in her purse as though they belonged to her. Could she even remember what it had meant to be a clever thief?

"I don't know Dad," Lucy said. "Maybe you *should* consider some sort of home." That's why he was calling, of course, for permission. "There's that place with the Russian nurses you heard was good."

"Everyone at work tells me all the time to look into it," he said again. "But I'm going to wait a little longer."

"Yes, wait a little more," she said. "It might not be—"

They both were shamed to silence then, shamed for that secret wish for a clean break, one that meant they would not have to choose to turn away or not.

"Maybe you can talk to her," he said. "About the stealing. I never had to notice until now, Lucy. All those years, I dropped you off; I picked you up. I never said a thing."

The frozen bottle in her chest was crackling again. She could almost hear it crack-crack-crack. The clock on her mantle read 9:08. She imagined the man whose features she couldn't remember, sitting at a bar, jangling the ice in his drink, waiting for her, a faceless figure on a stool, twirling a little red straw in a glass.

"I have to get going," she said and tossed the necklace on the coffee table. She snatched her keys and slammed the door behind her. The stairwell seemed shabbier—the mosaic tile floor caked in dirt, the window ledges thick with soot and flaking paint.

"You know better than anyone," her father said, just as she prepared to hang up. He was whispering into the receiver, as though he knew she'd left the privacy of her apartment. "You know how she gets."

But he was wrong. She'd never thought of it as stealing once they stepped out onto the street. As soon as they left those little windowless rooms and walked through the double glass doors, it was as though the theft had never happened.

She took the steps down two at a time and thought now of the one thing she had stolen on her own, the year before. It was hidden in her dresser drawer at the house. That afternoon, she'd gone to the store in the hospital lobby to find something to put beside her grandmother's bed, but once she stood between the shelves of shiny shellacked items, the need to choose exhausted her. She lifted a mesh sack of glass marbles, each one a different color and shape—a blue diamond, a yellow star, a red heart. They glistened and she had the urge to hold them unobstructed in her hands. Lucy had widened the netting with her fingers and coaxed the red marble out as quietly as she could. She hid it in her fist, slipped it into her pocket, its weight against her thigh as she walked calmly past the cashier, through the glass door to the elevator, up to the cardiology unit where her grandmother was snoring, a tube snaking into her nose. It was only in her grandmother's room that her nervousness caught hold of her. The glass heart gave a tiny thud as she draped her jacket across the seat next to the bed and she worried it might fall out, that her grandmother would see it and know what she had done. In her room at her father's house that evening, Lucy wrapped the marble in a Kleenex and hid it in the box her necklace had come in. She snapped it shut.

The door to her apartment building banged behind her, rattling its frame. Lucy wanted to pry that box open, to hold the marble in her hand and let it catch and bend the light through its prism of glass.

"I'll try," she said to her father. "I'll try to talk to her."

She reached her hand into the street to hail a cab.

"Okay," he said. She heard herself passed off between their hands— her father and grandmother's voices muffled under the sound of city traffic around her.

A black livery car pulled to the curb and Lucy got into the back.

"*Allo?*" she heard her grandmother's voice on the other end of the line. "*Allo? Allo?*" the voice called out, but Lucy was silent. She snapped her phone shut.

"Crime" Theme Contest Winner – 1st Place

62

Family History

Sarah Giragosian

No god is more inscrutable than ours.
Think of how our century began: red fistfuls
of pomegranate blossoms knuckling the windows
in the early dawn, a warning missed and a call to rise.
And at the doors—the early monsters
of modernity, trained to be meticulous, expedient,
propitiated neither by suffering or the skirl of exile.
Think of your grandmother with her rabbit-beat heart
who knew something about hope's atrophied muscles
and the secrets of rubies. She scooped pomegranate seeds
into her pockets, lined her body with an invisible god.
During the march, he roosted in her inner ear and whispered back
such strange flashes of memory: the first clean *A*
she played on her spiked fiddle, the last goat she skinned,
the wet cord that tied her to her son, the gleam of her sister's scissors
that snipped it off, the gleam of the bayonet that killed him.
She watched her daughter's ribs peek through the skin,
and in time, realized that god is anonymous
and intimate as a nurse who can deliver pain
or take it away in the same breath.
What do we say? Our family history?
A death sentence, and yet—
you breathe. You tell me the rest.

"Crime" Theme Contest Winner – 2nd Place

#ponytailforjail

Adam Carpenter

On Sunday at 7:06 pm, she took her mug shot. Or, rather, she had her mug shot taken.

Look straight ahead, ma'am. Now look left. Now right. Step over here. #justlikethemovies

They cuffed her again while she signed her name to the list of her belongings. A roll of ankle tape (half-depleted), a pair of Nike Overplay's (black), spare laces (black), backpack, a collection of Anne Sexton, a Swiss Army Knife. The booking area was grey with forest green accents. The other cop was texting someone and smirking. She snuck a glance. Ew. His girlfriend did not look good in a bikini.

The silence in a booking area is leathery. It's a sticky, miasmic vacuum. A parched desert of sound lustily thirsting for something other than the cluck-clop of the best shoes $58,067 a year can buy. The TV, had it not been muted, would've been the perfect backdrop as the news anchor pretended to look even more excited than he was above the scrolling headline, "College-bound Southie High honors student arrested for attempted mur . . ."

Her mom always said, "Cawps work hahd," followed by the Bostonian semi-colon of pursed lips and a silent snort; then the inevitable, "They don't get paid enough. F'gawdsakes." Even when her older sister got arrested for the Craigslist thing, and the cawp pushed her head into the cruisah with a "watch y'head, sweethaht" while checking out the rise of her miniskirt, mummy just said, "they work so hahd." #smh

The pea stew-thick silence made it hard to breath. A joke. A sexting crack? Nah, too soon. A yo mamma joke? Nah, both of these cops are white. But not Southie-white. They won't get it. The one who put the cuffs on was the kinda cop who tried to be nice. He tried to pretend he wasn't next to someone who had just asphyxiated her physics teacher. With a rope purchased at Home Depot for $23.97 cash.

What he said next was an alley-oop. Even if she weren't looking for a joke opportunity—even if she were mad about the nail she broke off in her physics teacher's neck and not in the mood to talk at all while being processed for jail—his slow, easy lob off the backboard would've yanked her out of silence with a whiplashing, noose-snapping yoink. Here's what he said: "Lemme know if the cuffs are too tight." She blinked to give him a chance to awkwardly take it back. He just glanced up at her, looking for a response. Her face exploded into the same smile she's had since she was five years old. All teeth. She paused for effect, then grabbed the ball and cocked it back over her head.

But then she paused, unable, for some reason, to slam it home.

The fat cop on his phone grabbed the rebound and kissed it off the glass. "That's what she said." She glared at him. "What?" he chuckled to his buddy, "did I offend ah little engineeah?"

Five minutes earlier, at 7:01, wearing her new connected bracelets in the back of the police car, she observed an irony: her sister, the Internet whore, might have sat in the same car wearing the same bracelets. Why hadn't she just snitched her way out? What was she so afraid of? But whatever, cuz she'd gotten'm back. Could that be a defense strategy? Momentary insanity? She made a mental note to Google that.

Six minutes before that, at 6:55, she wondered if the bleachers incident was in the police's records. She pictured the text of the report: *Suspect assaulted classmate claiming classmate called her "trailer park." Victim pushed into gym bleachers. Shin broken. Fourteen stitches.*

That same evening, Sunday at 6:47 pm, she checked her Instagram on her way upstairs to get her coat, and her pic already had 7 likes. One was from Keith Motley, the guy who liked her from English class, and one was from her ex- who refused to leave her alone. So that made it six legit likes and one extra. Her mother was asking the officer if he wanted something to drink. She didn't cry the way she had when her sister had been arrested. Weird.

That same evening, at 6:46 pm, a cop car pulled up to their apartment building, its front tire popping what sounded like a half-filled 20-ounce soda bottle. She peeked out the window in time to see the second cop kick a rusty can out of his way as he flicked the strap off the top of his holster.

That same evening, Sunday at 6:44 pm, she cropped a selfie, decided on no filter, and posted it to IG without a caption.

On Sunday at 6:43 pm, she took a selfie in front of the bay window of her house with the blue lights of the cop car pulling up in the background. #smuglife

On Saturday, the day before, at 7:07 pm, the lab results came back with a positive DNA match from the fragment of real nail that tore off when her falsie snapped off in her teacher's neck.

The day before, Friday, at 3:36 pm, she smiled.

Friday at 3:17 p.m. She got off the bus and called her father's college roommate who was a lawyer.

Friday at 3:15 p.m. she thought maybe he didn't die. Shoot. That means he'd snitch. She cut her hair a few inches and put it up with an elastic. #ponytailforjail

Friday morning at 8:32 a.m., she realized he wasn't in school. Of course. But, I mean, you never know, right?

Thursday, at 7:27 pm, she woke up on the damp grass with a sore finger on 87 North Oak St. in Somerville, Massachusetts. She had blacked out and fallen off the chair.

Thursday at 7:25 pm, she grabbed him by the neck with one hand, just beneath the rope, and squeezed as tightly as she could, glaring directly into his bulging, twitching, bloodshot eyeballs, only blinking to avoid the spattering froth foaming then flying off his flapping stuttering thin lips and scraggly beard. Without knowing why, she found herself hissing in a silent scream, calling him everything she could think of and sputtering threats she had just fulfilled and the phrase "ever again" kept spilling out and "my sister" and she didn't cry at all because it didn't hurt at all in any way and her father was right all men are dogs and her little brother must never know and . . .

Thursday at 7:24 pm, she screwed the pulley—with the Home Depot rope that cost too much already in it with a noose at one end and knot in the other—into the lowest branch on the tree in his back yard by stepping up on a chair. Then she put the noose around his neck and tightened it. Because a pulley effectively divides the weight of what's on the other end in half, she could hoist him up if she put all her weight into it. *Effort equals load divided by mechanical advantage.* He was passed out, so he wouldn't fight. He stunk of vodka and sweat. She had put her shirt back on but not buttoned it all the way because she was still a little drunk and a lot nervous. His back yard was black and only the half moon provided any light. At first, as the top half of his body came up, it was a really easy pull, but as more of his weight left the ground, it got harder and harder. But she did it and tied the rope around the trunk of the tree so he would dangle. Then he started to twitch, and that made her mad, so she got up on the chair she brought down and got in his face.

At 7:17 pm, she threw back her fifth shot, and he threw back his fifteenth. "A real man can drink three times what a woman can, never mind a high schooler." She checked her skirt, making sure it was convincingly crooked. Then she lied and said she wanted to continue the night under moonlight. He said he was too drunk to get up. She sweetened the deal with a pouty face and a promise to give him a lap dance outside. He was too drunk and perverted to question it—never mind be the first man in history to turn down a lap dance.

At 4:32 pm that Thursday, she arrived at his house for their "study session" with a bottle of vodka.

Wednesday afternoon, she told her parents she had a study date and went to Home Depot instead. But before that, she parked two blocks from his house, walked down his street casually, tiptoed around the neat hedges of his neighbor's house, climbed his fence, skulked between his perfect forsythias, and saw the tree. Before that, she told him she had thought about what he had said, and he was right. But moreover, she hadn't even threatened that. She was just shocked when he made his move. It wasn't a problem at all. And would he mind helping her with some physics at his house Thursday. He said, "That's tomorrow." She said ditzilly, "Oh, right, derrr," then, looking into his eyes, "So you wanna?"

The day before that, he brought her into his room again. She was shaking. He said if she ever told, no one would believe her, and her name would be in the papers for months. And plus, she had no evidence. She was silent.

The day before that, while she was asking for help on review question number 16 in chapter three, section four, he put his left hand on her lower back so she couldn't move, huskily whispered, "Say hi to your sister," then slipped his other hand up her skirt.

"Crime" Theme Contest Winner – 3rd Place

Fall 2015

Our Father, the Lost Geometer

Cal Freeman

Down near the creek, Euclid Avenue floods
with brown-green water. I rest my right hand
on his *Elements* and swear that my life
will always be this circumscribed and small,
              a rite that goes by many names,
among them allegiance, temperament, weather.
My sister wanders out in a fog of obtuse angles.
She wears a Gore-Tex slicker to bear
the heavy rain that's falling from the north.
                Cataracts echo in the culvert;
the submersible pump emits its steady hum.
Last August I watched the mud of the creek bed
            dry to shaved ridges of bone
from the west-facing doors of my mother's house.
These drastic riparian shifts drown
and erase the stories nobody wants told.
I keep referring to Euclid as our father.
I keep guessing where the edges of this life
fall off into ensoulment. In bisecting
          the city he made us who we are,
a terminal series of squares and birthing lines,
as if this town were the geometry of grief
              and we were blameless.

To Be Sung at Certain Funerals

_____

Cal Freeman

Black trusses of the drawbridge
gleam in river mist, that span

of iron work between Trenton and Grosse Ile.
My friend Brad Morris

drives his VW Rabbit forever
from the mainland to nowhere

listening to mix tapes and considering
the wild anachronies of heaven.

~

Radial tires of the procession
rumble over grates.

The Trenton Channel
swifts around the jetties

toward the big lake.

~

The family asked me to play guitar
and sing at the funeral. I hadn't spoken

to Brad in nearly ten years.
I felt like an impostor.

I wouldn't have wanted me there
if I were them. His father

was moved to tears,
explaining that I was a real friend

to Brad because I hadn't been
his friend during the bad times.

Some version of tough love,
some mess of grief and logic.

~

In the middle of the night,
in the floodlit shadow of a spire,
Brad pulls into a parking lot

and sees a deer's glowing eyes
in the shallow woods
behind the church. Votive candles

light the stain glass windows
of the atrium. He scrolls
the contacts in his phone,

looking for a high school
girlfriend's name, thinking he
has typed her in and she will

show up here, halated
like the dawn, to nurse him
from narcosis, that inveterate

track marks might sew themselves
of the needle's wake.

~

I picture him turning blue
after injection and the jaundiced woman
with the face tat and lip rings
shoving an ice cube
up him while dialing 911.

~

Each song is a vague guess
at its own meaning.

~

He is in in in
the many predicates
such as spirit, and night

predicated upon several
hours of naked daylight,
which leave us translucent

as gobies or saints,
finds all that inheres
and all that only seems

to disappear until somebody
breaks into sobs, or sings.

Piedmont

Stephanie Ellis Schlaifer

EF-4, Winter, 2011

From the Cumberland Plateau to the coastal plain,
the forest seems nothing but pines—
loblolly, longleaf, shortleaf, and slash,
nothing but overstory.
Silhouetted, tall clear trunks,
high-branched, rough-barked, and heavy-boughed—
everything at right angles.
No dogwoods or redbuds heralding beneath
as a portent in anaphora. And the comfort is in
the uprightness of the vegetation.
But the land half-cleared in Ringgold stands as proof
some things cannot be stopped by mountains,
and the stand becomes a cemetery in stumps and needles.
That the tornado would not hit has showed itself: a myth.
That the Confederate army would afterward prevail, mercifully untrue.
I cannot see the mountain without the breach,
but I cannot cede the mountain either.
The mountain foot leaves everything oblique,
and I am oblique to the land
that I can't live without.
A bright sky intensifies the color of the soil,
which isolates the red from iron,
where once the sea came in and out and in and vanished
as the fall line, as Lookout Mountain,
as Chickamauga, as something screaming.

Performance Art

Adam Clay

Like illumination, the light flatters our bodies
past the point of forgetting.

Remember how children careened
off their bikes into the void

of the avenue,

their skin holding back their bones,
despite the force of brick

upon the fragile human form?

The moment one goes from feeling
immortal to not feeling optimism

must be blurry,

I think, turning the nightstand lamp
off well before nine, imagining

the sleeping life blurring into the gestures
of the body, the way shaping the world

can shape our place within:

a lilac blooming before spring
and finding its way before its time.

The House Winter Built

John Sibley Williams

This is the gap
between houses
spiked by fences
where certain birds gather
into a crowded warm plural
while others—today it just happens
to be a blue jay—are as kindled by solitud

*

Standing here, divided by glass from a dawn
clouded as an early Polaroid, I count
two strands of footprints helixed for a while
ground down to one then to a faint red after-stain, everything
gradually erased by snow. In time

a becomes *the*, as in *a fawn used to eat*
the green from my lawn, as in *all the deer*
are gone now. I am haunted

*

by the space my body fills
and how little it matters
when my breath on the window
cools to winter.

If home is an invented place
why does it hurt so much
to leave?

*

There's a pool of bells in the distance.
The knitted spine of a sycamore naked
and gray. Above the fence a thin slice of sky.
Above the sky a single galaxy uncoiling into millions

of lights. Many of the birds are as silent as light
but today on the fence between us there's a blue jay
bold and alone, like someone I know I will lose
and still burn for.

Regret and Other Bodies

Marlys West

The electrocardiogram showed of one of the heart valves,
I don't know
which one and this is the longest set up for one tiny image
to the point where I have to question why I bring it up,
only let me be clear it's to point out my own loneliness
and face wet with tears,
which has nothing to do with the valve waving
itself like
a white branch. Each heart contraction starts with a little
tree perfectly still then fluttering madly.
A cartoon of a twig waving hard over blood then nothing.

Perfect, said the doctor. How do I look at my daughter when
she wants to go home and play without me? I look at her
with a face full of love and distraction. Is my phone ringing?

Everything I am now trying to play standard isn't working
but this is false, I already went over it with a dear friend

who says the time to question your life is never
seven days after someone looks at you and says he can't,
he just can't, it's
all so tiring. It's so bad his hair is falling out. Meaning me.
Meaning him. Meaning I ignored the signs
even as I dragged
my feet on other important things as all humans do.

Who gave us consciousness?
Enough of this, I have to shower and go to work and put
my children in the care of the nanny who is young and full
of promise. That ship has sailed, we said.
There are some opportunities
that never come again but are we not inhaling
the air as I write and you read? Are we not alive and able

to lift our heads even slightly? Where is hope, that sharp
fork that puts the sugar over everything like rain wets
earth telling every weed's seed and grass root to come up
because now all drought will be forgotten, never again
the long summers without someone watering and watering

but we know this isn't true. And yet we go on sprouting
and cutting our hair and wondering if this goes with that
does it go?
if the countertops should be granite or poured cement or if
tile is what we should be thinking, every new place in town
using the longer white tiles for now but you know it will wash

up on the beach in ten years, chips smooth and round as
teeth; the children picking them up and asking their mother
if they can keep it. She says put them in your pocket
and stop collecting everything, she says
there is sand in your hair
and everywhere;
lunch is gritty that took me an hour to pack up
and where is your father and why
am I picking apart every second and when she stands up

to dip her own body in the water every harsh word is nearly
forgotten because she is up, the mother, heading
for the breaking edge of the white water.

A miracle then, her body, and how she doesn't care
about the spit and spray,
cuts through all that pounding water with her arms and legs
she who brought us forth with equal parts love and shouting.

Louise Bourgeois to Her Husband, on Love and Her Father's Mistress

Katie Knoll

Robert, you might not remember but once, drunk,
you told me of your first time: you were twelve; it was brief.

Like houses collapsing under wind, and like you,
my young father gave too quickly. To my mother—

his house, a ring, my brothers, me. To me, his name, Louis.
Like a runt, Sadie came last, received little.

I'd like to say she got nothing, but there is the burning house
smell of her curling her hair at the bureau, laughing

when Father came from behind, cupped her eyes,
set before her a chocolate wrapped in gold foil.

Robert, we will have no daughters—I learned early on
how a house will give under too many girls.

Of my mother's death, the reports say *consumption*,
but it was a house that fell on her, and when it fell

she burst, and steam came, and burned my father,
and his Sadie, sweet governess, who taught us the words

on loan, and to fold a crane from foil left after chocolates
have been eaten. Robert, I can promise you only houses split

with guillotines, iron spiders who in my voice say your name,
and my stomach rounding to you, filling our house,

and also our sons, someday, with stitches from thrown rocks
and our love. *This is love*, we will say, showing them a flower

with two heads, x-rays after accidents: how broken bones
rebuild cells, coming always back to each other.

Persephone's Blues Song

Megan Grumbling

The blues, down there, got dark.
Slate-blue, bruised cobalt. Worse than the usual
solemnities, the chilled goblet and robe.
Nightshade and coal. Cold sentences
of *cannot*.

The blues leave blind spots.
Somewhere between the blue of need
and the blue of want, my eyes cease
to adjust. To abide my milk-blue cast
in the glass.

The blues send me above for a dose
of solace. Robin's egg and gold.
Summer freckles, honey and rose.
This town's ever warmer harbor
nearly green.

The blues beg bright things freed.
Larkspur in my brow, lemon
in my blonde. Inklings far too fair
and far too fleet to be kept
in the dark.

Persephone's Winter Feast Song

Megan Grumbling

I went such long winters in want
of pea shoot, corn furl. Now, I gorge.
Torpor, tumor. Pods and ears
by the trough.

Lately I long only to feast
on bowls of stones, spoons of light. I starve
for dark. For starving. Our revels now
are endless.

At picnics, I can taste dwarf lumps and cleft
tassels in the Xtra Sweet. Dopamine.
Cobalt and ultraviolet.
Split atoms

that shriveled and sugar-cured the seed.
My mother's meals turn shame into starch.
Each raw ear leaks a milk so sweet
it scours.

But Nothing's Fair after Love

Stevie Edwards

Because I was a bad finger to tie his ribbon to.
Because I was a bad sky
to look up at—
not ugly, but bad. Because I threw myself
into myself. Because I threw
the sky into a suitcase
I left in New York. Because I never learned
to drive myself. Because I needed
a guide out of the woods. Because I lost
my way, sat down in the middle of brambles
so high above my head but didn't say
come, didn't say *come get me*, not once.
Because he said *take care of yourself*
on the voicemail I deleted.
Because I thought that was taking care
of myself. Because I was cruel with honey,
lured in the ants to squash. I can't
resent them for coming.
I can't even step out of my bedroom without
ruining my shoes: I am the wrecking ball
and the closed factory. I am what swings.

Mr. Kimberk's Kindness

Gabe Herron

When I found Mr. Kimberk downstream, he was leaning against a Douglas fir that had fallen across the river. He was all wet down one side, smoking shag-tobacco, and eyeing the riffle on the other.

"My legs listen to me about as good as pond turtles once my feet get cold," he said. "What happened to your chin?"

"It was a black hawthorn, I think." I'd run chin first into a thorn when stumbling off a log. I'd forgotten about it—let the blood drip dry.

"They'll do that," he said.

I opened my creel with my free hand—two brook trout uncoiled on watergrass. He asked me where I'd caught them. I told him. He gazed at the tip of his cigarette as if he could see the exact place I'd taken them from—a curling wisp of smoke turning into a spumescent waterfall. He didn't tell me about how he'd gotten half-wet.

I didn't ask.

"I found this." I held out the bone.

"I see that."

"Can you say what it's from?"

"Well, where'd you find it?" He scrunched his cheek up against his eye and scratched the side of his neck.

"Stuck in a sandbank below the logjam."

Mr. Kimberk thought about that. You could use his mouth as a level most days, but today he pulled down on his chin and forced a smile." Mind if I have a look?"

"No, sir." I handed him the bone.

He held it away from himself to let his eyes work over it. "Below the logjam?"

"Yes, sir."

"Could you show me?"

I was happy to have found something of interest to him. Mr. Kimberk's spent his whole life up here, except for when he was in France and Germany, so it's hard work showing him a thing he hasn't seen before.

He followed me upstream, his eyes on the streambed, moving as his age allowed. I showed him the sandbar I'd plucked it from, but he could tell that much for himself. My meandering tracks leading to a little hole in the earth where they'd deepened due to my pulling efforts.

"Here's where," I pointed.

"I see that." He nodded—looked around himself, and then upstream to the tangle of logs, "You think you could help me up in there?"

"Yes, sir."

I think that's about the only time I'd heard him ask for help. He hadn't even asked for help the day I found him pinned upside down under his quad machine. I think he asked me where his hat was. But I knew enough not to spend time looking for it. He told me to stay away—he was hurt bad—just get the hell away from him. Then he asked for a drink off my grape soda. Then he spat it out and screamed at me—a curse. Anyhow, he doesn't remember any of that, and I don't remind him either. It was just luck I'd found him out there at all—trespassing as I was on his land, hoping to find some morels to cheer my mother with. She'd fry them in butter, sometimes with breadcrumbs and parmesan cheese.

After that, Mr. Kimberk and I got to be friends.

"What do you think it is?" I asked.

"Can't say, not exactly . . . on second thought, I can make it on my own."

I watched him work his way around a boulder. He crossed over to the clay flat on the other side, where the water is shallow and slow in the summer, and then back over to the logjam. He moved in and out of the sunlight, green leaves glowing above his head, shadows scrolling down his back—gossamer and bugs floating through streaks of light. No one had ever been so kind to me as Mr. Kimberk. I vowed that if his own didn't move back to care for him once he got too old to cut his own meat, then I'd do that much for him myself.

It took him a long time to reach the parts of the logjam that interested him. He spent a longer time poking around up there. I got distracted by a school of minnows that didn't seem too bothered by my standing in their living room. He was halfway back to me before I looked up again. His face was leaden, so that I thought he'd caught a chill.

He was moving careful as he walked down with the current.

"What'd you find?" I asked.

"Can't say." He looked at my hand, reached out with his own. "Let's tuck that back where you found it, son. I'm awful tired today."

I was so pleased that he'd called me son, I couldn't think beyond it. There was lots of stuff I'd have liked to ask, but my dad had me in good trim as far as not asking many questions. It was my habit to spend a long time puzzling a thing out for myself before I'd dare ask a question. That didn't much work to my advantage in school, or hell, anywhere else for that matter.

I followed Mr. Kimberk down water until we got to the path that leads to North Mill Road. We could walk back to his place from there. He didn't say much. He laid his hand solid across my shoulder. He'd never done that before.

"You're a real good boy, Peter Green." he said. "Don't let no one tell you different."

I felt I might float out of my squeaking sneakers with his unexpected praise. I may have too, if not for the heavy of his hand holding me to the earth.

~

He kept the dogs off me while I cleaned my trout next to his garden.

"You staying for supper?" he asked.

It was strange to be asked. I ate supper with him about every weekday. He'd stopped having to invite me a year ago.

"If it's all right?" I smiled down at a row of mounded potatoes.

He smiled too, "Always enough for one more."

It wasn't just the he fed me dinners most nights, but he fed me good dinners: beef and corn, trout and baked potatoes, soda biscuits with thick gravy from pan drippings, pork he'd traded for beef, beef he'd traded for chicken, chicken he'd traded for venison, venison he'd had made into sausage by trading the butcher for butter, all of it served with baby carrots and peas in the spring, or parsnips, turnips, and other roots in the winter. The kind of dinners that could stand you through to the next, if you didn't run across breakfast or lunch along your way.

"I was thinking you might stay over the night. You could take that old army cot, go and sleep under the stars by the pond, or up in the hayloft. It's good sleeping up there summers—stay up late and watch TV if you want. Hell, I don't care."

"I'd have to ask."

"Of course, after dinner then. Run and get me a pint a green beans outta the cellar. I've got bacon we can fry these fish with."

"Yes, sir." And I did run when he asked me to fetch a thing. He'd tell other grown men I could out work them. I'd believe it too. What a fine way of praising a boy while insinuating the laziness of a man.

He was on the phone when I got back, and stayed on it a long time after, longer then I'd ever seen him talk on it before—even to his own daughters.

We sat down to supper.

It wasn't long before there was a knock on the door. It was Sheriff Quick. Mr. Kimberk put on his barn coat and opened the aluminum screen door. Sheriff Quick nodded towards me. I nodded back. I knew him from answering about a million of his damn questions about my mother after she left us without a forwarding address. I wasn't sure how to feel about him now, but more and more, I was starting to think he was better than all the things my dad had to say about him. Mr. Kimberk seemed to think he was okay, and there had to be some good to him for that, because Mr. Kimberk wouldn't like a person for no reason. In fact, lots of days went by where he didn't like anything at all, not unless it was absolutely necessary.

Coffee was offered and refused.

They stepped outside.

I decided I'd stay up in the hayloft that night. I knew Mr. Kimberk didn't think much of the television, other than for watching baseball, and there wasn't any baseball on, so I wasn't going to stay up late watching TV. I could do that at home. I didn't much want to stay alone out by the pond either, with animals coming in for water all night, although I'd never admit such a thing to Mr. Kimberk.

The hayloft was almost empty—awaiting this year's hay crop. I followed Mr. Kimberk up a ladder that was a little loose all over at once, as a good homespun ladder should be after too many years of service. He swept a bare spot on the floor with his boot; dust rose to the evening light. He stretched out the army cot, and opened the loft doors, so that I could get a good look at the evening sky. It smelled like a hay barn does, but less so after the doors swung open. A summer breeze blew through, going real gentle, carrying the good sweet evening air in on it.

"I forgot to call my dad," I said.

"I called over. He said it's fine." This was mostly pretense, because we both knew my dad didn't give two-shits where I slept or ate, so long as it didn't get in the way of whatever he was doing next. Mr. Kimberk started down the ladder, and then clamored back up. "Almost forgot." He reached into his barn coat and pulled out two Payday candy bars.

My favorite.

"Thank you."

"You need anything else—you come on inside. You won't wake me 'cause I don't hardly sleep." There were sirens coming up the valley from the junction road. "You're a good boy, Pete. I wished my own had turned out as good as you."

I didn't know what to do with such praise but turn my face red with it. I'd always suspected he liked me all right, buying me my first fishing pole back when he'd discovered no one had bothered taking me fishing—things like that, but he'd never said so much aloud before.

"Sleep good." He clicked down on the dusty cotton string hanging from the only light bulb. The sounds of his descent into the darkness. I clicked on the flashlight he'd set atop an apple crate. I turned it back off so my eyes could get used to the night. I heard him opening and closing the side door—the sounds of his dogs following, the closing of a screen door. I stretched out across the top of the sleeping bag. It smelled like a pillowcase that had been stored in a cool dry place for a long long time. The warm evening breeze made it so comfortable up in the hayloft, I almost fell to sleep without eating my candy bars; the sweet grass and tree pollen mixed together, crickets calling, frogs croaking, a view of the stars above the ragged blue ridge behind the tawny fields—deep-space stars so dim you can't hardly see them at all.

I used my thumbnail to cut into the candy bar wrapper at the notch. I pealed it back as softly as possible; took a bite—chewing, holding on to all that perfect salty sweetness as best as I could—knowing how good it all was made it even better.

I rustled around.

The cot squeaked.

I felt good under the weight of my own tired muscles.

Mr. Kimberk brought this cot back home after the war, wood and heavy cotton duck, better than the bed I slept on at home: a blow up mattress with a slow leak, so that I'd have to wake up nights and blow into it if I didn't want to awaken on the hardwood, which I did most mornings, minding the hardness less than the effort of inflation. I ate the candy bar as long as I could and decided to save the other. I fell off to sleep better at nights if I knew there was something good about the coming day, something certain, something that can't be taken away like a promise. I heard more sirens coming up from town and wondered what they were about.

I fell off to sleep.

That night they surrounded our place and hauled my father off for the final time. Of course, there was a whole bunch of stuff about it in the papers. I didn't read the papers. It would take me most of that summer to get the rest figured out for myself. There are some things people simply will not tell you to your face—even people paid for telling others the worst—things like: who it was hung up in that logjam, and whose femur it was I'd held in my very own hand, not recognizing it for what it was.

Mercifully, that kind of knowledge moved into me slowly, so that I had time to forget the true size and shape of it, to where I couldn't perfectly remember its waterlogged heft, or how it had darkened to green at the one end, and become tobacco stained in the middle—the slickness of the ball on its end. It was the kind of knowledge that did not move swiftly at first, but came on slow, like an afternoon thunderstorm from a long ways off. How you make good plans to find yourself some shelter, a big fir a few bends upriver, a rock overhang in a quarry about a quarter-mile off. You believe you've timed the storm's arrival with your own, but somehow it always moves a little faster than you'd expected, so that you're caught out in it, and just a little surprised by it every time.

Last Song

Annie Reid

Something rolled in the trunk as Leonard pulled the Mustang onto the gravel shoulder, knocked heavy against the back seats; a deft, quick thud. An elbow, perhaps, a knee. The police car pulled in right behind him, close, the flashing lights hammering the twilight. He closed his eyes, but those lights did not stop penetrating, sinking through the thin skin to his sight. Like salt in the membranes.

Hindsight being 20/20, it was a poor time to consider that he really ought to have tied the body up with some rope, might have at least weighed it down so it wouldn't roll around, knocking into the tire iron, the briefcase, the steel lunch box, making so much noise. And of course there was the faint possibility—despite all that had occurred back at the little cottage over on Elm Street, despite the length and vigour of the discussion, despite its energetic conclusion— that Sprocket was still alive. Stranger things have happened in this wide world; far stranger things do indeed happen each and every day, and so it will continue, long after we are all good and gone.

The cop got out of his car. Leonard chose not to accelerate away, spitting up a haze of stones into the man himself, nor did he throw the car into reverse to crush the officer of the law between the two vehicles, although each of these options played out clearly and without pitfalls in his mind. Leonard regretted the lack of initiative his mother had ceaselessly warned him about over the many lukewarm dinners they had shared together, waiting for his father, watching the meat cool, salivating while a thin skin formed over the open skull of the gravy boat. But it had already been a long and ugly day, and he wanted things to go easy. He wanted to go home, have a cold beer, and put his feet up. And the gun was still within reach, underneath a tweed jacket on the front seat of the car, a tiny blue ukulele sitting atop them, comical and obtrusive as a groomed lap dog.

The cop eased up slowly, like they do, checking out the car, assessing the man at the wheel, rendering judgement. Leonard knew himself, and he knew himself to be a bad man, but he was a bad man with a clean driving record. The Mustang was twenty-three years old, and didn't even have a dent.

Leonard rolled down the window. The cop was nearly there when there was another thud from the trunk, louder. Sprocket was definitely alive. Leonard had been sloppy; he saw that now, full of reprimands for the person he had been an hour ago. Leonard put this down to his own sentimentality, his own lack of conviction. He had once liked Sprocket, and had not wanted this job. He had specifically requested a pass on the assignment, despite the needs of the organization and Sprocket's own poor life choices. But the boss was unyielding, and now Leonard was here at the side of a lonely highway at sundown, a live man in his trunk and another one at his window, the fate of many lives hanging in the balance. Given the current, sad condition of Sprocket's face, it was unlikely that he could speak, but there are other ways of making noise. There is always a way.

"Sir," said the cop. He wore mirrored aviator sunglasses despite the hour of the day, and a wide-brimmed hat that resembled an airliner settling in for a landing on his skull.

"Officer," Leonard said.

"Do you have any idea how fast you were going?"

"Oh, at least ninety," said Leonard. "Regrettably."

The cop said nothing, his chin sharply outlining the quieting blue sky above them. Leonard noted not a trace of stubble.

"Possibly ninety-two," Leonard said. "Distracted. Absolutely my fault." Honesty might get a man a bit of leniency. And he was unfocused, just as his mother had always said. He was thinking about Ellen all those years ago, about the ukulele. But a man cannot afford a distraction if he wants to do quality work; a man must be nothing if not consistent.

"Ninety-five," said the cop. "Is what you were doing. Are you aware, sir, that the limit on this road is sixty?"

"There is no excuse for my behaviour," Leonard said. If Sprocket were conscious, he must surely have heard the sirens, the distant murmur of the dispatcher on the radio back in the cruiser, static breaking through the crisp fall air like a failing heartbeat.

"License," the cop said. "Registration." And there it was. The faintest tap.

The cop heard it too. He froze, like a lion that has heard the faint, fearful shift of prey in the bush, the merest quiver of the blade of grass in the windless savannah. A good cop has good instincts.

Leonard began to tap his feet.

"Nervous?" The cop paused, smiling with delight at Leonard's failure to answer. "Anything else you want to tell me?"

Leonard held his breath. He waited for another tap, a thump, a knock, the faint whimper, for Sprocket to sing one last song to finish the both of them. It would be all over in just a minute now. All these years he'd never gotten to the inside of a penitentiary, all these years he'd been cheating the law, playing just a little bit close to the open flame. Perhaps it would be a relief. At least there'd be three squares a day, and he'd never have to do something like he did this afternoon again, not to an old friend.

Leonard looked over at the ukulele, the gun sitting just underneath the jacket it rested upon. So many things could happen, just now. The squeeze of the cold metal in his hand, going all hot as everything burst around him, a thousand miles of highway until the border and one long night ahead. All the quantum possibilities of the universe seemed poised to occur, spread out like the bellows of an accordion just before the big squeeze.

"Got a song in my head," Leonard said. "One I was making up. Trying to get a feel for the tune before I forget. Reminded me of a woman. I lost track of things. You know how it is."

"You're talking like a man I should be giving a sobriety test to," said the cop.

"Oh, I'm sober, officer." It was true that he and Sprocket had enjoyed a last glass of scotch together before getting down to business, but in practical terms Leonard was not drunk.

"Oh, are you now?" The cop leaned in the window, surveyed the back seat, and took a theatrical sniff. His eyes stopped at the ukulele.

"Maybe you can play me a little something if that's the case," said the cop, smiling, and not without a bit of pleasure, in Leonard's estimation.

Looking back, Leonard was not really certain what had provoked him into returning to the dark cottage to retrieve the ukulele from the tumble of furniture on Sprocket's floor. Leonard hadn't played in years, not since Ellen. This one was blue, had been tucked away on a bookshelf that held no books, dusty with age and neglect, an impulse buy of the past, someone else's quaint regret.

Leonard himself had smashed his own ukulele shortly after Ellen had blown her nose into the white linen napkins he'd purchased just for the occasion, that dark evening in October she'd returned his engagement ring, twenty-three years earlier. It scared her, the way he broke it to pieces, this thing he loved and she loved too, and she had fled the house, tears shining on her face like she'd been stuck in a heavy rain. She did not return. He had learned to play, years earlier, because she liked the sound of it, sweet and sad both at once, like a woman laughing even as she was crying. He had not played a note since Ellen had left him.

Ellen had disapproved of his work, asked him to reconsider the future, find another occupation. Piano tuner, she suggested, baker, handyman – an honest trade can be learned, she said. It doesn't matter about the past.

Unless you get off the road, you'll arrive exactly where you are going, she always said to him, in the mornings when she would walk around the kitchen, her robe hanging open, just a bit, just enough to tease. He would shrug, pour another cup of coffee for the long day ahead, admire her long neck that always made her look so good in pictures. What she said didn't sound so bad.

But it made him sad, how inadequately she understood him. He would hold out his meaty hands to her, showing her their lack of delicacy by the very way in which they moved, never mind the thick and awkward fingers, their muteness in the presence of all but the loudest blows, the music they could only make when clenched into fists. That was his only gift. An ugly one, but the only one. She shook her head, suggested the integrity of a simple and honest calling. A musician then, she said, looking at the ukulele. You don't know how good you are.

Now he smiled up at the cop. Twenty-three years he hadn't played, not for anyone but Ellen. Leonard picked up the ukulele, strummed it, adjusted a few strings.

A musician, he had scoffed at Ellen that night twenty-three years ago. I'm a thug, he'd told her. A high school dropout. I'm lucky you even looked at me twice. But the organization. We'll take care of you, he told her. They take care of me. Of us.

She shook her head. All you have to do, Leo, is start over.

The policeman put his hand on the driver's door, leaned his weight against the car, waiting. Leonard smiled, gave a nod, put his head down. He strummed. He fumbled the first few notes. Puffs of dust rose like the tiny ghosts of his own doughy fingers from each string he plucked. The policeman's smile under his mirrored eyes became thin and tight.

Leonard's index finger dropped and the others followed the instinct into a chord, sad and sweet—a beloved piece of rare glass breaking, then miraculously becoming whole again. Leonard closed his eyes. He felt the shift of the car as the policeman took his hands off the driver's window and stepped back. Giving him room, giving the music space. Leonard played, a song he didn't remember knowing, but each note came to him like a distant memory sparking to life, the way a smell in a stranger's kitchen could remind you of one moment from a summer night in your childhood long away.

The tips of his calloused fingers stung from the sweet pressure of the strings, the hollow curve of the box nestled against his ribs, beating. The cop was silent, Sprocket motionless in the trunk, dying. Each note drifting for a moment through the air, heard, then unforming itself again, waves and matter untangling as though never present at all.

Finally Leonard stopped playing, remembered where he was and who was present, all of them. He opened his eyes, the light too bright, even though it was nearly dark, his face frozen.

"Damn," said the cop.

Leonard forced himself to smile, and reached out to take back the license and registration the policeman was handing back to him.

"You're a talented man," said the cop. "Might want to keep your speed down in the future." The cop kicked the front tire of the Mustang.

"Sounds like she needs a tune up," he said. "Have a nice day."

The policeman finally took off his glasses. It was night now, and the man was older than Leonard had thought he was a few minutes earlier, now that he could see the lines around his eyes. He walked back to his patrol car and got in. The patrol car peeled off the gravel with an urgent moan.

Leonard sat there for a few minutes, the ukulele cradled in his arms, watching the cruiser grow smaller in the distance. The blue and ruby lights flared up as it reached the horizon. Emergencies were everywhere; they could not be avoided.

There was a shift in the trunk—quieter, calmer, as though the song had been a comfort, even though they were both bad men, the two of them. Even then there could be comfort. Leonard knew he should turn the key in the ignition, to get back on the road and drive away, but he found that he could only sit as the night deepened and think of Sprocket, trapped in the heat and the dark of the trunk, too wounded even for rescue to amount to anything.

Ways to Mourn an Asshole

Venita Blackburn

Once is not enough. Believe in Santa and Jesus and Clark and Bruce but only 'til daylight. Remember not to be a child. Pretend to be ill. Wear black slacks. Pray. Cut your hair without a mirror. Buy a casket. Use the casket. Invite all of the friends. Invite no one at all. Bury the empty casket. Collect the ashes. Hold the ashes. Kick the ashes with your heel. Be glad the plastic did not break. Put the ashes away for later. Play basketball. Write an obituary. Remember not to be small. Go hunting. Go mountain climbing. Remember to be very strong. Look at your muscles. Touch your abs. Remember to be proud. Take out the death certificates. Make copies of the death certificates. Draw penises on the back of the copies. Draw faces on the penises. Put the originals away for the insurance company. Open the ashes. Smell the ashes. Cough. Feel a little sick, and shake it off. Put the ashes in glass containers. Pretend they are Canopic jars. Pretend to be a pharaoh. Pretend these are the organs of ancestors. Pretend to come from greatness. Remember not to be afraid. Put one jar outside for the rain. Kill ants outside with an index finger while the rain falls. Remember to be big. Go inside. Open the plastic bag from the hospital full of clothes. Take out the wallet. Pocket a hundred and sixty eight dollars. Look at the driver's license. Pull out the belt. Wear the belt. Remember to get fat enough to fit the belt. Collect the jar of wet ashes. Drop the license inside. Take the license out and wipe it off. Put the jar of ashes and rain in the freezer. Take it out of the freezer the next day. Sit it out on the fence. Find your hunting rifle. Fire one shot. Miss. Fire again. Don't miss. Remember not to care. Remember there are other jars left.

Big-Headed Anna at the Ice Cream Social

Stephanie Dickinson

1911. Basswood leaves powdered with dust overhang the courting couples and the table of sweet ices. Farm girls fragrant as peonies in their white mutton-leg-sleeves stroll the country church lawn. In stiff collars and middle-parted hair, the farm boys pitch horseshoes. I wear an apron and my wide-brimmed hat. Between scooping, my hands splash in the wash bowl. The ice cream I helped churn with rock salt breathes its cold kisses into the July heat. I know the seed swells inside me. I hum to myself as I pare the apricots thin and chop the ice fine. The horses unharnessed from the ice wagon graze the blue grass that thickens next to the creek. Couples share the stereoscope and view picture cards of faraway places. They spoon ice cream perfumed with orange blossom into each other's mouths, they touch breath as they sort the picture cards. Snap snap goes the fingers of the pastor's wife. *Big-Headed Anna, fetch more ice, then more churning. Anna, we need the wooden crate brought from the water.* I kneel next to the creek, fishing for the cream crate. A waggle of boys follows me. They skip stones at the tree stump in the stream's middle that raises its half-drowned massive head, as if a dog lifting its moss-painted muzzle and snout. *That's you, Big-Headed Anna.* I press cold palms to my flushed face. They see my belly, but will not believe. *Who would do that?* I wasn't expected to take in the air of this world long, I was left to expire beside my dying mother, and now I carry life inside me. I will name my child after the giant trees that rain insects onto the water, so he or she does not forget the budding and singing in tree-time and insect generations, its chitter and scat. He won't be born in an overcast of sadness, a dead mother in its thickness, and the deeper his childhood rows him, he'll find no weeping. I listen to my heart beating its small river of footsteps. I hug my stomach and wonder if my son, safe in womb-water, will like the color red, the bleed of cherries and mulberries, or will it be green my baby loves, the forest world of frogs and grass. I'll name him so that he will be ever thankful to life, which comes from the giver. If God walks on this earth, He is water.

Big-Headed Anna Gives Birth in a Pasture

Stephanie Dickinson

1911. I still bleed where you came at the beginning of fall and broke from me like innards from a chicken, there in the pasture grass among the green walnuts and water trough, with no doctor looking on, only a grazing horse crunching a wormy apple. No one besides you, my son, my little seed, believed. *Big-Headed Anna has swallowed a wind baby. Her belly is all in her mind.* My scowling great-aunt thought me asleep when there were chores still to be done. There I lay in the glary sun and you on my belly, the cord between us yet to be severed. A leaf sound seeped from you and it looked as if you were trying to climb with ten toes. I wondered if your bright eyes were watching the ladybug crawl up the grass blade, which grew next to us. Where did she think she was climbing to so frantically and fast with her fat little body? Was she the same ladybug who clung to me as a wee one? I rocked you ever gently, so you would feel safe in my arms. Little seed, I carried you to my breast, putting your jelly mouth there. At first your lips didn't take suckle, and then they did. How beautiful you were! You'd seen me from inside a thousand times, mornings, afternoons, nights. Now you saw my outside and I was frightened. Would you one day feel shame at the sight of me? Once I understood you were coming, my feet and ankles figured it out too—swollen like civet cats, and my toes, lumps of dough. I threw up and couldn't stop hungering for bacon drippings on sop bread. I touched hands to my belly, searching for you. When I felt a kick, I danced. A dark tree bloomed, dazzling flowers. My heart floated big and soft like a cloud of hyacinth petals. Now I rub the reddish-gold hairs on your head that feel like corn silk only softer, much finer. I tell you stories of the world when fish were birds that flew in the water and trees were the tiny children of the long grasses. I patty cake your hands that are warm as hot red peppers. My nostrils inhale the perfume of you. A white fragrance. You'll never hear how a cow kicked your pregnant grandmother in the stomach, I'll never tell you how she died in childbirth from my head large as a calf's trying to live. My father could not abide me. Not an hour old and I was already a murderer. Look at that dragonfly so suddenly huge.

Caedra

Zana Previti

I own a photograph of a road in the Tagab District, in Kapisa Province, in Afghanistan. It is not a good photograph. It is a very brown photograph. I imagine the person who took the photo—a man—and he is very hot, sweating so much that he is wet inside his boots and pants, and he is taking the photograph because someone—a woman, with a gap between her front teeth—tells him, "You must take a photograph of this road," and he is annoyed because it is sweltering and there is nothing spectacular about this road, and it is ugly, actually, and he snaps pictures, one after the other, of the soft crumbling shoulder, the brown stones, the blowing sand. What an ugly place. Huge. Huge and ugly. It was not worth it.

~

I met the actress Blane Kronborg, for the first time, four years ago. The meeting, at her request, was held at a restaurant bar in Laguna Beach. It was a Wednesday morning. The place was called Fin and when I sat down she asked, "What do you think they mean? Like a fish? Or the *end*?"

"Both?" I said.

"Ah," she said, and I did not know if she meant she liked ambiguity or did not like it, or if she had any opinion on ambiguity at all. She smiled at me. Her teeth were false and perfect—no gaps, no chips, not a single flaw. She said her name. I said mine, and we shook hands. Blane explained, very efficiently and deftly stepping around the obvious emotional mines, that she had taken a film role—the role of a recently bereaved twin sister —and she thought that I could help her.

"Okay," I said. I looked around the bar. She had chosen a desolate time of day. It was eleven in the morning. Some of the chairs were still hiked up on the tables, and the lone bartender, a thick blonde block, leaned her elbows on the bar and watched us. Blane Kronborg was absurdly beautiful. Her skin . . . her complexion was too duskily perfect, too unearthly and glowing, to be in a bar, to be in a bar at eleven in the morning, to be sitting next to someone like me.

Blane sipped a martini. I drank orange juice. We admired the surfers who dotted the waves outside the window. Outside, the dishwashers and busboys, in long white aprons, smoked in the parking lot. When Blane spoke, I had trouble listening, and really understanding, because her voice sounded just like *her*—just like her movies, the ones I had paid money to go to see on the nights they opened. I owned two of her films on DVD, the one about the submarine and the one where she plays Marie Curie.

"What do you want?" I asked. "Not to sound rude. But what can I do to help you? I don't know anything about movies."

Blane rubbed her thumb and the tip of her forefinger together. No more than a few interviews, she told me. No more than ten hours, all together. Arranged around my schedule, she promised, and she would be happy to have a car come and pick me up from my home or my work. Her assistant would call later that day to arrange everything.

"Okay," I said. "That's fine with me. But I took my lunch a little early, so—"

"Of course." Blane Kronborg stood up and for a moment I did not know how to operate my legs or voice. There was a machine inside of her, one that calculated my qualities like an avenging robot from a science fiction film. It was the machine that had made her into such an good actress, probably. Blane Kronborg could take what she needed from my inventory of skill and emotion and biography and create art from it. It is a rare thing, to see your own worth in the eyes of a genius, and to see it amount to so little, so quickly.

She smiled and shook my hand and left before I had come down from my barstool.

~

Caedra disappeared in Afghanistan in 2007. I stopped working for a little while. I became a staple on television news programs. But when the news cycle tired of her, I found that I had nothing to do, and so I began to eat. I ate studiously and seriously. Within a year, I had gained almost a hundred pounds and my doctor told me that I was killing myself.

Three years later, I felt very tired, and one day I looked in my bathroom mirror and could no longer see a face that I loved. With all the fury and coldness with which I had put in on, I set about taking off the weight. When I lost the weight, I took a position as a weight management counselor at a Costa Mesa health clinic. I still work at the same clinic, though in a different role, and look after many of the same people who came to me in those days. I am not slim, now, but I am recognizable to the people who knew us in our youth.

~

Around this time, when I was meeting with Blane Kronborg, the clinic was very busy. I had begun seeing teenagers in group sessions, and one of my bosses had just had a baby so we were coping without her and without a replacement. I had begun taking classes, at night, toward my master's degree. Once a week I saw my mother, and we went to church and to T.J. Maxx and we steamed chicken and vegetables for our dinner. Sometimes, on a Friday night, a friend from the clinic and I would go salsa dancing at a small nightclub near the beach. We gossiped and danced and sometimes invented a romance. I did some online dating but nothing came of it, and soon I decided that it was not worth the anxiety, so I canceled my subscription and spent the money on an elliptical machine for my living room and did not regret it.

~

I have a terrible memory. Once, I slipped and fell down the few concrete steps leading to the door of our duplex, and my mother, having seen me fall, asked me why I ran so wildly out the door. I had lived in that duplex my whole life, all nine years of it to that day. I could only respond that I had forgotten the concrete steps and ran so wildly because, in my mind, they were not there. My sister laughed and laughed.

My twin sister is Caedra Margolis, the journalist who went missing, along with a British photographer and their interpreter, during a trip to Afghanistan in 2007. She is the elder by seven minutes. When we were young, she lurked in the backgrounds of things: birthday parties, in the corner with a new toy, in the den—not on the sofa with me, watching television—but on the floor, leaning against the heating vent, half-obscured by our cat sleeping in her lap, photographs in which she is only an arm or a shadow. In photographs, now as then, I look surprised and out of place. I am always caught moving, my mouth open and my eyes dull, swimming to the point I ought to be. And when I look at these photographs, I can hear Caedra, laughing laughing and laughing, off-stage. We slept in the same bed until we were ten.

~

Blane Kronborg's agent offered me a great deal of money in exchange for a series of six conversations over the course of the next six weeks and so, the following Tuesday night, I met Blane at a hotel in Los Angeles.

"Look," said Blane, "here is the crisis."

She spoke like that: "here is the crisis." Her voice, when she was not acting, was low and monotone. And she rarely used the muscles of her face. I never even saw her raise her eyebrows. I felt as though she was saving up all her emotions for when she needed them, the way that singers sometimes speak in whispers on the day before a big performance. Except that Blane did not do this for one day. It seemed like she did this forever. I remember thinking that it must be a very carefully housed life, Blane Kronborg's life.

"This is a small little film," said Blane. "But I want to do it well and, of course, I think I'd do a better job if I could understand a little bit more about the relationship between twins. Twin sisters."

"What is the movie about?" I asked.

"Me. I play a woman—about your age, a little younger—and my twin sister overdoses on heroin and dies. And then the crisis is that her sister is dead. So she's in mourning. And the movie takes place in the weekend she goes to her sister's house, to clean it out."

"No one else could have done that? No one else?"

"No. The sister who is dead lived alone. I—my character—lives with her husband and two small children."

"I do not have a husband or children."

"Good for you. I mean it. Keep it that way."

"Do you have a family?"

"Could you, do you think, clean out your sister's house if she were to die?"

I nodded. She had decided to speak as if Caedra was still alive.

"Why do you say that so readily? You have absolutely no doubt? Wouldn't it be painful for you?"

"I have already done it. Caedra had a small apartment. My mother and I did it together."

Blane nodded and made a note in her little book. "Can you name some of the things in the apartment that made you especially emotional?"

"She had left a hamper full of dirty laundry." Blane had perfect skin. Perfect olive skin, smooth as cake batter.

"How did you feel about that?"

"I thought . . . my mother wouldn't have liked seeing that Caedra hadn't done her laundry before she left. Stupid. I knew she wouldn't be mad, but I still wanted to do it . . . do the laundry."

"Did you do the laundry?"

"No."

"Did you feel closer to your mother during that time?"

"I have always been close to my mother."

"Do you feel that your sister is the same person as you?"

"Of course not."

"But?"

"This is not possible to understand unless you have a twin, I think."

"You *do* feel that your sister is the same person as you."

"We are very different. Caedra was very strong and very bold. I am not that way."

Blane smiled at me and said that she, too, was very different than who she was. I suppose I should have given her more credit. She might have understood something I could not say or even coherently feel. She was a very good actor.

The film, Blane went on to explain, is about how, as her character is cleaning out the sister's apartment, she finds evidence of a wholly different life than the one she thought her sister had been living. And she becomes obsessed with finding out who her sister really was. Did I think I really knew who my sister was?

~

Six years ago, some teeth and part of a jawbone, later identified to be those of the British photographer who had accompanied Caedra to Afghanistan, were found off a road in Tagab District, in Kapisa Province. His name was Tallent Oakes, and he had no brothers or sisters. His camera was eventually found and purchased in a stall market by a German tourist.

~

Blane received a telephone call from her child's father, a man called Michael. He had been called out of town unexpectedly, and so Blane would have her son for a few days. She became happy and sent me away with many thanks and a box of very expensive chocolates, and I did not see her for more than a week. I had to throw away the chocolates after I had eaten one, a caramel. Food is a razor in my palm, some days.

~

It was a full two weeks before I saw Blane Kronborg again. In that time I went to work, saw my mother, wrote a paper for my management class, and watched television. My favorite show was one that focused on a small team of crime investigators who flew around the country and worked together to solve horrifying murders. There was an interesting balance on the show, I thought, between the gruesome slaughters and massacres that the camera loved and the tight-knit camaraderie of the detectives. They often referred to their little group as a family, and the episodes always ended with a shot of two or more of them together, smiling or even embracing. The show's producers meant, I suppose, to temper the blood-lust of their audience with an element of wholesome community, so that it could be argued that the program centered on the triumph of the human spirit over darkness. I watched the program every day. I watched an episode every weeknight at seven o'clock as I ate my dinner.

~

When Blane called again, she invited me to her home in Calabasas. A fat white woman wearing green running sneakers walked me through a cavernous and cool house, and we came outside again into Blane Kronborg's backyard. Around the periphery stood a cheerful militia of citrus trees—grapefruits and lemons and oranges—and ensconced in the green lawn was a small clear pond, swarming with golden fish. A trickle of water gurgled down a pyramid of stones. Blane sat by the pond, in one of two sturdy Adirondack chairs, in a yellow bathing suit, drinking ginger ale from a can.

"Hello," I said. "Sorry. I got a little lost."

"Where do you live? I should have sent a car."

"No, no. It's fine. I live in Costa Mesa."

"My god," Blane said. "I knew that, and forgot. I'll send a car next time. You'll be on the 5 forever, going home. What do you take? The 5? The 405?"

I did not like talking about roads. I said I would decide later, and that it was not a big deal, anyway, but that we should get started so that I did not waste any of her time. Blane stood up in her bathing suit, and though her body was beautiful, I felt concern for her. I am not sure why. She was very thin, of course. With some effort, she pulled the second chair into the shade of an orange tree and I sat down in it. There was a small table between us, and on this sat Blane's little notebook and pen.

"I want to talk about some experiences you had growing up," said Blane. She pulled a loose white t-shirt over her head, and then she pulled her hair out from the collar. "Some things that I could perhaps find similar experiences to in my own life. I really would like to understand your feelings and the complexities of the relationship between you and your sister."

"Caedra," I said.

"Exactly. Do you remember a time when you were angry with her?"

"Loads," I said. I thought, *this is why her films are so successful.* I would watch this woman do anything. Wash dishes. Cut her toenails. Count grains of sand.

"Really, really angry. Terribly angry. A time when you may have said, 'I hate you,' or 'I want to kill you.'"

The fat woman came outside and handed me a cold glass of orange juice. I thanked the woman but she did not look at me.

"When Caedra first went missing and we got the news, we were watching television. We learned from the television. I was with my mother. I was very angry with Caedra. That she had decided to go to such a dangerous place. She should have known what would happen. She was stupid. And she ruined my life because she was stupid. She had broken my mother's heart."

Blane looked at me. I could see her swallow. She was wearing sunglasses, but she took them off and immediately shielded her eyes with her palm.

"What about," she asked evenly, "when you were kids?"

I sipped my orange juice. It was very good. Someone had spent the time to squeeze oranges, and I guessed that the oranges came from these trees.

"This is good," I said. "Thank you."

Blane smiled. Caedra had a large gap between her front teeth. I have this gap, as well.

"We got angry lots of times," I said. "Once I fell down the stairs. We were nine. I was rushing and I stepped outside the door like the stairs weren't there, and I tumbled down them and cut my cheek. And Caedra laughed at me. She laughed at everything. I was very angry at her. I said, *Don't laugh at me when I hurt myself.* And she was laughing so hard that she was crying. I felt betrayed. I felt very betrayed and I thought I would never speak to her again."

"Did you speak to her again?"

"Of course."

"How soon?"

"I don't remember. Probably that afternoon."

"Why do you think she laughed at you?"

I finished my orange juice. I felt even more thirsty than when I had arrived, but I did not want to ask for more. "She asked me to cut her cheek, to match mine. But we only had a butter knife and it didn't work very well," I said.

Blane squinted at me. She had the pen and her little notebook on the table, but she did not pick them up. I wanted to stand up and walk away, slowly, through the orange trees and the grass and the clear, cold water through which the fish darted like flashes of gold. She watched my face with the kind of focus that turns coal into gems. "Now that she is gone, do you still feel angry at her?"

"No."

"Why not?"

"There is no point. There is no one to feel angry at. Or with. We were always together until she was gone. I did not become a person by myself, and so it is not the same as it is for other people, being people." I felt ugly and I was confusing myself.

"You are still alive," said Blane. She wore the most impressive mask of humanity I have ever seen. I wondered, if I came across her in a year, would she remember who I was? I folded my hands on my stomach and let them rest there. I am still a little bit fat. I will always be a little bit fat.

"Yes," I said. "But . . . yes. I spend most of my days trying not to be fat."

Very slowly, Blane reached out and picked up her pen. She uncapped it with her teeth and wrote a few lines in her notebook.

We spoke a long while longer until I left her there, in the sun. A man in khaki shorts, walking his Dalmatian on the street, watched me leave the house. I knew that he thought I was a maid.

~

At the clinic, a few days later, my boss visited with her newborn baby. His name was Zachary, and he had been born after more than twenty hours of labor and an emergency Caesarean section. He did not seem to care, however. His little red face turned unconcernedly to all of us cooing and crying over him. He looked like his mother. My phone rang, and I returned to my office. Blane Kronborg's agent asked if I would be available for one last interview, but I told him that it would be impossible, and he did not press the point. He told me that Ms. Kronborg would like to send me a gift, and so I gave him my home address. The following week, a man in white pants delivered a baby orange tree in a blue bucket.

~

The following year, my mother died—complications from diabetes— and the year after that, Blane's film came out. I went to see it at the big theater in Pleasant Hill, with a friend, the same one who went salsa dancing with me, and afterwards we talked about how beautiful Blane Kronborg was, and how much the movie had made us cry, and how the landscapes in the movie—snowy, ice-colored landscapes—had been so unlike what we saw here in southern California. We decided that the following winter we would learn to ski, take a trip to Big Bear and ski in the snow, maybe. And then I went home and I watered my orange tree and then I washed my face with soap and water and then I went to sleep and dreamed again of coarse brown sand and coarse black heat and something, something clawing our face like an animal, and then, the next morning, I stepped on the scale, looked in the mirror, and wrangled down the pandemonium of joy that rose up like steam upon seeing her face, and I said hello, hello, I miss you, come back, to my sister.

Mr. Longley's Paper Suns

Eliana Ramage

Mr. Longley has black hair and green eyes and he grew up in the contiguous United States. I learned that word through context in a chapter book last week—contiguous means the lower 48 and context means never having to use a dictionary.

Mr. Longley won't be here forever. Just two years, to teach at-risk Alaska Native youth. At-risk means being on the free-lunch list in the school cafeteria. I wait for Kevin to get his food and go sit down, because if I don't then I'll whisper to the lunch lady "Jess Ticasuk" and then Kevin will say, "Hey Jess, you didn't pay!"

Mr. Longley says he's Indian, but we had expected someone darker, longer haired, colorfully feathered. We had expected someone more exotic than Mr. Longley with his puffy sweater and skinny red tie peeking out the top. But Mr. Longley says there are more than 500 tribes, and us Inupiat are only one of them. Mr. Longley says we should use encyclopedias to read about the diversity of Indian Country. Dad says I don't need an encyclopedia set for my tenth birthday present, because anything I want to know I can just ask Mr. Longley. But Mr. Longley won't be here forever.

Mr. Longley gets grouchy on November 18th, and I worry he might stay that way through January. November is when the sun goes down and doesn't come back, so he takes up a whole math class making us cut little suns out of yellow construction paper. We tape them all over the storm windows, triangle rays overlapping, criss-crossing, blocking out the blackness behind the cold glass. Mr. Longley slumps at his desk and grumps about the weather. He says we should've had fall, when you get to jump in leaf piles and we should've had summer, when you lie on the beach till your skin falls off. I don't think Mr. Longley wears enough sunscreen in the contiguous United States. I keep cutting out suns and I think about rubbing sunscreen on Mr. Longley's back. I keep cutting out suns and I think about me and Mr. Longley jumping in leaf piles.

Mr. Longley is a good man, and I know it because of the way he treats me when I finish last in the class on the math quiz and most of my answers are wrong and I cry a little bit until Kevin whispers real fast are-you-okay and I know I've hit rock-bottom. I want to go out in the snow and cry as loud as Dad did when Mom took the baby and forgot us at home. I want to leave, too. I want to move to a town in Florida with no Kevins and no multiplication. I want Mr. Longley to come with me and tape paper snowflakes on the kitchen windows if I ever miss home.

Mr. Longley says it's time for lunch. He gives me a nod that it's my turn to stay and do work. Me and Mr. Longley are alone.

Mr. Longley takes out his tomato cheese white-bread sandwich, which must have been very expensive because Dad says all three of those are on the list of foods that take five plane rides to get here. I brought my own lunch because it's my birthday, but Dad says outsiders are fussy about whaling. I'm embarrassed to eat muktuk in front of Mr. Longley.

Mr. Longley must know that's what I'm thinking, because he asks me about the food here and he says he's only been here a few months but he is already addicted to seal and beluga whale. Sometimes you can use "addicted" like that and it doesn't mean like Mom was, it just means hyperbole, which means not telling the truth. I unzip my purple lunch box and offer him some of my muktuk and he smiles.

Mr. Longley and I are sitting across from each other, smiling, and it's the happiest I've been since payday when Dad brought home candy that took five flights from the contiguous United States. Mr. Longley has a dimple and he says he likes beluga whale and it's the happiest I've been since Dad said he'd buy me a ticket to college in America if I do really good in school. If I do really well.

Mr. Longley asks me multiplication tables, the easy 10s and 11s, and then some hard ones. He asks me to pass a napkin and then right quick when my hands are still in the air he whips out another hard one. I can't count off my fingers so I give each one a little twitch, 56, 57, 58, 59, 60, 61, 62, 63. I tell him 63.

Mr. Longley doesn't say anything about me counting on my fingers. He doesn't say that I'm in fourth grade already, that I'll never make it to college if I can't keep up with the simple times-tables. He doesn't say that I'm getting dumber, that I'm trash, that I should get less fat because one of these days I'll have to be a whore just to feed my bastards. I don't know what all of that means, but Kevin seemed like he meant it and the dictionary definition seemed like what Dad used to scream at Mom when I was door-closed, under the blankets, under the bed, don't say a word.

Mr. Longley doesn't know any of that. Mr. Longley thinks I am perfect, with a little bit of a math problem. Mr. Longley smiles with his dimple and he asks what I'm reading. I tell him *War and Peace* because that's the smartest book I know. He says he's reading *Harry Potter*, but I don't have to worry about spoilers because he's read it so many times before. So I don't worry about spoilers, and me and Mr. Longley talk about all our favorite parts. He says he doesn't like how Harry had an attitude about Remedial Potions, because the book made it sound like it was so bad just to need some extra help.

Mr. Longley offers me some extra help. He gives me for free a times-table book with lots of activities and puzzles you can only figure out with math. He asks me if I have a long walk to the bus in the mornings and I tell him yes, I live by the old research lab and it's only connected to the rest of Barrow by a little dirt road. I don't tell him that I get cold and alone and afraid of the noises the wind makes.

Mr. Longley says I should do my times-tables while I walk to and from the bus each day. He says if I say them aloud to myself just twenty minutes a day then I'll get faster and better and he really thinks I can be one of the best in the class because he knows I'm smart.

Mr. Longley knows I'm smart, and I know that I will love him simply, quietly, always. I know that I should enjoy this moment, when he eats a piece of my beluga whale and finishes off his chocolate milk and says I have an impressive vocabulary. I know that behind the sun-windows it's forever twilight, dark till January, and on my walk home Kevin will hit me with snowballs and call my mother names. I know there will be more Kevins, more snowballs in the face and times-tables and bastards and whores. I know there will be nights that last all day and then days that last all night and just me, alone, in bed with a book, with a flashlight.

Dream Car

Matthew Hobson

I was eight the summer my father brought home the Porsche 356 from the scrap yard. Primer-gray, dented, and mottled with rust, the car had no doors or wheels or even seats. The restoration process consumed two years of my father's life, but when it was finished the car gleamed like a green and gold scarab. Every Saturday, he washed and waxed it, massaged oil into the leather seats to keep them supple. When he wasn't driving it, the car stayed cocooned under a dust cover. I didn't even have to be told not to fool with it. About a year later, my father woke one morning before the sun, drove the car into the Carbon Canyon foothills with a garden hose and duct tape, then sat behind the wheel while exhaust took him from the world.

"Maybe he's not really dead," a friend tried to comfort me. "Maybe he's in that Witness Protection thing."

I didn't really believe this, but I was an imaginative kid with a penchant for mysteries. The thought of my father living a secret, shadow life somewhere was tantalizing. And, back then, before I'd ever heard terms like "manic-depressive," the Witness Protection theory made about as much sense as the truth. At night, I constructed wild scenarios about what my father might be doing. Sometimes, he was hiding out in some ramshackle, roadside motel along a desert highway; other times, he was living a solitary life in a white clapboard house surrounded by acres and acres of corn.

We kept the Porsche for several months before my mother sold it. Only a few hours after the advertisement appeared in the Penny Saver, a man showed up with cash. After he paid, he pried the shield-shaped Porsche emblem from the hood. "Keep it," he said, handing it to me. In my memory, he winks conspiratorially. Probably he was being kind—I suspect my mother explained our situation—but I imagined he was going to deliver the car to my father in his new life.

These days, my father visits two or three times a year in a recurring dream.

I wake to a knock. It's early. My wife and children are asleep. When I open the front door, it's him, dressed in a white t-shirt and washed-out

501s. He's smoking a Marlboro. His hair is as dark as the day he died, his chest broad and back straight, his face not riven with the passing of years.

"Where have you been?" I ask.

He turns to leave, like he doesn't recognize me. Like he's knocked on the wrong door. I follow, trying to think of how to persuade him to stay.

This is where I wake up.

But, if I could re-enter the dream, re-write it from inside, he'd say something like, "Let's go for a spin," and point to the Porsche parked at the curb.

We drive with the windows down to Angelo's, a Southern California carhop with waitresses in hot pants on roller skates. A classic car show is in full swing. He backs into the space beside a purple roadster with ghost flames. From the glovebox, he takes a soft cloth, then moves around the car, breath-polishing the chrome. When he reaches the front, he frowns, noticing the Porsche emblem is missing from the bonnet.

I reach into my pocket. "Here," I say, dropping it into his open hand.

"I've been looking everywhere for that," he says, popping it back in place.

We stroll around admiring the classic cars. I've never been much of a car guy, but I try to share my father's joy as his knuckles caress fenders and bumpers and flaring tailfins. I think about my son, nearly a man, and how I always meant to show him how to replace an oil filter; and my daughter, nine, and how it's never too soon to learn to fix a flat. Later, my father and I eat cheeseburgers that drip down our chins and milkshakes so thick we need plastic spoons. Sated, we lean against the Porsche and pass a joint back and forth. It's the kind of moment that would make a perfect memory if only it were real.

"We should do this again sometime," he says.

I've held on to a few memories of my father—shooting baskets on the hoop above the garage, watching a baseball game at Angel's Stadium, sharing a ski lift on a rare family vacation—but not many more. He was distant, unapproachable, forever at the office or in the garage endlessly tinkering with the Porsche. I couldn't name it then, but I always sensed something volatile inside him, something violent in repose that might, for reasons I couldn't anticipate, explode.

In the end, he left silently as smoke.

"I'd like that," I say, glancing at my watch. "But I'd better get home before my family starts wondering where I am."

Engraving

Elena Kua

Sometimes I doubt that it's my father I'm trying to save. What I'm really trying to save, I think, is one particular memory: Batu Pahat in the 1940s and '50s, my father's hometown in the southernmost state of Malaysia. I'm already coming to terms with his losing a grip on other things. It isn't Alzheimer's—or isn't a full-blown disease yet—but it's too early to know exactly what we're dealing with unless he relents and sees a doctor. He finds it laborious to match names to faces; he forgets what he ate before; the dishes of green and yellow served for dinner elude him as to what they are called. Even as these memories slip like windblown dust off a cliff—a cliff he walks inexorably towards—the Batu Pahat of my father's childhood remains chiseled on stone face. It will remain, I hope, long after he leaves this earth, a marker of long sunny days and cool breeze licking the face.

In reality, though, Batu Pahat itself is slipping away. The sleepy rural town I knew from yearly family pilgrimages in the 1990s and early 2000s has since boomed into Johor's "Northern Shopping Paradise," and I find myself mourning for an eroded Old World charm I never knew.

~

The general store owned by the Kua family in Batu Pahat always had a giant kettle of coffee ready for the pouring. Customers and family friends lounged around a heavy marble-topped table with mugs of coffee and the daily paper. When the kettle ran dry, they ordered one of the children—my skinny-legged father or his cousins—to scuttle to another store for coffee powder. Throughout the day, my father refueled himself on caffeine. He drank much more coffee than water, like it was gasoline to his engine.

During the day, Dad hung around the store or played in the field or slipped off to swim somewhere off-limits. At night, he and the rest of the Kua clan slept in rooms above the store, children lying side-by-side like a box of cozy cigar rolls.

Folks were always coming and going. They wanted rice, sugar, soap, cigarettes—the essentials—and biscuits, F&N orange drinks, and ammunition. The Kuas sold rice wholesale. There were bags of it piled at the back of the shop with crates upon crates of F&N bottles. Dad snuck biscuits into his pocket. Or cash from the money jar. He'd pop into the back and open an F&N bottle, drink it partway, and return it to the center of a crate with the lid snapped back on. There were hundreds of bottles; who would miss one?

Not so with the ammunition, though, which the Kuas stocked for wild game hunters and plantation owners. By law, every bullet had to be accounted for. Customers who wanted to buy more were required to bring the expended shells of previous bullets. These local residents, including Grandpa, hunted wild boars and flying foxes in the jungles around town; Grandma made pork floss from the wild boar Grandpa shot. The Kuas' was the only other store besides Frank Tan's licensed to sell ammunition. Obtaining that license took a good reputation, connections with the higher-ups, and a secure strong-room that had been inspected and approved by the police. The Kuas' strong-room sat at the back of the store, locked at all times.

Also at the back of the store was its sole bathroom, terrifyingly dark at night—no light bulb. Dad thought a ghostly hand might reach up between the stair gaps and seize his legs on the way to the loo. He enlisted a cousin to escort him on these nocturnal business trips. The cousin sat on the staircase and exchanged jokes while, in the bathroom, Dad squatted on a platform with a hole in the center.

A waste bucket sat directly beneath. In the late evenings, a night soil carrier came around and yanked the bucket out through a metal hatch in the shop wall and emptied it into a *tong*, a metal canister three feet high. The soil carrier had two *tongs*, balanced on the ends of a pole. He sold the waste as fertilizer to farmers.

The upper-floor bedrooms housed several units of the Kua clan: the store was run by Grandpa and a handful of brothers. Dad addressed them as Fourth Uncle, Seventh Uncle, and Eighth Uncle. He called Grandpa not "Father" or "Dad" but "Fifth Uncle." Grandpa was the fifth of thirteen siblings.

Living together meant that Dad's best friends were cousins instead siblings, as the children roved together in gangs of the same age. Living as a collective also meant that an errant child could be disciplined by any uncle or aunt. A whole troop of cousins were sometimes punished for the crime of one, to ensure they caught the lesson quick or to prove the uncles and aunts didn't play favorites.

The Kuas outlawed, for instance, swimming in the river. Since the riverbank lay right across the street from their store, far too exposed, Dad opted for swimming in the monsoon drain. This, too, was forbidden. The drains were gigantic, about twelve feet across and at least four feet deep. Almost every monsoon season, young and old died from misstepping into the torrent of an overflowing drain. But in dry seasons, the drainwater rose only two or three feet high. When the water was about three feet high, Dad and his cousins biked to the outskirts of town where the drainwater wasn't as dirty because it hadn't passed through town and picked up waste yet. Further downstream were orange peels, dead chickens, and floating excrement.

When they found a good spot, Dad jumped off his bike, stripped bare, and splashed. His hair was crew-cut short, and everything dried so quickly in the sun and wind that, by the time he had pedaled home, he looked as clean and fresh and brown as ever.

~

Lately, Dad seems subdued, almost melancholy. He's acquired a frozen shoulder this year and still gets hit by a bout or two of vertigo. So, he walks quietly, slowly, around the house.

He perks up if table talk turns to history or theology like his engine's revved to start. If the engine's kept humming, he'll offer famous names, dates, theories, and even dominate the conversation. But if we begin to talk about people we know, the engine sputters. His words falter, and he places a hand to his temple and squeezes his eyes shut, as if this might help him grasp at wisps of knowledge that may no longer be there. It doesn't help that Mum, my sister, and I conduct table talk the way people play table tennis. The ball, light and airy, shoots back and forth and back and forth, and poor Dad can't keep up, so he stays quiet.

~

I've seen the old family store, now empty and dilapidated. A ficus tree has grown into one of the brick walls, shattering it in increments. In the evenings, it is more despondent than ever, waiting on the abandoned corner of a shop-row by the Riverside. On the upper floor where Dad and his cousins once slept, tall windows betray rooms' vacant souls. Window shutters that were once bright-blue are missing or ajar on broken hinges, like a row of weary eyelids.

Across the street from Dad's old house is a zinc-and-tarp-roofed marketplace on the banks of Batu Pahat River. As a child, I loved Dad leading me to the riverbank while a duck hawker set to preparing our dinner. Dad showed me decrepit rusty boathouses bobbing on the water. Some were half-beached into a thicket of grass. There were ruins of huts built on stilts over the river. I imagined boat adventures, gobbling luncheon meat from a tin can, and hiding in smugglers' caves. We came to the Riverside every time we came to town, like a ritual. For me, it was the ritual of eating soft stewed duck I never found back in the capital. With duck-gravy drenched rice, I had orange juice and *otak-otak*, a spicy fish cake wrapped in coconut leaves that had been charred crispy over a grill. Not until I was a teen did Dad point out his old house across the street. Perhaps he assumed he had told me before. Only then did I realize the ritual wasn't just mine but his as well.

What did my father see when he looked up at those windows?

~

Perhaps he remembered leaning out of the windows at high tide, when the Batu Pahat River overflowed its grassy banks and waves lapped at the store's doorstep. Giant bluish prawns flopped on the flooded road. He'd fling a fishing line from a window while, below, children splashed among the thrashing fish. Some folks had planted poisonous tubers further upriver that made the fish groggy and easy to catch with bare hands.

Something sinister also crept downriver. Rumors of fighting. In 1946, when Dad was three, the first post-war racial riot was anticipated to strike Batu Pahat. Town residents patrolled the riverbanks in event of an attack by boat. Each patrolman carried a thick stick and a trash can lid in case he needed to sound the alarm. Though originally established by Malays, Batu Pahat was now populated mainly by the Chinese. Malays and Indians made up the new minority, with many Malay villagers living on the outskirts. (The town council, however, consisted largely of Malay officers and a few English-educated Indians, appointed by the British administration and overseen by a British District Officer.) The Chinese who had settled in Batu Pahat were descended from China's southern provinces, particularly Fujian and Guangdong, bringing with them the Hokkien and Teochew dialects.

Migrant laborers, they worked in plantations, iron mines, and retail. Eventually, they dominated the banking industry and enjoyed enviable success in business.

On those tremulous evenings, steam wafted from the entrance of the Kua store. The Kuas made cauldrons of hot porridge to feed night patrolmen. Before retiring on those nights, as well as on rationing days, the Kuas secured their front door with twenty planks that fit into twenty vertical grooves. Across these planks, they slid two heavy horizontal bars. It took ages to lock up before bed and to let customers in the next morning.

It was such a bother to unbolt the door that the Kuas threw open their upper-floor windows and lowered a basket of money by rope. In exchange, they hauled up breakfast and supper from hawkers walking the streets. Come evening, the Chinese *wan tan mee* seller struck a pair of bamboo sticks to announce his passing by, and the Kuas hauled up his thin, sauce-drenched noodles with red slices of pork. In the morning, a turbaned Indian man walked by with a wide, shallow basket on his head, and they bought his *roti*, a floppy flatbread.

In the late morning arrived the duck noodle seller Pak Nang, whose name means "Somebody Else" in the Teochew dialect. When Pak Nang was older, his son took over the pushcart, and townfolk cheekily called him Pak Nang eh Kia, "Somebody Else's Son." Many hawkers carried their stores with them, like Pak Nang did with his pushcart which ferried a charcoal-powered stove and a sloshing pail of water for doing the dishes.

When Dad wasn't in the store chugging down coffee, he gambled against street peddlers—the beef-ball-soup seller, the tangerine seller, and the ice-cream seller.

The *ais krim potong* seller, who carried a Wheel of Fortune contraption on his cart, hailed Dad over to play for popsicles or bars of ice-cream sandwiched in wafers. For an extra ten *sen*, Dad could yank a lever to set the Wheel's arrow spinning furiously across hand-painted numbers. If the arrow fell on a zero, Dad lost his money. If it fell on a number, Dad won that many ice-cream sandwiches or popsicles. After a game or two, Dad indulged in sticky, wet, glistening ice balls—the iconic artifact of his generation, now extinct in mine. They were made of shaved ice, molded into spheres and sometimes stuffed with red beans, then drenched in syrup and condensed milk. The syrup was tricolored: rose-red, *pandan*-green, and sugar-brown. Dad cupped a tricolor ice ball in his hands and suck at the dribbling, melting goodness. Never mind that the peddler who spun that ice ball had also rubbed his fingers on grubby *ringgit* notes without washing his hands.

Eating an ice ball was messy. And heavenly. And so cold that Dad kept switching hands because it stung his fingers.

Back in the store, Dad loved watching the uncles and aunts gamble at *mahjong*. Their marble tiles slid and clicked across the round table for hours. The adults didn't like Dad and the cousins hovering over their shoulders, so they ordered them off constantly to fetch coffee. They didn't want the kids giving their hand away.

Children weren't officially allowed to gamble at *mahjong* or cards, so Dad and his cousins flocked hungrily to the cart-pushing, pole-toting peddlers who doubled up as mobile street casinos. I can imagine Dad dancing on his toes and rubbing his hands together, savoring the golden seconds which luck takes to unfold.

~

Dad, once keen on games of all kinds, taught me the basics of play: This is how you hold your breath underwater, this is how you mount a bike, how you serve in badminton, how you flick the ball in table tennis, how you open in chess by controlling the board's center. But he never taught me *mahjong* or poker. Not even blackjack—it was his elderly Twelfth Aunty that did, when she journeyed from Batu Pahat to our home in the capital, beckoning me to bring real coins for betting.

At family reunions, I've tried teaching Dad the new-fangled board games my brothers like, but I think he prefers old classics like Rummikub. Besides, he seems ever more tired these days. He prefers to sit in front of the TV, which doesn't demand anything of him. Even speaking is an effort.

I wonder if I should be dusting off the Rummikub box more often and getting Dad away from that TV, which his brain has been snoozing in front of for the last ten years.

It's like his mind is falling asleep, slowly, gently, into a bed of snow. I want to shout, "You have to stay awake! Or you'll never wake again." I don't know if he'd hear me. When something crashes into his reverie—like his many close shaves with other drivers—I think it should jolt him back to the world but it doesn't. He's on cruise control, driving steadily into a fog.

I wonder what these waking dreams of his are. Do his thoughts wander to some lost, beloved place?

~

Business dwindled. The store closed. Dad went to live in a long, narrow single-story house on the outskirts of town. The house I would grow up visiting every Chinese New Year's Day.

The house was built on low ground, twenty yards from the concrete road. To compensate for its low altitude—a definite liability in the monsoon season—it had raised foundations. As a child, I thought Grandpa's porch roof so wonderfully high. Up there was where the family hung their clothes to flap in the breeze. In the yard stood a *rambutan* tree of sprawling canopy, lovely for shade but home to a swarm of mosquitoes. Beyond the yard were the attap roofs and fruit trees of Malay neighbors.

Post-store-closure, the Kua clan dispersed into separate homes, though these rested in the intimate proximity of adjoining courtyards. In this little complex, the Kuas tended bougainvillea, cacti, and other potted flora, and visited each other daily. They shared a badminton court until Small Uncle and Fourth Uncle quarreled. Fourth Uncle built a stone wall between their houses, right across the badminton court. I don't know what they quarreled over, but Small Uncle's children might have had something to do with it. Their noise and pitter-patter aggravated Fourth Uncle's nerves. They tramped around his garden, which he kept meticulously neat. He thought them ill-disciplined and a menace to his fish pond and flowers. Behind his back, Dad and the cousins nicknamed him "The Terror" and called his stone wall "The Great Wall of China." Even so, they were genuinely afraid of him.

Of all the uncles in that compound, only Fifth Uncle—my Grandpa— still lived when I was born. Grandpa was a gentle, stooped man with a large Adam's apple and a deep velvet baritone. He loved to sing. Dad says Grandpa was so good a singer that during the Japanese occupation of Malaya in the early 1940s, Japanese soldiers roped him in to entertain their officers.

I can still hear him and Dad crooning in their twin baritones:
Roll back the curtain
of memory now and then
Show me where you brought me from

and where I could have been—
Remember, I'm human, and humans forget
So, remind me, remind me, dear Lord.

It was Grandpa we visited two or three times a year in Batu Pahat until he died of a ruptured aortic aneurysm when I was sixteen.

~

Only after Grandpa's passing did I suddenly want to know all about him, so I pressed Dad for details. Now, as Dad turns seventy-one, I am seized by a need to find out all he knows before it is lost for good.

He's a reticent man on the subject of his personal life, but Batu Pahat is the one thing he'll talk about. It surprises me how animated and quickly he talks when he's waxing nostalgic. And how much he remembers of a long-gone world.

He'll tell the same Batu Pahat stories again and again like a tape on loop: how frightening it was to visit the bathroom at night, how he swam in the forbidden monsoon drain, how Fourth Uncle was "The Terror." He forgets he's told it before, either a year ago or a minute ago. Dad's telling and re-telling of tales once chipped away at my patience, but now I see that it's also left me a legacy, an engraving.

~

After Grandpa passed, we undertook the trip to Batu Pahat only once a year. It takes three hours by car from the capital, Kuala Lumpur—a long distance by Malaysian standards. The drive always had me fidgeting, especially when my father began to play at overtaking other drivers on winding stretches. Close shaves with roaring trucks nearly gave my mother a heart attack as we sped through the land of oil palm plantations. These lonely roads stained red by clay earth on truck tires were punctuated only by utility poles and very few signs. That marked the entry to sleepy-town. But it was not to remain sleeping for long.

The pilgrimage culminated in stewed duck, eating by the river, and, if it was Chinese New Year's week, red-paper packets of money. But Batu Pahat also meant no computers (much less the Internet) and no friends my age, for the relatives had mostly migrated.

Grandpa's tiny TV set crackled and occasionally drowned in snowy static. If it was Chinese New Year's Day, which is when the TV channels played crowd-pleasers, I re-watched classic blockbusters like *Once Upon a*

Time in China, featuring kung-fu king Jet Li as the folk hero Wong Fei-hung, marred by fuzzy colored lines across the screen. There was little to do outside, especially when evening drew near and mosquitoes emerged to feed, and especially when I grew older and could no longer amuse myself with leaves and pebbles.

I explored Grandpa's dust-choked bookshelves. They looked ancient, untouched, abandoned. Dim lighting fell upon the books from a skylight, and the whole corridor bathed in perpetual grey. This corridor ran the length of the house, connecting the dining room on one end with Grandpa's TV room on the other end. In between were these bookshelves. I was a little scared of the corridor at night, which had not a single lamp. But in the day, I picked out decades-old issues of *Reader's Digest* and looked for joke pages and stories about being bitten by sharks. I hunted for Judge Dee detective novels that some uncle or aunt had left behind: mystery murders and clever heists set in Tang-dynasty China.

While time crawled by in Batu Pahat.

The town itself, I thought, had been left behind in the pre-electronic age—almost pre-electric. Men still bicycled to town; children spent hours kicking ball. Folks dozed on recliner chairs or lingered at coffee shops without a glance at the clock.

But just as Dad's old Batu Pahat was being erased and written over, so was mine. When both Grandpa and Uncle Kia Mien passed away, Dad and the cousins sold the land. They bought two houses in a brand-new neighborhood that had not existed until I had gone to college and returned.

The new houses had bathrooms with electric-powered showers. Grandpa's old house had only a small faucet, installed above a stone well from which we drew water by bucket. The new houses, bought side-by-side so that Aunty Lena and Aunty Yu Sim could keep each other company, had smooth tiled flooring. No longer would my phobic brother Jonathan be terrified of Grandpa's hole-pocked cement floor. My mother no longer needed help lifting wet clothes to dry, which meant my skinny arms no longer ached thrusting a forked stick to boost the clothing-draped pole across the beams of Grandpa's porch roof. In this bright new world we now pegged clothes to a drying rack behind the kitchen while peering at the houses of unknown neighbors.

Within the year, the Kuas' old plot of land was bought by an aluminum business, which razed the old homes and trees and replaced them with a large warehouse. It was as if Grandpa and the Uncles and their dusty books and flower pots had never existed. Even Fourth Uncle's Great Wall was demolished.

Today, just a minute's walk from the new Kua residence, an Internet café has appeared, large as the Goodyear tire shop. But who needs to go looking for the Internet when the Internet has come to us? Aunty Lena has gotten a DSL modem. The broadband connection is sporadic and isn't the top speed we're used to at the capital, but it's brought the whole world to Grandpa's doorstep.

~

People say that you never forget how to swim or ride a bike, that these motions are imprinted in our bodies. But the wind gives, and the wind takes away. I find myself wondering if anything endures, like the name of a loved one inscribed on the heart. Or a small etching of home, nested in primordial affection.

Maybe this is what it takes to remember, even if only for a time: A telling and re-telling. A humble engraving. Chipped, smooth, or fading—let it be.

~

Everything's slowed down with Dad except the driving. Mum tells him, "You've *got* to drive slower so you can read the signs and *think* for a moment before asking me, 'Where now?'"

Mum yells at him on the road, for his own good apparently. He gets confused and anxious and grouchy. I think he feels, for the first time, truly lost and out of the loop. One night, after years of driving the same route to church forty-five minutes from our house, Dad found himself disoriented on the night drive home. Since then, Mum rides with him as often as she can.

But he hasn't forgotten the way to Batu Pahat.

The Crystal Lattice

Amy Wright

During breeding season, male eastern fence lizards begin a push-up regimen. Flexing their forelimbs, they pump their sunbathed bodies in a rhythm herpetologists call "jiggling." They flash bright blue side patches like Sons of Anarchy motorcycle jackets. Pigmented cell layers in their dermis and epidermis mirror blue and green wavelengths whose underlying crystalline structure Kinsley refers to as "the crystal lattice."

An undergraduate biologist, Kinsley, has applied for a research grant, and I am a professor on the granting committee. Female lizards also have patches, she explains, though white or lighter blue and more often at the throat. As the sexes evolved, some females developed more coloration, but biologists don't fully understand this morphing sexual dimorphism, or sexual differentiation, she wants to study.

I'm in. Any other semester real-time scrutiny of evolution by confocal microscope would earn my vote, but now it reflects the gender spectrum illumining our classrooms.

~

Leah requested on the first day that we call her Luke, an assertion of masculinity delivered with soft-spoken voice. I looked up from my roster, noting this name preference, searching for distinguishing facial characteristics, hair, clothing, before smiling into the eyes and moving on. I might have gone the whole semester letting this student shuttle in my mind not yet *beyond* gender, as the prefix *trans-* suggests, but between or inter-gender. Except. A sentence arose requiring a pronoun. I knew it was the wrong one the moment I spoke, scrambling to revise my antecedent to mean the author we were reading rather than Luke's comment about her work.

When class was over, I strode to the office of our university's director of Women's Studies for guidance. "Ask the student," she advised.

"I didn't know we could be that direct," I said, both relieved and intimidated by the conversation to come.

"As long as you phrase the question with respect," she said, "she/he will appreciate that you want to know."

~

The name of the genus *Sceloporus* originates from scent glands located at the fence swift's thighs, the species *undulatas* from the ripple illusion created by its crossbars. Its name implies why gender is so compelling to study, since undulate, "to cause to move in a sinuous or flowing manner," sprang from bars—places bois might shiver past or clock some former lover, dual as light that moves as both a particle and a wave.

~

Lizards show their strength in order to reduce threatening encounters by ruffling their lapis lats. Prompted by circumstances to show my colors, I can only imagine how Luke feels.

"There are brilliant reasons for making gender an active decision," I begin my logistical heart-to-heart. "Since the name you've given us to call you is traditionally male while the one on my register is traditionally female, what are your preferred pronouns?"

"He/him," he answers. Later, a SAFE Zone counselor says I can assume pronouns match the chosen name's gender, though to do so propagates the binary some seek to dispel. Not Luke. He contributes more afterward to class discussions, lowers his hoodie away from his face, perches higher in his desk.

~

Kinsley states her theory so clearly, an interdisciplinary group of mathematicians, physicists, artists, and geographers agree to fund her project. She wants to prove that the number of irridophores beneath any individual's skin is not the primary basis for its shading. Instead, compounds on the surface filter a prism of rungs from which only the brightest blues escape.

I look up "crystal lattice," knowing it refers to more than my family's wooden-slatted patio, and it does mean specifically "a set of infinite, arranged points related to each other by transitional symmetry." Still, I picture the crosshatched diamonds I peered through as a child, scraping laceworks of frost with my thumbnail. That thin skin peeled, melted beneath my fingertips so cold it felt like hot candle wax. I touched the pads together again and again, sensing the riffle between apparent opposites.

~

In the wild, jiggling begins mid-April. Males competing for territory gorge their throats and flare dewlaps like chins jutting for a fight. They eyeball each other, circle, and if pushed, push back, tails whipping like snapped towels. In a few years Luke will lash out if his defense isn't honored, to prove himself a man among men.

* Students' names have been changed to respect their privacy.

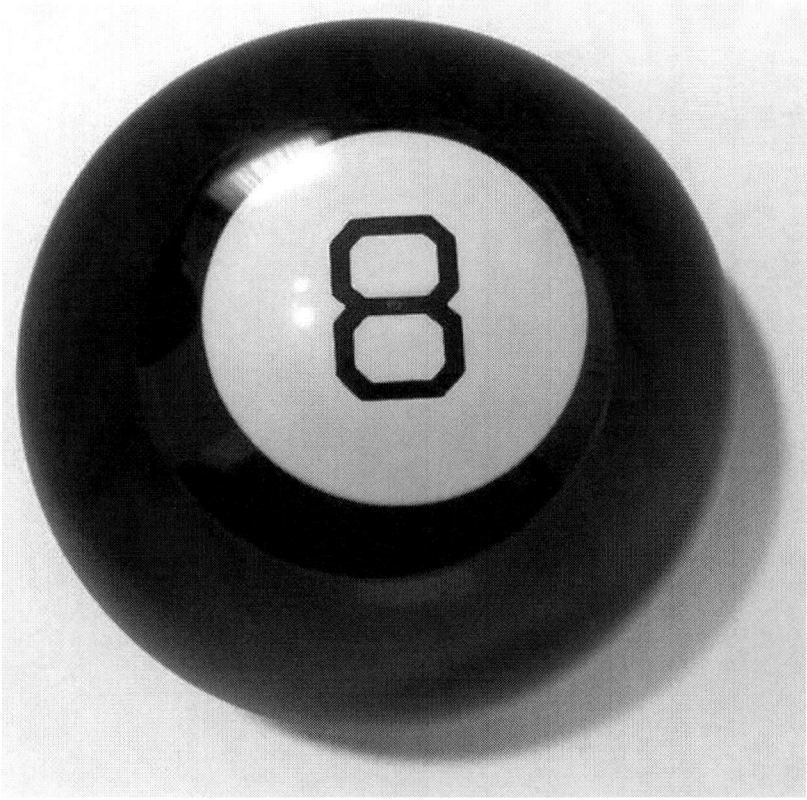

Winter 2016

I Love You, John Maynard Keynes

David Kirby

"Every point on the earth," said 13th-century Franciscan
        friar Roger Bacon, "is the apex of a pyramid filled with
the fires of heaven." I wonder what he meant by that.
                Probably that there's all this power under our feet and that
        it's up to us to figure out how to unlock it, which, for you

writers, means to write as though your life depends on it,
        because it does. Put yourself in Dante's shoes: in the Seventh
Circle of hell, there's a river of boiling blood and a forest
                of souls that become suffering trees, not to mention centaurs,
        including Nessus, who fires off a couple of arrows but then

gives Dante and Virgil a ride out of there on his back.
        You can't make this shit up, folks. You have to be there,
see it, write it all down. Otherwise, you're just turning
                the Magic 8 Ball over and over: "Most likely," "Outlook
        doubtful," "Try again later," "My reply is no." That's why

top-shelf British economist John Maynard Keynes said that
        "words ought to be a little wild, for they are the assaults
of thoughts on the unthinking." Actually, I like the Magic 8
                Ball and use it often to make decisions which aren't very
        important, which, let's face it, most decisions aren't.

Should I eat at Wo Fat's or Waffle House tonight?
        "Concentrate and ask again." Do I need to take a shower
or just paw myself with a washrag? "Better not tell
                you now." John Maynard Keynes, I love you so much
        I want to call you John Maynard the way Southerners

call people Sue Ellen and Billy Joe. You're so much

smarter than the Magic 8 Ball. But words shouldn't
be wild all the time, John Maynard! What if words
                  were wild all the time? Either we'd be overwhelmed,
         like people slathered in whipped cream, then given

hot-chocolate enemas and wrapped in live electrical
         wires before being tossed into tubs of stale chablis mixed
with rancid mayonnaise, or else our senses
                  would become so dull that, instead of jumping around
         like somebody wearing a jacket made of mice

and a pair of cheese pants who's standing under
         a molasses shower as pygmies with blowguns shoot darts
tipped with sneezing powder at us, we wouldn't react
                  at all, and the words wouldn't be wild any more:
"dynamite" would be no more powerful than "filtered tap water,"

"ecstasy" the same as "nap." You writers make these
         little buildings of mud and diamonds that most readers
will never even notice, much less enter the way Wilbur,
                  the neighbor's cat, waits on our deck till I let him in,
         saunters through every room in the house as though

he's thinking about buying it, and then walks right
         past me without even looking as he leaves, as though to say
"No catnip farm, tuna pond, milk river?" In addition to
                  John Maynard Keynes, I also love Keats, silent upon his peak
         in Darien and thinking about his next poem, thinking hard.

Mortling

Matthew Landrum

When a sheep is found dead, sprawled on its side
in the winter grass, flies droning about its still form,
one eye pecked to a bloody root by carrion birds,
its coat may still be salvageable. Shorn of curled fleece,
the cold sheepskin will reveal itself—grey and inelastic,
shot through with purple veining. The head will loll
when the body is flipped to reach the remaining wool.
No sense letting it molder in the Atlantic mists,
scatter in clumps among the stones, or snag on barbed wire.
Lanolin that could not keep out privation, disease
will hold in the heat of a new body. Deft hands can knit
socks, scarves, sweaters from the last gleanings of animal life,
but pull a thread and they will unravel, unskein, unspindle
to seafog, sunlight, lichened rock, starved grass.

An Accident of Nature

Kate McQuade

Through the glass: July. Bright, teeming, the dead
middle of the thing, leaves so charged they flicker.
No bruisy wintry blues now, just a lawn edged

with shadows, and that little yellow shimmer
can't be fall yet—only blight along the border
of the green. So we tell ourselves. Picture

me at the kitchen window, looking over
all we've tended. Seething, urgent green. The kind
that says *today*, green of arbors, ardors,

malignant green, frantic with now. You've called
to tell me no, they didn't find the gene
in your bloodwork, the one that might forestall

the tumor's growth, explain its lineage—might mean
history, might mean future. *Just a little
accident of nature.* Your voice is reeling

between laugh and car crash, a throaty middle.
Across the yard, years ago, a thick branch fell,
snagged in the armpit of the old maple

on its way down. It's still there, balanced, swelled
with moss and moths and little buds, tender
shoots taking root in decay. As though the knell

of thunder or God—whatever rendered
it broken—could just be undone. As though
that maple were enough, those arms as slender

and fissured as any body. Noon. Shadows
in the grass are shrinking, the phone cord's caught
and tangled in my hand; later, slowly,

daily, we will stretch them back out. Once, we thought
we'd know when it was time for life to shake
us down. The difference between growth and rot.

The clarity of falling, its vibrant stake
in gravity, that suck into earth's keen
and hungry mouth. And yet it hangs there. Raked

and raw and rootless as any in-between,
as violent in its brightness, its ruthless green.

Injection Ending in a Bible Verse

Destiny Birdsong

Peel the wax paper backing from the plastic case, but leave the syringe inside as the medicine thaws. You haven't cleaned the countertops in weeks. Don't think about the intern you saw earlier today, who is neat and beautiful and ironed, even her hair. How her kitchen must sparkle like her engagement ring, which slides along her finger as she turns over your peeling hands, asking if you've ever been diagnosed with psoriasis. Have you ever cared about the word *comorbidity* before now? In the days when the pain was negligible, would leave quickly to plague the people you saw on television. All those sterile commercials, all those lined, white faces. Hearing the black box warnings, you wondered: why no grapefruit juice? Now you know. Your uncle says knowing is the price we pay for not dying young. He is a black man who knows that even old accounts must be settled. Be careful when handling; this medicine costs more than you make in a month. Your mother would be proud to know this. You might not have a good job, but at least you've got good insurance. You have arrived. Don't think of distances, of home, of all the people who are not thinking of you because they've been taught how to avoid being afraid. Hold the syringe up to the light. How little it takes. How clear the solution. Don't think about lymphoma. The clouded X-rays. That this could kill you faster but you could leave with your whole body. Don't wonder about whether that makes sense. Good sense is wasted on the young; they still die early. Play your favorite song on your phone and then wash your hands because it's your phone. Don't worry if you cry a little. No one else is here, but don't think of being lonely. Instead, tell yourself no one needs to see this. Maybe, when your elbows aren't swollen and you can lift your arms to comb your hair— maybe then. The alcohol pad and cap removal are easy. Just don't touch your phone again. If the song ends before you're ready, hit replay with your knuckle. Then, count to three. The pain is never as bad as you think. In fact, this will one day become a thing you do all the time, even in the middle of doing other things, like dressing for brunch. In this way, you'll achieve a stinging normalcy. You'll become a person who takes for granted that being healed means being pierced. Push the button, watch the plunger sink towards your flesh. It's OK to wonder if this is how faith is supposed to feel, a closed circuit of questions: the body, the dosage, the body. You might remember that you didn't pray, and you can do it now if you like. Just be honest; God can see right through you, how you've been wanting to ask: *are you still considering the birds?*

Ballycotton

Roisin Kelly

It was on a July evening last summer
that I realised the impossibility
of owning another person. I'd spent
too long in the city, in a state

of nauseous heartbreak, and as the streets
filled with the dust of people
coming home from work, my friend
drove us out to the country,

to the Ballycotton cliffs. We walked
apart—I was some way
behind, watching her long hair
brush her back like grass that reached

from either side of the path
and was swept aside by her knees.
My bare arms and the shorn fields
were evening-light golden

while the sea below
crawled in and out with
the sound of water in darkness
because the cliffs were already in shadow

and young boys from the village
poised to jump from a rock down there
were shivering, all lean
white chests and skinny arms.

As the lighthouse in the bay
slowly opened its red eye, I watched
the boys and thought about one of them
growing older; wondered

if he'd ever hold a girl to him, if
she'd listen to his heart and if, without
his knowing, she'd love him
in the way a man can be loved.

I wondered, too, if she'd ever be this
summer evening to him:
at once the oily water, the cold
plunge, damp rocks echoing

with his friends' cries, and high
above him—the day's last shreds,
the silhouette of an unknown woman,
an amber sky.

Dad's Last Entrechat

Patricia Colleen Murphy

We've entered
      a gentle collaboration.

You've agreed to be
      dead. I've agreed

to re-wind your 30-
      year clock, its brass key

all cool and pre-recession.
      Later I'll realize

I don't know where
      I am. I'm in a large car

somewhere between
      two geographical points.

Point A is known for
      its crying that sounds

like laughing. Point B
      has a river in the shape

of a noose. Now
      I can't imagine speaking

to a child with kindness.

I Won't Be That Foolish (Domineer, Devour)

Virginia Smith Rice

> *And now, O Lord, Behold, these nations which are reputed as nothing, domineer over us and devour us.*
>
> – 2 Esdras 6:57

My mother's bones are soft, softer. Ten children
take turns pressing into her
humerus, her uncertain wrist. We are kind about it

sometimes (blue underfoot,
under our nails.) If she could have been her own
parent there would be more ribbon

and hospital corners. My mother and I
understand one another—
we stay wary, holding a fear in

common: that she is doing it wrong. Now,
each child cannot stop caring
about who leaves the deepest depression.

That woman is no longer ours.
She is busy reclaiming who she was
before us. I bury my mother daily

and with a flourish I become her
resurrection. Once, when I was five, green-
loud noonlight hurt my eyes

and I wished for the sun to go away.
It left for forty days. Even then I knew that
if I could order the world, I would

do a terrible job. Mother, you are queen
ruling all the starlings. They are your own
murmuration—*come home, come home.*

The house is empty. Your birth bench weathers
open air and trellises the wild
dog rose. On the hillside something whistles,

hidden in razor grass and cineraria—*go in, go in.*
Mother, you are growing small and smaller. Soon
you will fit in a keyhole the size of a church.

Sitting on a Fallen Cedar

Michael Johnson

It has taught us sway, unsway,
to mimic its crown
browsyful in the banqueting wind.

The last storm laid it down, here,
where dew nests in the grass
like the eyes of a field of serpents.

There must be a word for how light finds one
sitting on a fallen cedar,
the stand in their burled tongue

adding a verse in the dusty croon of us,
the moon candling in the clouds
and wandering through the trees,

everything painted shades of soot
and raven, of obsidian and snakeback,
the wind a suggestion of cello,

the low chorus of rot building, a vigil of ants
marking the mossroot concourse
through lilytongue and hellebore —

if you slow their song, the crickets become
tremulous, vibratory, haunting as a choir
where no choir should be,

where the ants gauge our footfalls,
everything bated,
and as we move, they move.

Heir

Michael Johnson

It was the field, rock by fucking rock,
hauled fenceward, and the field, finally, fenced
and the tender blessing of their knickering
out there in the grass, the tympani of hooves
flushed from the barn, the moon and shadows
pennons in their nightly cantering.

It was hayrakes tidying the mower rows,
the muscled teens by chugging balers cursing
the dogged days, dreaming scantyclad river drifts,
heaving horsefeed onto the roving balecarts.

Later the gnawn fruit and garden growth
bribed from the deer and bears
with apple husks and squash rinds,
pumpkin skins oozing in the compost.

And the lowtide mussels sunning like butterflies
plucked and broken by gulls from their heights
across the saltskeined bedrocks,
the snow waning across the tattered ridges
and cedars playing their shadow theatres
on the mossy skins of stones
and ravens singing old myths and lusting
after salmon eyes in the gasping shallows.

It was the dreaded cellar door,
hay bale hives and gunnysack itch,
potato pile scree in the bins, horse pucks
petrifying in the nightshade stalls,

the shelves specimened with mason jars
like trophies from some orchard apothecary.

It was the 20° below, mice treading
the tunneled walls with mousely abandon,
wind bawling on the roofcorners,
the ache of coveted window displays,
Sears catalogue fantasies,
everything envied, everything craved.
Through the brittle bones of our want
there were kingdoms we wished for.
Keep them. I have my kingdom.

Where Are They Now? – La Llorona

Paul David Adkins

Same place as always:
the bars and the cars,
the bridges and gullies,
sunning with gators in sawgrass.

She claims to have lured
Weldon Kees to the bay
with a wave
of the arm,
and a smile.

Why wouldn't we
believe her, believe
she's marked every one of her drownings
with the plunk
of a flipped centavo?

Every boy that she claims,
every girl that she culls
from the arms of her mother

is another step down
on the treadmill to heaven.

She's still
crashing the parties on Cinco de Mayo,
Dia de los Muertos,
sucking the sugar skulls shapeless,
tucking razors in Halloween apples.
Still the shiz-nit, she claims,
"but I'd love a Hollywood Star."

She's working the crowds,
mute as a Disneyland Pooh.

She hooked up last March
with Freddie Prinz.

The accent's ditched – a flowered Microbus
in Laredo.

She wants a job with the gringos.

She's not getting
any older.

The same beauty mark which drew
Cortez' teeth

lured a boy who thought
he had balls
for some action.

There's something about her.

Even her bones are tattooed.

Her autographs
are worth Marilyn Monroe's,
circa 1987.
She's still
in the same B movies.

She's still in the room
with a star on the door

(Don't bother knocking),

rolling a peso
tight on her thigh,

alone

snorting coke
the color of bronze,
dry blood she's crushed into powder.

A Not-Conversation with Patrice Lumumba

Paul David Adkins

I want to talk, but you're dead.
There is no voice left.

And me?
I just thumb through pictures
in a library book
on The Cold War.

Mobutu roped you,
drove you vanquished through Stanleyville
in a battered Mercedes truck.
He burned your wrists himself
though his toughs yanked the burns
white into your skin.

You have no voice for me.

You are
your bronze Kinshasha statue:
raised fist, flapping tie.
Silent as a dust mote strung on a sunbeam,
dancing
though there is no music,
no beat to master.

You swing off a griddle of mirages,
the panting of a pride at noon.

The last of your burned and pulverized corpse,
the very last fleck
of one hundred trillion flecks,

wafts off without a voice,

but detects
even the infinitesimal tick of hyenas
padding the distant capital,

strains to hear,
then hears as it floats on the drafts,

the slow stretch and twist
of all the brown necks
of the hanged.

Watchdog

Nick Almeida

Our mother had a tattoo. A blue dog under her shoulder blade, no bigger than the pit of a plum. When she let us, we ran our fingers over it and howled.

She cooped herself in her bedroom for quiet, lights out, hours at a time. We were animals. When he got home from the job site, Pap told us, Shut up. You're making her nuts. Most of the time she hid it, but in summer she let the dog out. We saw it sweat in the sunshine, bound to her back by a bright bra strap. Later, she left for Montana with Neal—the man from the computer, Pap called him—and the dog went too. In time, we left. Some of us for jobs, or school, or nothing at all. Some of us forgot about our mother and her dog.

Our sister had a tattoo but never showed us. She deployed and our brother forwarded us a video she'd made for Thanksgiving. Deek Roomy. Arabic for turkey. When she turned and laughed, there it was. A little dog behind her ear. I imagined that was where a helmet might rest. She turned up later, quieter than our mother had been.

My grandmother had a tattoo. Cleaning out my brother's apartment, I found her photograph pressed in a stack of *Motor Trends*. In the picture, my grandmother has little charcoal eyes. A pinup queen. Shoulders back, a hand wrapped around her neck as if holding it up. The picture is old, but you can still see the little dog on her wrist. Everything else was sold or thrown away.

Some nights, as I lie in bed next to Gloria and feel her breath on my shoulder, I think of dogs. Our daughter sleeps in a crib against the wall. I stay awake for the two of them, listening to my wife sleep, counting our child's breaths, praying everything is as it should be. I tense up at every car horn, every shuffle of feet on the sidewalk outside. Now and then, I look to the door. No one gets in, no one gets out. And in those dark hours between asleep and awake, I think, maybe I am one of those dogs. A dog perched on the slender shoulder of a woman I love. I am a watchdog watching skin, watching silence, watching the permanent ink, watching, so you can't leave, you can't take me away

Ebbing

Robert Edward Sullivan

Saturday morning Dad will make the choice—who gets to go with him to pick out a new bed, mattress, and whatever other random gloriousness IKEA has to offer. It's his special one-on-one trip with one of us four kids, to ask how's school, how's life, pretend things are hunky dory, and slowly replace our furniture. I'm the only girl in the family and I don't know if that hurts or helps my chances. No one knows Dad's system of choosing; it's probably convoluted, intricate, possibly organized. We don't know why he chooses the eighty or so stale miles to get to a Swedish furniture store to have "quality" time.

I hope it's me. I need a mattress made out of marshmallows and puffy cotton clouds, mashed potatoes and grandma sweaters. One with more tightly coiled springs than all the stars in the universe. It's only the first few months into the school year and I don't want 9th grade to be a repeat of 8th grade. I need sleep, good sleep, so I can "imagine my success" as my counselor says on the rare occasions I talk to her. Just imagine it Abbie, that's all you really need to do. She probably believes it, has faith in her own bullshit, as if the imagination holds some sort of magic. She probably would've said that even before my mom killed herself.

There's cheering coming from downstairs, more hoots than hollers. My brothers are in the TV room watching Monday Night Football. I'm in Dad's room. The Seahawks must've scored or fumbled or something. Tyler, the senior, only watches for his fantasy football league; Josh, who is one grade ahead of me, watches because he says it's just like war; and Kyle, who just turned six, likes fierce birds and lime green. Dad is working late again, apparently. He comes home at odd hours, quiet, and smells like peaches and cigarettes.

I'm digging around the back of one of my dad's closets, which used to be my mom's closet. Still is mostly. Her clothes, all of which now fit me perfectly, even her bras. Her records. Her books that aren't on the family bookshelf. Boxes. Bags. I'm looking for one of her necklaces. It's the Star of David. My mother told me she used to be Jewish. Used to be. She never really said anything more about it and I never thought I could ask. I didn't know it was something you could choose. I've been looking for the necklace for thirty-three months and ten days.

I pause to listen. I'm hoping for fumbles, touchdowns, bullshit pass interference calls. Anything to tell if my brothers are still down there or not. They get weird when they see me in here.

I emerge from the closet and go over to my dad's bed. His room is cavernous and echo-y and you could fit like five king-size beds in here. Above his nightstand is a painting my mother did and it might be the last one she finished. It's a twisting, barren tree in the bright moonlight. I lean over to look at the blue in it.

More noise from the TV room. I open the top drawer of my dad's nightstand and find a shit-ton of condoms. I decide I'm done looking for now.

~

Later, I'm in my lumpy mashed potato bed that's full of rocks and marbles. Can't get comfortable, can't drift, there are too many swinging shadows in my room, too many dark corners, too much bloated emptiness. Tried humming myself to sleep, but no tune comes to mind. I am my mother's daughter, I suppose. She couldn't sleep either. Some nights I used to crawl out of bed and find her on the couch, not awake, but not asleep. Some nights I'd find her in her studio, just staring.

My mother was a painter, a former model, *Just a few catalogs when I was young*, she'd say. She listened to Billie Holiday, Joy Division, Morphine, and other moody things. She would unearth a record religiously from a crate and play it loud while she did the dishes. I liberate records from her closet and play them on the rare occasions I'm home alone. Dad gave me an iPod last year. He said we don't need records anymore.

The sheets are strangling me and I throw them off and then beat the shit out of my pillow. I jump out of bed, and in the dark, I flip the mattress over for the third or fourth time this month. Tires me out. I hum low notes until I fall asleep.

~

In my dream, as with most of my dreams, I'm with my mother. Maybe they are rooted in memory, or maybe there's just nonsense neurons

155

shitting all over my brain. In this one, I'm in her studio, now my room. She is painting.

Abigail, she says, I can't get this fucking color of blue right.

She steps back from this swirling, cloudy, blue dream-mess. Maybe it's an ocean. She is the perfect version of my mother. Fantasy-novel body, auburn hair so auburn it's twinkling. Her clothes look part rock and roll, part smoke and flannel.

It's more of blueberry blue, she says.

Gross, I say.

We both have a serious disdain for blueberries.

She turns to me and she has no face. As always.

~

I'm eating breakfast in our brown and orange kitchen. It's like a Thanksgiving explosion. Dad's work papers of crazy scribbles and numbers cover our gravy brown table. I won't sit on one of our turkey brown stools, but lean against the counter. Kyle stumbles in wearing his motorcycle pajamas. His hair is messy like the pile of clothes on the loveseat that I've yet to fold. I'm not sure his eyes are open.

"Is there any Life?" he says.

"Life is all around you. Live it up, Champ," I say.

He yawns. "What are you eating?"

"Steak and eggs, hold the steak and sub the eggs with oatmeal," I say.

"Who do you think Dad's going to choose? For IKEA?"

Kyle has never been on an IKEA trip. Although he did see the Space Needle with Dad, but he barely remembers that. He doesn't remember much of our mother, except what I tell him. He doesn't know about the tiny mole on her neck. Or that she had told everyone she quit smoking, but I'd see her in her bathrobe out on the back porch, smoking almost every morning. He doesn't know that she put sour cream in our mac and cheese, and that's where I got the idea.

"What do you want to eat?"

"Can I have popcorn for breakfast?"

"Sure," I say, and throw a bag in the microwave.

"Do you think Dad will pick me? I'm trying to imagine it, but I can't."

The kid can't keep still. He's the opposite of Tyler who sometimes will only move to turn the page of whatever he's reading. Kyle is bobbing his head. He gets up. Sits back down, hops up again, starts pacing, he wanders out to the hallway. I lean around the corner to check on him. He's staring at a photo on the wall. I know what photo he's staring at. I do the same thing each time I walk by it. It's a black and white photo of me smoking, but it isn't me. It's Mom.

Lately, people tell me I look like her.

You sure got her green eyes.

You talk with your hands just like her.

You totally have her nose, her ears, her sass.

Don't have her voice apparently, as I can't sing for shit. I can't paint as far as I know. I don't think I'm going to play tennis any time soon and if I do, I'm sure I won't have "the serve from hell" as Dad says. I doubt I'll learn French, and I'm sure I'll never be able to make chocolate walnut cookies that could only be called divine.

I never believed the comparisons, not really. Not until I looked at that photo.

The microwave beeps. "Come eat your popcorn."

The refrigerator starts to hum, filling the silence while Kyle waits for his popcorn to cool.

Kyle doesn't know she hung herself. I don't know why I went straight to the basement to look for her that day. I saw a kitchen stool, out of place in the basement, knocked over, and found her swaying gently, her whole face pale blue.

Kyle looks at his popcorn, says, "Can you put some milk on this?"

~

Dad's Tuesday night meeting was canceled or something. I found it odd that he had meetings at night anyway. He has a DVD from the library and throws it on the kitchen table. Josh and Kyle are watching me stir soup with my big wooden spoon.

"*The Chosen*?" I say, looking at the DVD. "Really?"

"Your mom loved the book," he says, but makes that face, like he just swore.

My eyebrows are somewhere up in my scalp. "Don't we own this?"

He doesn't answer and goes upstairs. The movie will play to a mostly empty room, like every movie. There aren't enough seats for all of us anyway.

Josh says, "Is that a Jewish movie?"

"What the hell is that supposed to mean?" I say, and he looks up toward Dad's room.

Josh snorts. "Whatever," he says, walking away.

"No whatever," I say, following him around the corner, to the hall. I'm holding my spoon like it's a torch. "What the fuck is that supposed to mean?"

"It's not like we're Jewish, Abbie."

I narrow my eyes at him.

"What? We're not. Dad said so," he says and turns around. I look over at that damn photo, where I'm smoking, and looking off. I go back to the kitchen and resume my stirring.

Kyle asks, "I know Mom used to be Jewish, but what does that even mean?"

"Is your room clean?" I ask.

"Was Dad ever Jewish?"

Dad would probably say he's somewhere between a failed Catholic and an atheist, if he said anything at all. If he talks about religion, he'd have to leave out why we only really have one set of grandparents. Not because Mom's parents live way the hell across the country in New York, but because they didn't want her marrying Dad, didn't approve of her modeling, her choice of schools, her art, and according to Mom, her.

"So, is your room clean or not?" I ask.

Kyle doesn't say anything, just blinks fast.

Dad comes down the stairs holding the tree painting from his room.

"I was thinking you should put this in your room," he says, holding it out like it's on fire.

"Why don't you want it in your room?"

"I'll put it by your dresser and you can decide where to hang it later."

~

Wednesday, 3 a.m. but still Tuesday night in my mind. I hear a voice, murmurs. I get out of my bed, crawl on the floor, thankful I vacuum every other day. The voice is coming from Dad's room and I feel, for whatever reason, this has something to do with who he's going to choose on Saturday for IKEA. I get close to the crack at the bottom of the door, the light spilling into the hallway.

"Yeah," I hear my dad say. Then again, "Yeah."

His breathing is rhythmic and sounds like it's coming out of his nose, like he's jogging.

"Mindy," he says.

Who in the fuck is Mindy?

I hear what sounds like someone slapping hamburger patties repeatedly. And then, a female's voice. A female voice that is not my mom's. One that turns into a female moan, also rhythmic. I realize all that breathing is, I guess, what two people do at three in the morning. I can't move.

Then Dad sighs. Big. I hear more murmurs. Footsteps. I hear something about using the bathroom. The bathroom that is right behind me.

I crawl in reverse all the way to my room, to Mom's old studio. The room I demanded be mine. Once in my bed, I bite my lip and taste iron in my mouth. I stare at the twisting tree painting leaning against my dresser. In the dark, it looks abstract and blurry. I hear the toilet flush.

~

Wednesday at school, after lunch, though I didn't eat again today. The only thing that sounds good is IKEA meatballs. It's the only meat I'll allow myself to eat. And I have a very specific craving for it as of late. I used to think my mom was the same way, until Tyler told me it was matzah balls she loved, not meatballs.

"Miss McKay," my teacher, Mr. Jefferies, says. I might've been napping or staring.

"Yes?"

"The question I just asked you. The one we're waiting for. Is . . .?"

I can see all those ellipsis spilling out of his face. His grayish hair is not balding, but I can see the on-ramp. He's leaning forward, his glasses sliding ever so slowly down his nose.

"I don't know, actually," I say.

I really wish I had the answer, or at least knew the question. I had been trying to remember if I ever heard either my mom or my dad use each other's name. It was always Babe this and Baby that. Unless it was an argument and then it was her shouting Jerk this and Asshole that – which I found some strange comfort in, knowing it was far better than her silence. A silence that arrived in waves, an abstract thing of dark matter that no one could predict when it would crest, when it would ebb and recede.

I'm waiting for someone else to shoot their hand up and answer so I can go back to the window, to beyond, to deep space.

Mr. Jefferies has pointed his forehead directly at me, his eyes perched above his glasses.

"Shit, I don't know," I say. "How about the Declaration of Independence?"

The class erupts in laughter, and Mr. Jefferies frowns like his eyebrows are trying to hide in his nose. I look over at the board. Written on it is something about *To the Lighthouse*.

"Does anyone else know the answer?" he says.

My face is hot and soaked in battery acid.

Class ends.

"Miss McKay. A word. If you will."

My classmates' eyes lower and they shamble out of the room. I'm the third McKay kid to come through Mr. Jefferies' class. Josh had him last year. Tyler had him the year Mom killed herself.

"I'm worried," he says. He takes off his glasses, puts them back on. He knew my mom on the few occasions she subbed as an art teacher, even though she was never asked back after she made some kids cry with her Rothko rants and her swearing. "I'm worried that you might be unprepared for Monday's test."

"Test?"

"The one that's twenty percent of your grade?"

"Oh, the *test*," I say, making my voice go as low as it can. "I just need a new bed and maybe a good lamp. I'm getting them this weekend. I'll sleep better. I'll be able to read in bed."

There's another bell ringing. He looks at me, beyond me. His lips are pursed, but not like I'm in trouble.

"I'm sorry I said 'shit' earlier," I say. I don't wait for his reply or any more words of worry asking me if "I'm okay" in that super serious, quiet voice that adults use. I walk backwards, slow motion, into the river of classmates rushing through the hall.

~

Dad won't be home for a few hours. The light is better in the living room and the couch is comfy, so I have constructed an intertwining nest of blankets, pillows, and an ancient *Star Wars* beach towel. Josh finds me in full nest mode.

"What are you doing?" he asks. I don't hear any venom in his voice. I don't look up. I don't believe it, but I still hope that if I ignore him, he'll go away.

He says, "Are you making dinner, or is Dad? I'm hungry."

"If Dad doesn't bring something home, I'll make dinner."

"What time's he getting home?"

I look up after some silence. He's chewing on his lip. He sighs. I never know if my brother who used to be my co-conspirator, my co-pilot, my "co," is still in there. Or if it's only post-Mom Josh, who gets angry at me, who sighs at me.

"I'm trying to read," I say.

"You've been on the same page this whole time."

"Exactly. I can't read with all your escaping air."

"Here's some air for you." He sits on me and lets out a musty tuba fart.

"Fucking gross, Josh." I push him over. He's laughing.

"You have such a potty mouth."

"What the fuck do you want?"

My nest of blankets has fallen to the floor. He takes my book.

"Give it back."

He looks convincingly confused. "What am I supposed to give back?" He holds out the book. I reach for it. Miss. "Oh, this? Is this what I'm supposed to give back?"

"Just fucking give it back, Josh," I say.

"You got this off Mom's shelf, didn't you?"

I take a breath and he dives in and tickles me. I hate—hate—that it makes me laugh. That my body betrays me. I laugh out, "Please."

He drops the book and uses both hands to tickle me. My stomach, my armpits, my sides. I'm laughing hard. Both the quiet laughter, and the loud one. I breathe-laugh in, breathe-laugh out.

"Stop," I say, but I'm trapped. Laughing. The more I laugh the more he goes at it. My neck, my calves, my feet. His hands are dark spiders, and they miss ticklish spots but find equally sensitive ones. My chest, between my thighs. My body betrays me again. Jolts of pleasure I absolutely do not want. I am struggling for air.

So, I go to deep space. To the edge of the known universe, where time and matter are all whatever I make of them. To Josh and me building cities in the sand, Mom sitting with us, her tummy full of Kyle, while we waited for Tyler to get out of school. Not the Josh who looks perpetually confused and angry.

I knee him right in his crotch. Hard. He gurgles and coughs and plummets like a sack to the floor. It was a solid connection. All of my knee. All of his junk. He's coughing and rolling around.

Tyler comes into the room, jerking his head to the side to get the hair out of his face.

"What the heck's going on?"

"She," Josh spits, "kicked my balls."

"He ..." I clench my fists.

"She was just sitting and staring at nothing." Josh moves to the couch, in fetal position.

"I was trying to read. He took my book."

Tyler grabs it off the floor. "*Tropic of Cancer*? Really, Abbie?"

"It's better than reading about fucking dragons all day."

"Dad's going to hear about this," he says as head snaps his hair again.

"Or fucking space ships."

"Abbie," he says.

"What?"

"You look ..." He grits his teeth. "You look terrible."

He swallows hard and walks away with my book.

Josh stands up, though hunched over.

"I hate you," he says. He plods out.

"I know," I whisper to an empty room.

~

Dinner is KFC, which means just mashed potatoes and coleslaw for me.

"Sorry, Abbie," my dad says. "I keep forgetting."

Kyle is trying to scoop up gravy with his fork. "Who ya going to pick to go to IKEA?"

I'm impressed with his nonchalance, even though his leg is shaking. He must've been thinking of when to ask that the whole day, saving it up.

"Not until Saturday morning," Dad says, grinning. I think if he didn't draw and drag these things out, we probably wouldn't care. I mean, it's not like kids usually get excited about couches and end tables and such. The choosing seems random at best. There might be points. Might have something to do with school, with grades, not arguing, not swearing, not making a mess. He says it's an opportunity to *talk* to him, just him. It's mostly silence the times I've gone.

"Abbie kicked me in the balls," Josh says. He must've been saving that up for the right moment, too. Dad looks at me.

"Yup," I say. "Sure did. More like a jab. A knee jab. He was misbehaving."

Josh says, "Just because you wear her clothes and read her books doesn't make—"

"That's enough," Dad says. "What were you doing, Josh?"

"What? Me?"

"Do you expect me to believe that Abbie just randomly kicked you in your balls?"

"Knee jab," I say.

"I was trying to make her laugh," he says. He tears off some meat and sinks into his chair.

~

Still Wednesday. 11:58.p.m. according to the clock, the blue digits illuminating my room. I crawl by each door. Josh and Kyle's lights are off but there is flickering light. Josh is probably playing *Call of Duty* or something and Kyle is pretending he's asleep but watching. Tyler's industrial fan is on, which means he's out cold.

I crawl by Dad's room, thankful no lights are on and I don't hear any harlots giggling. But there's light from the kitchen. I stand up at the pictures lining the walls, at the me-that's-not-me-smoking one. There hasn't been a photo added since Mom killed herself. I'm the only one that says that. That she killed herself. My brothers, if they say anything, act like something random fell from the sky and crushed her, like a piano, or she stepped in a hole. Something accidental. Something she didn't plan. Didn't choose. Dad refuses to say anything.

I walk into the kitchen. Dad leans over papers that cover the entire table.

"Go to bed, Abbie," he says without looking up or turning around.

He puts down his pen. I see the book I was reading amidst the piles. Tyler must've debriefed him while I was doing laundry earlier. I reach for it. He stops me.

"Abbie." He turns. His eyes are red and he takes me in. It's like I take all his breath when he looks at me, or like I'm stabbing him, like I'm twisting a dull blade back and forth. It physically hurts him to look at me.

"I was reading that."

"You're a little young for this one."

"Have you read it?"

He nods. "Yeah. Your mom liked . . ." He keeps nodding. "Yeah."

"I've already read half of it. So, I've already been corrupted or whatever."

"It's for adults."

"Oy, I'm not some dopey little kid. I've seen the word 'cunt' before, Dad."

"Jesus, Abbie," he says, shakes his head. Slow.

He pushes the hair out of my face. I can tell he's pleased it's growing back now and it's auburn again. Not watermelon pink.

"What?" I ask. "Do I still have gravy on my face? I know it probably wasn't vegetarian gravy. Is there such a thing?"

He does his smile-grimace. There are more lines on his face than I remember. I'm still twisting the blade, apparently.

"Will I lose points for this?" I ask. "Are there even points? Because I need a new bed. Maybe a new reading lamp. Possibly a new wooden spoon."

When Josh went last spring to get bookshelves and a coffee table, he ended up with this reading lamp that looked like it was made out of gummi bears. It's amazing. He doesn't even read.

"Go to bed," he says. He hands me the Miller book, and turns back to his papers.

I wait for a few beats, a few pauses, and then do what I'm told.

The sun is coming up when I fall asleep.

~

Thursday and I'm in the stars. I'm seeking out horizons and studying them. It's a drift day. I float through school, ignore questions and looks, concerns and ridicule. I ignore my brothers. I manage to take a bath in the upstairs bathroom without a single knock on the door, or without any rolling thunder of steps, or stampedes. I don't snoop around Dad's room, don't look for any of Mom's necklaces, or records, or clothes, or old grocery lists. My tongue is fat and I vomit up everything I try to eat. I plant myself in pages and look at words from left to right, shifting and tossing in my bed, trying to find comfort, the right amount of light. So, I keep drifting. Just seems easier to ride waves to deep space as much as I can. I wait for the day, the night, to pass over.

~

Once upon a time, there was a Friday, near the end of the day, when the sky turned cosmic orange, copper, and licorice red. My freshly bathed mother in her yellow Big Bird robe was arranging flowers in her studio. She lit bone-white candles that weren't pumpkin scented, or vanilla, or cranberry.

"What are you doing, Mom?" I asked, standing at the doorway. She nodded at me and I knew it was okay to enter.

"I'm lighting candles." She smiled. She looked tired

"I know *that*. I mean, why?"

"Because it's almost sundown."

She pushed her hair behind her ears. Her eyes were my eyes. Green fire.

"It's something I used to do every Friday when I was a kid," she said.

"Are you going to paint?"

She knelt down in front of me. "No work. Just rest until sundown tomorrow."

"Can Josh and I watch a movie?"

She held my chin, held my gaze, breathed deep. "Yes, Abigail, if you want."

~

I don't light any candles on this Friday, but it's dusk.

We're having dinner. Our talk starts off so small it might as well be grunts. Dinner is some poor attempt at lasagna that my dad bought. But before I even take a bite, he says, "I got a phone call today, Abbie."

165

"That's great Dad. Thanks for sharing." I'm trying to keep my Jenga piece of lasagna from toppling over.

"From school."

"Uh oh," Josh says, "Abbie messed up *again*."

"They said I need to come down on Monday after class for a meeting? Something about your grades? Sleeping in class? About swearing?"

"Are you asking me or telling me?"

"Don't talk to Dad like that," Tyler says.

Dad holds his hand out. "Is there something I should know about?"

"I got a little frustrated and I might've said shit, or fuck, or go to hell you cocksucking motherfucker. I honestly don't remember."

Kyle drops his fork. Tyler starts eating even faster. Josh is smiling.

"Go to your room," Dad says.

"Why?" I ask.

"Because your language—"

"You asked me if there's something you should know, and I told you what I *might've* said, what I *might've* been in trouble for. I wasn't calling *you* a cocksucker."

He takes a big, *huge* breath. My family, bags of air, the sigh-ers. He leans back in his chair and leans forward, puts his hands on his head, rubs his temples, and deflates. I don't wait for more deflating. I go to my room.

Before they finish eating, I turn my light off and pretend to sleep. Soon enough, I am.

~

I wake to the smell of bacon. Saturday morning. Sizzling and plates clanking, French Roast coffee, the microwave beeping.

My sheets are clinging to me. My skin has fused with them and it takes a good five or six seconds to peel them off. I'm raw, and pink, and newborn-ish. I get mostly dressed and tiptoe to the kitchen.

Josh sits up as soon as he sees me.

"Sorry about the other day, Abbie," he says, too loud and too formal.

"Sorry I had to knee jab your balls," I say. I yawn and sit down on the table, my legs swinging.

"Morning," my dad says. The plates are lined up on the counter. He plops some eggs down, all cafeteria style. He pulls out some fake bacon from the microwave, tosses it on my plate. Does the same thing with my brothers, except real bacon. Deals out toast like cards. Kyle is possibly still asleep, and yet he's squirming. Tyler is reading yet a different book with different swords and dragons, et cetera, on the front. Josh looks like he's praying to the bacon.

"Before you grab your plates and start eating," my dad says, stepping around the stove. My heart is knocking against my ribs. Kyle has perked up and his legs are bouncing. Tyler has closed his book on his finger. Josh is chewing his entire mouth. "I have an announcement."

Dad pauses. His pauses are the worst. They're dry, and solid, and stale, and time has been known to stop, as it has now.

In this pause, I try to focus, try to *imagine my success*, but instead I think of a moment when Mom tucked me in.

I was young, like four or five. Her necklace was dangling over me.

"What's that star?" I asked.

"The Star of David," she said, real whisper-like. Then smiled. Perfect smile like girls in catalogs have.

"Who's David?"

The concept of another male that wasn't one of my brothers or my dad was inexplicable. And that she'd be wearing a necklace of his was scary in an exciting way. Like there could be this whole other life, this whole other Mom that I didn't know about.

"Sometimes Abigail we make choices that . . ."

I kept watching the necklace.

"It's just something I used to—" She squinted. "It's just something I wear."

The pause is over.

"So," my dad says. "For the IKEA trip. I'm taking . . ." He looks at each of us. He is grinning. "I'm taking Tyler," he says.

"Fuck," I hear someone whisper. Me!

Everyone is staring at me.

"Fuck. Fuck. Fuck," I say, each one getting louder. My skin has melted off and someone just rubbed jalapeños all over my body, my eyes. Then I shout as loud as I possibly can, "Fuck!"

"Abbie," my Dad says, hands up bank robber style. Everyone is freeze frame frozen.

"I can't. Fucking. Sleep. She couldn't either. Don't you see that?"

Then I'm just screaming.

I grab my plate and toss it against the wall.

I take someone else's plate and do the same thing. Then again.

Then I'm kicking over chairs. Pushing over stools. Throwing papers from the table.

I run to my room, swiping the photos off the hallway wall.

I plunge through my door.

I pull my hair. Hard. I can't see. Everything is white and blurry and raw. Except that painting. It's bloated and the blue is grotesque.

"Abigail!" my dad shouts. Right in my ear. He wraps me up and holds me tight.

I turn into a puddle. An Abigail puddle. I have no bones.

He wraps me up tighter and I can hear humming. It's me. I'm humming. Like I used to do with Mom. When I'd come home from school and find her curled up on the couch in the same exact spot she had been when I had left. I'd nestle in next to her, wrap my arm around her and hum, and try and figure out how far away into deep space she was. And would she ride a wave back before anyone else saw her like that? Did she hear my voice? Maybe she did and that's when she would eventually smile. Next thing I knew, she became my mother again, said something like she wasn't getting enough sleep, asked about school, or have I seen the TV remote, or what should she make for dinner.

Dad rocks me back and forth as I hum.

He says, in a loud whisper, "My God, Abigail." He is choking on his words. He might be crying too, can't tell because it looks like the walls are crying, the carpet is crying, everything. He says, "I was going to say . . . Tyler, Josh, Abbie, Kyle. You . . . you all get to go."

My brothers huddle in and around.

"You okay, Abbie?" Tyler says, his voice cracking, the words thick in his mouth.

"I don't hate you," Josh whispers to me. "I don't." He is sniffling too.

Dad is saying he's sorry, about being gone so often, about how tough it must be, how he's doing a terrible terrible job with us. Something about being a team, about family, about sticking together, we'll get through this, all that stuff. I know what he's trying to say. Been almost three years since the first and only time he said it.

But I'm trying to imagine Mom. Just how far to the edge of deep space she went. Did she see the universe expanding into nothingness, did she know she could just choose to ride some wave to that edge, beyond it, and she didn't have to ebb back? Is that what she did?

And when the rope was around her neck, she had to know I would find her. Was she warning me? To know that the darkness is there, will be there, and I had better fucking be prepared. Better find a way to imagine myself out of it, in the ways she couldn't or wouldn't. Knowing that maybe I'd understand she was unable to cast back to earth, unable to imagine herself in the world, and unable to return to it?

Maybe it takes imagining to come back for real.

So with my father holding me and my brothers surrounding me, I try for now, for the moment, to ride the wave back. Maybe it doesn't matter. Maybe my life depends on it.

I take a heavy breath. I let the air fill every part of me. I imagine a belly full of meatballs, a test I'll at least pass, a necklace I will find and will wear every single God damn fucking day. And I imagine a mattress that will be like a lofty cloud, soft and infinite, one that enables me to sleep deep and long. Something that will feel pure and maybe a little bit holy.

Standstill

Dan Malakoff

Over the bridge and down the road to the gas station, where she calls her parents from a payphone. He leans against the brick, smokes and listens to her ask for one more hour, so that they can get dessert at Kyle's bakery out on Route 1. When she hangs up, he stubs his cigarette in the urn of sand. Inside he knows where to find a 99¢ condom. He reaches in his pocket for a crumpled bill and asks the cashier with the baggy eyes of a walrus to let him slide on the tax. She does.

Back on the road, she speeds with his hand on her thigh. He feels the grooves in her corduroys and her heat, and he feels cold but they are still together, the night isn't over. Outside his window, the newly frozen land swoops by; the snow won't melt until May. An occasional car passes, kicking up salt that crackles against the steel body of her dad's Volvo. When she can borrow it, she comes to him.

He hacks up phlegm and lights another cigarette from a depleting soft pack. He exhales out the window and the smoke blends with the fog in the shallows of the road. She looks over at him and swallows. He knows she worries her father might smell the smoke in the gray felt that carpets the roof, though he never has before. He pinches the cherry off the end of the cigarette and places the butt in his pocket to dispose of later, the way she insists he do.

The turn-signal ticks. He tries slowing his heartbeat to match it. They pull into the parking lot of the church where they've learned to come in their spring-summer-fall together. The police once found them in the park. By the ocean, too, the police knocked on the window glass. But the police have never found them here. She parks, leaves the key in the ignition. The light from the high concrete poles pushes through the windshield yet stops short of their faces. He asks, almost in a whisper, Baby?

He unbuckles his seatbelt, leans across the stick shift, and kisses her, his bottom lip dragging from her upper lip. A car swishes by on the wet road; he pulls away when her lips don't gather. He wishes that they'd been drinking. Then they'd be laughing and playing reckless and reveling in skin and letting thoughts of tomorrow slip down into the car seat, change for some next telephone call. Her eyes move past him, toward the road.

He dreams of eloping and building a house together in the woods. All he wants to do, all he can do is keep her warm. But tomorrow: A strand of her brown hair on his hoodie, an echo of her in a stranger's patter. He is too old, going nowhere, her parents say. It is too serious to let continue. In winter, the snow buries fall's leaves.

She touches his face, drawing her fingers from his temple to the tip of his jaw, a crescent to match the waning moon. She turns the key in the ignition, says, "My curfew."

The Girl from Texas

Maxine Rosaler

The only time Nick and I were in our apartment at the same time was when we slept, with me in the bedroom, where we used to have so much fun, and him in the living room, where three months ago he announced he was leaving me. When it was Nick's turn to be in the apartment, I would go to the Starbucks up the block to copyedit romance novels, which was how I was making a living at the time, and that's where I was when I met the girl from Texas.

A man at the table next to mine was talking on a cell phone. I recognized him as one of the wine salesmen who would come into Starbucks every now and then to hold their team meetings. Apparently his crew hadn't arrived yet and he was biding his time talking to a friend about baseball. One player was injured, another was being traded; he was thinking of going to his friend's house and they could watch the game together. That would be fun, wouldn't it? How nice, I thought, to be so easy-going, so casual. What an amiable guy, I thought. What a nice way to be.

I had just written in the margins of the manuscript I was working on: "It was never clearly established why Glory remained a virgin after her marriages to *both* Calvin and Ormand." I was a good line editor and good as far as content was concerned, but I had never managed to master the punctuation and all the other tiny particulars, which unfortunately happen to comprise 99 percent of the job of a copy editor.

Last week my editor had forwarded an email she had received from a romance novel fanatic containing an itemized list of fifty-three errors she had found in a book I had worked on called *Theodora's Heartbreak*. Elaine said that she was tired of doing both my job and hers and that if I didn't improve she wouldn't be able give me any more assignments. I felt so ashamed of myself and so hurt at the thought of a complete stranger going out of her way to put me in danger of losing my only client. What a mean thing to do. And what a stupid waste of time to have actually sat down and recorded all my mistakes, and who reads romance novels anyway, and wasn't the fact that Lord Mounteville finally realized that it was Theodora he loved and not that bitch Candice all that really mattered, in the end?

I had just added: "It might be conceivable for one man to put up with Glory's virginity, but two?????" to my comment when a girl sat down at my table. I took her to be about nineteen or twenty. There were two empty tables available, so I wondered why she had sat down at mine. She was a small black girl dressed in blue jeans and a red T-shirt that had New Orleans written out in big bold sparkles across the front. She smiled at me sweetly, and that made me like her right away. Then she looked out the window and laughed quietly to herself.

When I was standing in line to get my free refill I noticed that the girl had fallen asleep, her head on the table. I was worried that the manager might kick her out but when I got back to my table she was awake and laughing to herself again.

"I'm happy," she told me. She spoke so softly that I wasn't sure I had heard her correctly. A few seconds later she asked me to ask her why she was happy and so I asked her why she was happy and she told me it was because she had just gotten a puppy.

"What kind of puppy is it?" I asked.

"Just a puppy. What difference does it make what kind of puppy it is?" she said.

"I was just wondering, that's all," I said.

"I'm happy, but you're not happy," she said. "Why are you so unhappy?"

I was glad she asked me that. I wanted to tell her everything, but when I opened up my mouth the words refused to come out so I told her that maybe I was just made that way.

"You look like you need a hug," she said. "I'm going to give you a hug."

I thought a hug might do us both a bit of good so I stood up from my chair and she stood up from hers and we gave each other a hug filled with hunger and love. When we sat down again, she asked me where I lived and I told her I lived down the block and then I asked her if she lived around here too.

"I'm from Texas," she told me.

"What brought you here?"

"Doesn't make much difference, does it?"

"I guess not. I'm just curious, that's all."

"Curiosity killed the cat," she said and she started laughing to herself again.

"Where are you staying?" I asked her

"I'm natural," she said.

"So are you staying around here?" I asked.

"I got my spot," she said. And then she asked me if I had ever been to New Orleans. That made me sad because Nick and I had gone to New Orleans on our honeymoon. I didn't tell her just then that Nick and I were a thing of the past, a figment of my imagination, but I did tell her about the honeymoon.

"You're married? You got married? That makes you established. A real citizen. A true blue member of the true blue sea of drowning humanity."

"Not anymore. We're getting divorced," I said. I was ready to tell her everything now. How I had loved Nick since he was thirteen and I was twelve and then three months ago, one sunny evening in the middle of April in response to my casual lament that the days were getting longer now he had told me that life was a finite thing and that he was going to be thirty next year and he didn't want to spend the rest of his life with a woman who preferred darkness to light. Apparently this was something he had been contemplating for a long time.

"So how did you like it?"

"How did I like what?"

"New Orleans?"

"We were never any good at going on vacations," I told her. "We tried to have a good time the first day or so. We even took a tour bus to look at the rich people's houses, which made us feel like a couple of hicks. We had heard that the food in New Orleans was wonderful. The first night we got dressed up like a couple of newlyweds in our post-wedding clothes and had a jambalaya out of which came crawling a greasy cockroach. We got to wondering why we had gone to New Orleans in the first place. Why we bothered going anywhere at all. It was fun, just wondering about that. When we gave up on New Orleans we spent all our time in bed or at a café that sold those special donuts New Orleans is famous for, reading books we had brought along. Actually, we ended up having a great time."

"You brought books along on your honeymoon?"

"Nick never goes anywhere without a book."

"I'm from there," she told me

"Is that where you just came from?" I asked her.

"That's where I came from. But it's not where I *come* from. I come from Texas, like I told you."

"How did you get here?" I asked her.

"On my own. I got here on my own."

"But how did you get here? Did you come by plane? By bus? By car? By train?"

"Do you know where the psychiatrist hospital is?" she asked.

I knew exactly where it was and how to get there, so I gave her directions. "First you have to go to the emergency room," I told her, giving her the directions to New York Presbyterian, which was just thirteen blocks away.

"You might have to wait a while," I told her. "But they'll take care of you." I had waited on a gurney in the hallway for over ten hours. All night long a guard had stood over me. He was my own private guard, assigned just to me. He didn't let me out of his sight for a minute. Even when I went to the bathroom he was there, standing outside the door, making sure I didn't try to kill myself again.

"I like to have fun. What do you do for fun?" the girl asked me.

"Not much these days," I told her. "My husband was my only fun and now that he's gone there's no more fun for me. Well, he's not really gone, since he hasn't found an apartment yet. But he's gone in spirit, gone in mind. His heart is gone, gone from me forever. Where it is, nobody knows."

"Maybe we could have a race one day? That's a good way to have fun."

"I have a bad knee," I told her. But she wasn't listening to me. She was looking out the window again.

I went back to my copyediting. The man on the phone was text-messaging now. I was glad about that because it looked like Glory was about to lose her virginity to the gardener who was really a duke and these scenes could get pretty racy sometimes, but then the girl stopped looking out the window and asked me if I was a psychiatrist.

I told her I wasn't. "What makes you think I'm a psychiatrist?" I asked

"Just because," she said. Then she went back to staring into space and didn't say anything for a long time. As predicted, Glory finally lost her virginity. Now the salesman was back on the phone. He was talking about baseball again. The conversation was more or less an exact replica of the one that had preceded it.

"Do you know where there's a gas station around here?" the girl asked me. I told her that I thought the closest one was on Amsterdam and 169th, but then the salesman, after apologizing for interrupting, pointed out that there was one much closer, on 179th and Broadway.

"Why do you want to go to the gas station?" I asked.

"Just to get some stuff. I'm going to leave my bag here." And with that she was off. Could there be a bomb in her bag, which was a counterfeit Louis Vuitton, the kind they sell by the truckload on St. Nicholas Avenue for ten dollars apiece? Maybe all the craziness and all the compassion was just an act, a setup for an act of terrorism. What did she need a gas station for except to buy a can of oil to pour on herself, or pour on the floor, or maybe on me, and then light a match, and that would be that. But then the girl came back, holding two tiny white jewelry boxes.

"This is for you," she said, handing me a box with a white pin and matching white earrings.

"Thank you," I told her. "But I wouldn't feel right about accepting it."

"Why not?"

"I'm not good at accepting presents. This was one of the things my husband didn't like—hated, I guess, about me. For our first anniversary he got me a silk nightgown and when I found out it cost a hundred dollars I told him to return it. He never got me another present after that."

"Everyone likes presents. Why don't you?"

"I don't know. Maybe because I had an unhappy childhood."

"Then you should take my present," she told me.

"Why do you want to give me a present?"

"Because I'm nice and I want to help make up for your unhappy childhood. Get you started on a whole new road," she said. "I also got a present for the woman who was sitting over there. Did you notice her? The one with the blue hat? She looked unhappy too. Where did she go?"

"I don't know who you're talking about."

"Well I guess I'll have to wear it for her," she said, pinning a plastic pin that spelled out Mardi Gras in fake emeralds and diamonds onto her T-shirt.

"I'm going to wear this one for you too." And then she took the other pin out of its box, and she pinned it onto the other side of her T-shirt.

"Thank you," I said, regretting that I hadn't accepted her gift. It could have been something I would treasure, possibly for the rest of my life.

"Do you know where the psychiatrist hospital is around here?" she asked me and I gave her the directions again.

"Some people I can open up to. I like to open up sometimes."

"I know. It can help. If it's the right person," I said. I thought about the girl I met when I was in the hospital. She was pretty and nice like this girl. I wanted to be her friend. She had dozens of scars running up and down both her arms. I have just one scar on my wrist. I don't think I really tried to kill myself. I just wanted to know what it would feel like to have the razor blade cut into my flesh. But mostly I think I thought there was just too much blood in me.

"Any drugs around here?" she asked. "This used to be the spot."

"I know. It used to be. There used to be drug wars, when we first moved here. Once a bullet came right through our window. It went through the wall above the headboard of our bed, where we were sleeping at the time. All that's different now. Things are much more peaceful now."

"My man. He got shot. He's dead now."

"I'm so sorry about that," I said.

"Do you know where the psychiatrist hospital is around here?"

"Yes, I do," I said, giving her the directions again.

"Well, like I said I'm glad they took care of the drugs. It looks better and everyone seems happy here."

"Some people are happy," I said. "I guess some people are always happy. Or there is always someone who is happy."

"I'm fine. Like I told you, I like to open up to certain people. But I'm worried about you. It's you I'm worried about. You should have fun. Did you ever get your nails done," she asked, looking at her nails, which were bitten down to the tips of her fingers. Her cuticles were chewed to bits. That was another thing we had in common.

"No. I never have. I guess that kind of makes me unique."

"Ever get your feet soaked?"

"I did do that once. Someone on the street gave me a coupon. But the calluses on my feet were so tough they had to use a razor blade to slice them off. That cost me an extra seven dollars."

"I'm glad you got your feet done. That's a beginning at least."

"I suppose so."

"Where's the psychiatrist hospital around here?" she asked me. And I gave her the directions again.

"I'm going to go now," she said.

"I think that's a good idea," I said.

"Ain't no shame in my game."

"I know that, honey."

"Well, I guess I better be on my way."

After she went out the door, I noticed that she had left one of her jewelry boxes behind. The one that used to contain my pin, but it also contained a set of earrings. I ran out the door to give it to her. When I got back to the table the salesman said, "That was a close call."

"What do you mean?"

"She almost left that. It's a good thing you got to her in time."

"Yeah. I suppose so," I said.

"It looks like you two are really good friends."

"Yes, we are."

"I could see that," he said with a smile. "I'm good at reading people. That's one of my gifts. It comes in handy in my line of work." Then the first member of his team arrived. The place was pretty empty by now and he asked me if I would mind moving to another table so that he could push my table together with his, since he was expecting six more people. I told him I didn't mind and he helped me move my stuff to a table across the room.

There were just twenty-five pages to go. I knew that there was more trouble ahead for Glory, but that everything would work out just fine for her in the end. I felt a moment of true happiness when the gardener, after revealing to Glory that he was really a duke, explained to her the reason for his masquerade was because he wanted to find someone who loved him just for himself alone and that he was happy it turned out to be her because he loved her with all his heart and he always would.

Foreigner Manager

Leslie Anne Jones

"Yes.. Mm, sorry-sorry . . . Yes, understand." My coworker Wenwen is gripping the end of her ponytail like a safety handle as she speaks into her headset. I stop clicking through all the browser tabs of grad school programs and Internet news that I've opened, because I can tell she's on one of those calls she'll have to transfer to me any minute now. I pull my legs up and pretzel them. I tilt my head side to side until my neck cracks. I like to feel loose before I get on the phone.

Wenwen and I occupy the last two desks in a double column of work stations squeezed into our tunnel-like office. Besides us there are six other customer service agents, and on an average day each agent needs my "foreigner expertise" roughly twice. So in an eight-hour shift, my employment is justified fourteen times in three- or four-minute bursts. I sit in the desk nearest the window. Sometimes when the light is low I catch my own tired 24-year-old face in the glaze. I have my mother's pointed, white-lady nose, but my father's Chinese eyes, his dark brows and small mouth. Beyond the distraction of my reflection, the view extends into the smog-stained tower opposite ours, where more office workers sit at computers, like our twins from a parallel universe. I've never spoken to a one of them. I look over at Wenwen again. Finally, she pushes the mute button on her mouthpiece.

"What's up?" I ask.

She shakes her head, "He's talking very fast, I can't say anything."

"Okay, pass it over."

I adjust my headset. "Dane Arnold" appears on the incoming call monitor and I click to connect. Wenwen slumps back and fans herself, relieved. This is why my salary is three times hers. The biggest jerks are best appeased by a fellow foreigner. Even so, it's strange to be hardly out of college and make that much more than a woman four years older and seated across from you.

"Guangzhou Fine Food Delivery, this is Nicole. How can I help you?"

"It's the orange chicken," he says in a grating nasal plaint. Dane Arnold's voice reminds me of a dying piece of office equipment. There's too much garlic, he whines, and weird peppery things. He drones in paragraphs. It is impossible to get a word in edgewise.

We don't even make the food. We're just a delivery service that contracts with restaurants catering to Guangzhou's ever-growing and kitchen-estranged expat populace.

"Seriously though," he continues. "If you knew what this stuff was going to be like—why did you call it orange chicken? That's false advertising. You can't do it. Not even in China, you just can't."

I listen and listen until he runs out of steam, having repeated each point several times over, then I offer him an account credit and we hang up. I type his name into Google—I don't do this with all of our complainers, just the insufferable ones—I like to see if there's a profile post, a blog or article comment, some digital clue to the nature of their jerkiness. I can pull up a few details on most people, but Dane Arnold's results are limited. All I learn is that he teaches at the Regal Eagle English Academy. There are pictures of him on the school's website, in one he's dressed up in star-spangled pants and a blue top hat, like Uncle Sam or something. His eyes have a buggy, amphibious jut and his chin is an afterthought. He looks to be about forty. I bet not even his students think he's cool.

~

When I leave work, the sun is dipping behind the jumble of high-rises, but the air is still like soup and sweat trickles behind my knees. Guangzhou is suffocating this time of year. To combat the heat I have to remind myself that if I were in the U.S. I'd be pouring coffee with all the other humanities majors. My dad, who is from Taiwan, can't understand why I—bearer of citizenship in not one but two countries with clean food, high living standards and comparatively transparent government—choose to live in mainland China. My mom, who is from Bakersfield, kind of gets it. I plan to go back to the States next year, if I get into school somewhere. I'm hoping to land on some grassy college campus to complete my master's in China Studies. I'm mainly interested in the macroeconomic trends that preceded the Chinese Revolution of 1911. But for now I'm okay with being a food-service industry worker, at least here it's a desk job.

Two blocks from the office, I turn down an alley that goes most of the way to my apartment. It's quieter than the main road, which is lined with shopping malls and glutted with traffic. I pick my way through broken pavement and past ramshackle buildings strung with laundry lines. People are starting to cook dinner, and the air smells like ginger and garlic.

Around the first corner, I come upon an old lady walking with a little boy, probably her grandson. She glares and shuffles him along the far wall. This behavior irritates but no longer baffles me. My half-white, half-Chinese face has the same racial signifiers as that of the Uyghur ethnicity. Uyghurs come from way up in northwest China, the part of the country that touches Kazakhstan. They don't look Chinese at all, and they're mostly Muslims. Chinese people think they're all robbers and terrorists, and often enough I'm on the receiving end of this misdirected antipathy. "I'm American!" I want to say, but don't, because it seems too complicated and kind of irrelevant.

The woman and her boy scurry away. I continue past the homes, hear the scrape of metal on wok from the kitchens. Just before the alley ends, the cracks in the pavement turn into black rivulets, thick little rivers of human hair. They flow together, creating a kind of hair-highway leading to the courtyard outside Mr. Zhou's two-room house.

"Meiguo pengyou, ni hao!" *Hello, American friend*, his standard greeting.

Mr. Zhou is wearing a blazer despite the heat and smoking in his doorway. The long fuzzy pile of hair that runs along his exterior wall could be mistaken for a row of thick bushes were it not pitch black and flecked with cigarette butts and Q-tips.

Mr Zhou goes around the city buying the hair off salon floors. He sorts out the dirt and trash at home, then sells the hair in bulk to factories that use it to make some kind of protein used in food and pills and makeup. I passed his home many times before my curiosity finally forced me to ask about all the hair. The first time we spoke he told me that when he left his village and came to the city, finding work was difficult. The small jobs he did get were tiring and paid barely enough to live on. Then one day he ran into a classmate from middle school who'd also come to work in Guangzhou. The old friend told him about the hair business. Not many knew about it, and fewer wanted to do it. When Mr. Zhou first got started he used to itch all over his body when he lay in bed at night, but not so much anymore.

"Meimei!" he barks. A second later, his daughter runs outside in her school uniform, a red Young Pioneer scarf knotted around her neck. "Jiang yinwen!"

"Hello aunty, how are you today?" she asks.

"Doing good thanks. How about you?"

"I'm fine sanks."

Mr. Zhou claps his hand on top of her head. "She's very naughty." He smiles. "But today she won the school English contest." I congratulate them both. We say goodbye and I continue on to my apartment.

~

The next morning it pours on my way to work and my jeans are soaked in warm, polluted rain by the time I get to my desk. My pants are slow to dry and there's a sour, thick odor that wafts up when I adjust in my chair. I wonder if Wenwen smells it. She would be too polite to say. I open up a Word doc and am deep into a draft of a statement of purpose explaining why I deserve to study the fiscal preemptors of the Xinhai Revolution when Wenwen taps the desk to get my attention. I minimize Word and see that she's transferring Dane Arnold's call to me. Again.

"This pizza crust has a fibrous mouthfeel."

It's as if Dane Arnold is trying to impress me with the sophistication of his complaints. By now he ought to recognize my voice, but we haven't established familiarity. We are just two strangers connected by a wire, except I know his home and work address.

"I'm sorry to hear the mouthfeel was not to your satisfaction, but I'm not sure mouthfeel meets our standard for refunds."

"Bitch."

"Excuse me?"

He hangs up. *Mouthfeel, mouthfeel, mouthfeel.* I contemplate the tongue movements it takes to produce such a ridiculous word. An hour later, Judy calls me into her office. Judy is my boss. The only not-Chinese people she'd met before age 18 were a handful of English teachers, but now she's getting really rich selling foreign food to foreigners.

"Just got call from some customer saying something about our rude customer service—

182

"Me? That guy?" I start telling her about Dane, but she rubs her temples and checks email on her phone and I know this is just the kind of small-potatoes crap she's not interested in.

"Let cry baby have his candy," she says. "We still making money, so don't worry about that. Better to have the happy customer."

"Did you credit his account already?"

She nods.

"Okay, sorry," I return to my computer and tap his name into the search bar. I dabble in keywords: "AND asshole" "AND psycho" "AND divorce." Nothing pops. "AND mugshot," is also fruitless. It's strange. He's the only one of our annoying customers where I can't even peg where he's from. Everyone else has at least a tiny digital footprint—a prep sports article in a community newspaper, a signature on an online petition, a mention in some relative's obituary. Dane is the only one without origin.

When I pass Mr. Zhou's on the way home, he is tossing sacks of hair into the bed of a truck like hay bales. It must be delivery day. When he sees me he waves hello and lights a cigarette, asks how my work is going. I tell him bad customers are making it hard.

"Ah, I understand," he says. "I also have some immoral customers. They try to cheat me, and say my hair weighs less than it does. This is why I have bought my own scale!"

"My customers just call me names."

"Ai-ya," he clucks.

~

The rainy season persists and wet weather makes our customers crankier. They want their food hotter and faster. They want bigger portions of bread. Dane Arnold just wants everything free and too often, at least once a week it seems, he gets it. Every time he calls, I look him up, never finding anything more than I did the first time.

On a Wednesday, the rain pelts thick and fast and acts like a curtain, shrouding my view of the officer workers in the building across the street. Dane calls and recoups the full price of a "slimy" Cobb salad, and I finally have a watershed moment in my search-engine manhunt. I'm surprised it took this long, but it suddenly seems obvious after so many weeks of not-infrequent sifting through the back pages of Google results: Dane Arnold must be a pseudonym. Hence his only results have to do with his English-teacher job.

This is not a far-fetched conclusion: A lot of people come to Asia to hide. A month ago, *China Daily* had a story about an English teacher who was arrested when he was discovered to be a wanted pedophile from Canada.

I drum my fingers on the desk to get Wenwen's attention.

"What if Dane Arnold isn't his real name?"

"Ah?"

"It could be a fake name! How come I can't find him on the Internet?"

"Fake name?"

"Yeah, Dane Arnold!"

"Who?"

I leave her alone and start in on the Interpol site, clicking through thumbnails of thugs and killers. My search takes detours through the newspaper articles about their crimes. I bleed away the afternoon in the sordid details, but Dane doesn't surface, which is fine, my expectations for success are low. When it's almost five o'clock, I switch to the FBI's most wanted website. I kill another forty-five minutes on kidnappers before clicking over to white-collar crime.

"Holy shit!"

I look around the room, but the expletive hasn't penetrated any of my coworkers' headsets. I pull up the pictures of Dane Arnold teaching on the Regal Eagle's school blog, then I click between that and the FBI page. Top photo, lefthand corner. His hair was a different color, but the bulbous eyes and dough-ball chin are unmistakable. Dane Arnold is Steven Banks and he is wanted for mortgage fraud.

I go to the tip form. In my note, I include a link to the Regal Eagle's website. The page takes all of thirty seconds to complete and I get an automated "thank you!" at the end.

Wenwen stands up. She yawns and picks up her lunch container.

"Wenwen, I was right!" It takes several minutes to explain my discovery because I don't know the Chinese word for mortgage and she doesn't know the English one.

"Oh wow, bad man," she says when I finish. "China have a lot of people like this."

"You mean bad foreigners?"

"No! Bad Chinese man!" she laughs and makes for the door.

~

Over the following weeks, it becomes very difficult not to tell Dane that I know. He pisses and moans, and I listen and hold in my knowledge. I send off my grad school applications, hoping the tone of my writing doesn't sound too desperate to leave China to study China. After that's done, I have all the time in the world to read up on the details of his crime: Steven Banks convinced people who were scared about their homes going into foreclosure to put their houses in his name, then he took out equity loans against them to fund his "lavish lifestyle," the papers say. They say he bought caviar tastings and wines of rare vintage, that he'd throw dinner parties at Michelin-starred restaurants. I guess that explains his trouble with our Cobb salads and orange chicken.

The delivery business is doing better than ever. To celebrate record profits, Judy treats the whole office to a Saturday trip to Hong Kong to eat dim sum and see a movie that's not showing on the mainland.

It's an hour-long train ride to the border, and when we board the carriage and Wenwen starts to sit down next to me, a woman seated across the way frowns and shakes her head, she motions for Wenwen to move away from me and sit by her instead. It's the Uyghur thing again, I'm sure she thinks I'm about to steal my coworker's wallet.

"She's American," Wenwen tells the woman.

"Oh! Sorry, sorry!" the woman says in English. For the rest of the ride she tries too hard to make friends. I ignore her and look out the window.

The train cuts through the brown haze that obscures the factories on both horizons. Not much of a view, but it's the reason we're all here. This is the global epicenter of low-end manufacturing. Everyone I have ever met has touched something that came out of this industrial corridor, probably many things, probably multiple times every day. From where I sit, the factories just look like giant, faceless boxes. I wonder which are the ones that buy Mr. Zhou's hair.

When we get back to Guangzhou, it's not raining for once and I decide to walk home from the station instead of taking a cab. I start down the alley for the first time in over a month. As I approach Mr. Zhou's I see the hairy tributaries in the pavement, but now they lead to a patch of stony rubble where his house should be. I turn around in a circle, looking in every direction, like maybe I'll find him standing nearby to explain the situation, even though his home is gone.

"Hey!' I say to an onion pancake seller at the mouth of the alley. I point at the rock pile. "What's going on here?"

"Building a new building," he says.

"Where's Mr. Zhou?"

"Moved away."

"Where?"

"Don't know."

We didn't really know each other, Mr. Zhou and I. Casual friends, I guess. I've never mustered much anger over any of the other bull-dozed communities in the city. This time only matters because I can still picture him and his daughter standing in their doorway.

~

The next morning grad school rejections bomb my email inbox as if in coordinated attack. No. No. No. And a Yes without funding. Which may as well be a No in light of my undergraduate debt. I guess I will just be tracking the cycles of economic history from my desk by the window. When I look out I see they've added more cubicles to the office across the street. Evidence of forward progress. Noted.

I haven't had even ten minutes to marinate in my defeat when Judy calls me into her office.

"Here, for you." She pushes a cup of corn soup from KFC across her desk.

"Thanks." I put the plastic rim to my lips.

"We're growing very fast. Need more foreigners to do the customer service. You will train them. You will be my foreigner manager!"

I set down my soup. Things are happening quickly. The first thought to forms is: Every time God closes the door on grad school, he opens up a window to middle management. I don't know what to feel, so for the second time in under a minute I say, "thanks."

Judy tells me to take a day to think about an appropriate salary. I shut the door to her office, edge past my coworkers and drop back down at my desk. I feel like I have freshly-poured concrete in my stomach. I want to string these developments into a logical chain of events but it doesn't compute: I spent lots of time during work crafting my grad school applications. I didn't get in, instead I got promoted. The rubble pile in the alley forms a crown over my thoughts. I wonder where Mr. Zhou moved. I know that soon the rocks and hair will disappear too.

"Nicole," Wenwen says. She's pinching the microphone on her headset. "It's Dane Arnold."

"I don't want to talk to him," I snap.

"Oh." Her shoulders droop and she looked embarrassed, which is not fair: My salary is going up because of all the Danes of Guangzhou.

"I'm sorry, I'm just in a bad mood—I'll take it."

I put on my headset and wait for the call to transfer. It's been two months since I filed my FBI tip and so far no one has come rushing to save us from Dane/Steven's home-stealing and petulance. The no-show on swift justice doesn't really surprise. Economic crime isn't really a priority these days. My earphones buzz and Dane Arnold's name pops up on my computer.

"You call these shoestring fries?! More like an under-cooked hash brown patty, I mean seriously what the hell?"

I want to say. What? I want to say everything, to shout about it, to tell him off for being annoying and evil, to call his sins by name, but instead I say, "Gee, so sorry about that, how about we get you a credit for one of our dinner combos?" Because I'm fed up and I want to have a conversation. A real one. And it ought to happen in person.

~

After work I take the subway and get off at Keyun Road. I walk past all the motorcycle shops, pirated DVD sellers and tea stands until I see the gleaming entrance, double doors frosted with the silhouette of an eagle's head.

I arrive as a group of little boys are filing in for evening classes. They carry shiny book bags with plastic wings sewn on the sides. Through the door, I can see them walk into classrooms where they'll probably waste the evening memorizing long tracts of conversation and chanting sentence patterns. I wonder if I should go in or not. This starts to feel foolish and possibly dangerous, and I'm not sure what to say anyway.

"Ni hao, xiaojie."

The Chinese greeting blared from behind me comes in an atonal American accent. "Are you here about the teaching vacancy?" he asks when I turn. "Wo shi zheli de hiring manager."

He's shorter and chubbier than the photos let on, and I can't tell if Dane/Steven is trying to ingratiate or alienate me with his garbled Chinese.

"Um, yeah. I'm here about that," I say. I am unpracticed at confrontation.

"This is hen hao de xuexiao. Our school is very selective, the most prestigious in the city. Tell me, do you have any teaching experience?"

"No."

"Ah, too bad. Maybe you can try Leopard Academy or A++ School, I hear they take anyone."

"Right, thanks"—he reaches for the door, my chance to do something is about to slip behind that faceless eagle head, before he can step inside I spit it out—"I know you're Steven Banks."

"What?" His milk-mush face churns from confusion to fright.

I can't think of an insult to trump the naming of his true self, so I just elaborate. "Yeah, you're wanted for mortgage fraud."

"Fuck you, you don't know anything about me."

I shrug, but he doesn't see because he turns around and strides away instead of going into the school. He rounds the corner and zips out of sight—never looking back. I imagine within the hour he'll burst into his apartment, throw open his suitcases, grab his clothes by the handful. I wonder where in the world he'll peddle his dubious teaching skills next. Vietnam? Laos? Or maybe deeper into China, one of the backwater provinces—somewhere that our delivery service hasn't penetrated. Yet.

I head back toward the subway. On the way, I stop by a fruit stand to reward myself with something sweet. Pawing through a box of mangoes, I look up to see a mother and daughter, the elder whispers to the younger, "Watch your purse," loud enough for me to hear it. They squeeze their bags against their armpits and try not to look at me.

The shopkeeper is turned away, attention focused on his TV, which is playing some period drama. Those movies are always about the revolution. I glare back at the two women and pick up a spiky durian, always a pungent fruit, this varietal smells exactly like hot garbage. I heft it in my palm over the mouth of my purse and drop it inside, it makes a muffled thud when it lands on the fabric bottom. The mother gasps. The daughter's eyebrows shoot up. The shopkeeper never turns, still transfixed by soldiers dragging a bright red flag through gun smoke. I draw a menacing finger across my neck and the two women hurry away. And I can't decide whether or not to pay for this fruit I don't even want.

The Amazon

Therese Borkenhagen

There is a photograph of my mother as she stands in front of Evenes Airport. On the back she has scribbled, in round and swirly letters, *April 26th 1979*. She wears a black turtleneck sweater and a brightly colored skirt. Her hair is dark and thick, folding neatly on her shoulders. In other pictures from when she was young, her hair reaches all the way down to her lower back. I assume she's just had it cut before moving to Oslo—some idea of big city life perhaps. She wears eye makeup as dark as her hair, and under her heavy lids, two eyes shine with anticipation. Her lips are pale and almost invisible against that translucent skin. She carries the large leather bag I'll inherit one day. This is the last photo before the city changes her—makes her hard. Makes her my mother.

On April 26th, 1986, exactly seven years after she moves to Oslo, I am born with a bang. To my mother's disappointment, my birth is overshadowed by the explosion of the Chernobyl Nuclear Power Plant in the former Ukrainian SSR. Two people die in the explosion, twenty-nine die in the hospital, and a suspected million will die later from cancer caused by radiation. Just like the Soviet Union, she waits until April 28th to inform the rest of the world of her big news, but when she calls her family to tell them about me, no one picks up the phone because they're all too engrossed in the Chernobyl news coverage. Because my mother didn't tell anyone she was expecting me in the first place, she keeps my existence a secret up until my fourth birthday when she decides to throw me a party.

She invites my grandparents and aunts and uncles and cousins, but refuses to let them take my picture; she says they need to earn the right first. My grandparents, who have flown all the way from Northern Norway to meet me, snap a few shots anyway while my mother looks away or is in the kitchen, getting the cake.

As I grow up, my mother makes it clear that while the world owes us both, we still need to work for things, but we will never ask for charity. I'm OK with this. In fact, I rarely ask my mother or anyone else for anything.

That's probably why I'm so surprised the day she asks if I can take her to the doctor. I'm twenty-three. She says her head hurts

We take the 12 tram to Majorstuen where we switch to the 20 bus, which stops right outside the hospital. The doctor talks to my mother in private for nearly an hour while I sift through every magazine his waiting room offers. I don't know much about hospitals, but I'm fascinated by the quietness. I know things happen here, serious things, life and death things, but the only evidence suggesting urgency is the occasional rubber soles whimpering across linoleum and the swift tapping of a keyboard echoing against the undressed walls.

When my mother reemerges from the doctor's office, the physician's assistant escorts us both to a room where she takes my mother's blood. She then escorts us to another room where she and a young woman in a white lab coat perform scans. For a full body scan, they inject my mother's veins with a cold, tinted liquid and tell her to lie completely still for fifteen minutes. I have to wait outside. "Please try to lie still," I hear lab coat woman repeat as the door shuts behind me.

On our way home, my mother swears the full body scan lasted longer than forty minutes. She lost track of her limbs, and worrying that her hand had somehow disappeared, she moved it. According to her, the women kept her locked in the machine because she challenged their authority. "That assistant kept giving me the eye," she says, and demonstrates *the eye*.

Two days later, that same physician's assistant calls my mother to let her know that the results are in. She asks if my mother is free to visit with the doctor the next day. My mother tells her that no, she is not free, and asks if the doctor is free to meet with her the next day, to which the physician's assistant replies "yes," and schedules the appointment. Her voice resonates through the phone, and it sounds as though she's smiling. I bet that voice calms patients down, makes them feel welcomed and maybe even a little bit special, and it wouldn't surprise me if she was hired on her voice alone, but my mother is skeptical. "Voice like an angel, horns like a devil," she reminds me. I once asked her if my father had a nice voice, and she said that my father had both the voice and the horns of a devil, and that's what she liked about him; "At least he was forthright about it." I am pretty sure he was forthright about not wanting a child either; otherwise, I doubt my mother would have been so accepting of his absence, which is good, because it helps me accept it too. The only time my father's absence actually upset me was in middle school when my friend Ane asked me why I wasn't sad that my father didn't want me. Never in my life had I ever thought of it that way, and the idea that he *didn't want me* haunted me for a while, made me do some stupid things, until my mother finally explained that Ane didn't know "a goddamn thing about parenting," and that as long as I had a mother who loved me, there was no reason why I should need a father who didn't want to be a father in the first place. Parenthood was not a right, she said. It was a privilege.

~

When we return to the doctor's waiting room, my mother scowls quite visibly at the physician's assistant, who smiles back, seemingly unfazed, and tells us to expect a small delay. We mosey over to a familiar pile of magazines, and my mother gives me one of those looks that signal: *I told you so.*

"You're losing your mind," I whisper, and laugh as I sink into a chair.

We wait only ten minutes, which my mother still finds suspiciously long, and when we enter the doctor's office—my mother wants me in there with her—the doctor is apologetic about the wait. I attempt to wave away his apology, but my mother grabs my hand and leads me to the two chairs in front of the doctor's desk. Once we're seated, the doctor folds his hands in a manner so majestic and so poised, it must be the result of much practice. He then draws a deep breath and tells my mother she has grade three oligodendroglioma. Brain tumor. He explains the nature of such a diagnosis, but he might just as well be speaking a foreign language. Nothing makes sense. His lips are moving, but the sound they make is unintelligible, and when I finally realize that I'm probably missing essential information, I look to my mother to see if she's following what's being said, but she's watching him as if trying to evaluate his proficiency as a medical specialist, whether or not it is wise to believe him. I can't help her.

This time, on our way home, my mother doesn't mention her appointment, and I don't ask. Instead, she points at the young woman two seats in front of us preparing to disembark at the next stop. She has one of those little dogs, which she stuffs into her handbag before zipping the bag shut. My mother shakes her head and whispers "dog abuser" loud enough for the young woman to hear. She casts us one of those sideways looks.

"Dog abuser." My mother is louder. A beat passes before the young woman turns to us.

"Excuse me?" she says and attempts making eye contact. She is nervous, and I don't blame her. Sometimes I forget what my mother looks like to others: she's tall. She's tall without heels and she's tall sitting down. Much like an Amazon, my mother also has only one breast, and this is something she doesn't like to talk about and something the young woman can't possibly spot under my mother's thick parka, but I know that my mother only has one breast and that it gives her a forceful sense of pride. Yes, my mother has already had cancer once before, and out of all of her accomplishments, beating cancer is the one she dismisses most often. After the successful removal of the tumor in her left breast, one of the nurses gave her a button that read: *I'm a survivor,* which my mother refused to wear, saying she wasn't going to boast about having lain there, and in her words, "happened to survive." I remember telling her that surely, most people didn't interpret *surviving cancer* that way. She tossed me the button and congratulated me for making it out of the womb alive.

Now this young woman on the bus doesn't know my mother like I do, and looking at her neat camel hair coat, Burberry scarf, and the sort of bag other girls get from those bantam boutiques at the bottom of Hegdehaugsveien, I bet she's never even imagined that someone like my mother exists. Her inability to look my mother in the eye confirms my suspicion. And my mother, she says nothing; just sits there, stone-faced. She's not a bully, nor has she ever been one, and she's not cruel or domineering. My mother simply believes that people no longer respond to polite requests, particularly coming from strangers, and that some level of humiliation is necessary in order to change a person's behavior. It does not matter whether this woman tries to incite some sort of argument with my mother or continues the taciturn standoff that's developed between the two of them; my mother wholeheartedly believes that once this woman exits the bus, she'll unzip her bag and let the dog breathe fresh air. She won't do it on the bus. People are stubborn. But people also fear humiliation, and most are willing to go a long way to avoid confrontation. This is what my mother wants.

"Did you just call me a . . ." She stops. She can't say the words. It's like word magic. If she says the words out loud, then somehow, to her, and maybe to the other patrons of this bus, they become true. My mother isn't surprised and I am proud. She might end up saving a life today. I wonder if there's a button for that.

When the bus stops, the woman wastes no time scurrying off. The doors close, separating madness from method. The bus rolls onward, and the woman looks away as we pass her, but the handbag has already been opened and a little brown snout pokes out.

Over the following weeks, my mother is in and out of the hospital for miscellaneous tests. She doesn't want me to come with her. Says I should focus on my studies. All she tells me about her appointments is whether or not the physician's assistant was there, and if she was, how she sabotaged the entire appointment. I try to concentrate on my studies, but whenever I pick up a book or attend a lecture, the words *grade three oligodendroglioma* sit in my mind like old gum. After my mother's third appointment without me, and after missing the fourth lecture in a row, I Google the words.

Oligodendroglioma is a rare form of brain cancer, typically found in men, and is generally diagnosed using a two-grade scale: II (low grade) and III (high grade). At a three, my mother qualifies for numerous new traits such as severe headaches, seizures, and changes in personality. A tight rope ties itself around my gut, which is already bursting from an agglomerate of pain, fear, and disappointment. I'd be lying if I said her decision to keep me in the dark surprises me, but I'm pretty sure that the less she tells me, the more serious things are. She never spoke much about her breast cancer, and while I've always just assumed that it was due to my age, I'm not twelve anymore. But that all worked out fine. Perhaps my mother just needs to keep the wheel. I really wouldn't know how to talk to her about this anyway.

~

Before Christmas, the kitchen counter had only one item on it: a yellow KitchenAid Classic Mixer. This is my mother's most valued possession. She never uses it for cooking; never has, never will. But she claims it helped her quit smoking. "I wouldn't want to damage it," she told me. "Smoke gets in through the cracks and destroys the machine from the inside out." I'm pretty sure the mixer is a metaphor for me. Up North, people are very good at speaking "straight from the liver" as we say, but when it comes to affectionate communication, it's as if no one ever taught them the words. No one in my family has ever told me they love me, although my mother has said she's "very fond of me" and "God, how I love that mixer!" I am OK with this. I know my mother loves me.

The KitchenAid Classic Mixer used to be the only thing on the counter. Now, there is an added row of pill bottles, most of them orange, but one is blue and another yellow. The orange bottles are steroids and suppressants of sorts, the blue a special pain killer, and the yellow an over-the-counter iron supplement called *Fe-bulous*. Those are for the both of us, she said after pouring them into the yellow prescription bottle to make them seem more important, making sure we'll take them. Within these walls, swallowing pills is a strenuous endeavor. We've both had pills stuck in our throats for hours, and so we won't try swallowing a pill unless the other is there to oversee the situation and provide support. Pseudodysphagia: fear of choking. It's a real condition. Because my mother has to take at least one pill every third hour, I'm home a lot, and I'm OK with that, too.

I keep my phone next to my notes during the lectures I still attend. If my mother needs me, I'll leave right away. But she never does. At least she never calls. That's why standing in the kitchen with her every third hour has become my favorite time of day.

One morning, after we've both swallowed our *Fe-bulous*, I ask my mother the one question I've dreaded asking for weeks: "Are the medicines working?"

She sips her water slowly.

"No."

The rope around my gut tightens.

"I have to pee," I tell her and leave the kitchen.

"Remember to put the lid down before flushing," she calls after me.

As I'm peeing, I try envisioning my mother's tumor. I wonder if it's ugly, and if it's lumpy or if it's smooth. Where is it? Can she feel it sitting there in her brain? Can she feel it while she sleeps? When she eats? Or when she pees? Does it hurt her? I bet it's ugly.

The ugliest.

I wash my hands and put the lid down before exiting the bathroom. My mother is waiting for me in the kitchen.

"Does this upset you?" she asks.

"Yes," I say. "Does it upset you?"

"Sometimes."

"Sometimes is something," I say.

A part of me is relieved that my mother's high-grade tumor upsets her sometimes; it means I'm not alone.

Weeks pass and we don't talk much about cancer or hospitals. At one point, my mother informs me that she thinks the doctor may have misdiagnosed her, that this doesn't feel like cancer. The very next day, she's forgotten all about her suspicions, and makes a joke about removing one side of her brain the same way they removed her breast. I don't laugh along with her, and I tell her I don't like it when she makes jokes like that. I don't tell her that it's because when she does, I wonder if, for a moment, she actually believes what she's saying.

One night, two months after starting her medications, I wake up to find her sitting in the bathtub. There is no water and she's in her pajamas. She is filing her toenails with one of those coarse diamond files, and she doesn't seem to notice me until I ask her why she's filing her toenails at four in the morning.

"They won't let me sleep," she tells me. Her speech is slurred as if she's not completely awake. But she is. She doesn't look at me, and keeps filing. Her toes are white from keratin residue; I can't imagine she has any nails left. My stomach curls just thinking of the bare pink skin underneath. "That's OK, mom," I tell her and reach for the file.

"Get off me!" she screams.

For a split second I'm paralyzed. She's never screamed at me before.

"Will you stop?" My voice is shrill, and I have to restrain myself from grabbing the file. I want to get angry, to take the wheel, but this is the part Google told me to expect. I'm supposed to be prepared for this.

"These fuckers won't let me sleep," she cries.

"How are they doing that?" I ask, trying to sound sincere.

"Every time I close my eyes, they grow," she says. "Luckily I got to them when I did—fuckers were about to take our heads off!"

"I see." I reach for the file a second time and she slaps my hand away. We lock eyes and for a mere second, I see my mother staring back at me, helpless, begging me to get her out of this hell she's suddenly found herself in. I instinctively turn the shower on and she squeals as the water hits her feet, washing off the white powder. She pulls her hands to her chest, but doesn't attempt to climb out. The water heats up, and making sure it doesn't get too hot, I let it fill up halfway. Her baby blue pajamas darken as the water rises. She watches the water as it runs from the faucet, and when I finally shut it off, her eyes follow each straggling drop that lazily leaks into the tub. I grab a washcloth from the shelf and dip it into the warm water. Then, carefully, I clean her face: the sweat on her forehead, the stains in the corners of her mouth. The dark circles under her eyes are like ink stains on her pallid skin. I wash behind her ears and on her neck. I unbutton her shirt just enough to reach her shoulders, one at a time. Then I run the cloth over the pink line where her left breast used to be, and lift both arms to clean them up and down and in between the fingertips. I'm worried about the state of her toes, and I'm unsure if she'll let me touch them. Maybe she sees me looking at them, because she lifts up her right foot. She barely breaks the surface of the water and I place my hand underneath the ankle to hold it up for her. The wet pants cling to her leg and her toes are rosy, like raw beef. A sliver of nail is all that's left on her big toe. The toes on the other foot look just as raw, and I try hard not to hurt her; I just dab. When I'm done, I cover her with a towel and help her out of the tub. She lets me. I undress her and fetch her robe. Then I lead her back into bed where I will sleep next to her that night and every night that follows.

The following morning, my mother tells me she's going to have some minor surgery done that Thursday. I can come with her, but it's during one of my midterms so she'll be a lot more upset if I do than if I don't. I know she's planned it this way.

"I can get an extension," I say.

"It's better you're around during recovery," she says.

"I'll come over straight after."

"Sure."

Two and a half months after my mother is diagnosed with grade three oligodendroglioma, my mother has had most of her tumor surgically removed. When I first enter the recovery room, I am taken aback by how good she looks despite the bandages wrapped around her head. I'm probably imagining it, elated by the successful surgery, but she doesn't seem as pale as before and the dark circles under her eyes have faded. She's groggy, a bit disoriented, but comes to rather quickly. The physician's assistant says this is a good thing. Then the doctor comes in to tell us that he, the neurosurgeon, the oncologist, and the radiation oncologist have decided that she needs chemotherapy to control what's left of the tumor. When my mother returns home, the counter has three new additions. The bottles are named vincristine, lomustine, and procarbazine, and come in an orange, a green, and a yellow bottle. The first thing she does, is swap the *Febulous* with the painkillers, so I don't accidentally ingest an antineoplastic chemotherapy drug instead of an iron supplement. She laughs when she shows me this, and I purposely laugh along with her.

Chemotherapy makes my mother weak. She loses weight, and because of her height, she looms over me like an emaciated scarecrow. In the beginning, she tries to vomit only when I'm out of the apartment, sometimes sending me out to buy things we don't need when she feels it coming on. But as weeks pass, the vomiting becomes so frequent that she brings the radio in with her, turning the volume on high, sometimes also leaving the shower and fan running. A few times, I return from her errands while she's still in the bathroom; the thick coughs and guttural gasps for air echo throughout the hallway. When this happens, I seat myself outside our front door until I hear the toilet flush. After a while, this unspoken agreement becomes pointless. She can't eat without throwing up, and I tell her that if she doesn't stop pretending that everything is alright, I'm going to get her a button saying: *I fight for life.*

I stop going to lectures completely. I drop out, tentatively. I tell my professors that my mother is ill and they respond as sympathetically as they can. One professor asks when I plan on coming back and I tell him I'll have to ask my mom when she plans on getting better. She's proud of me for that one, she tells me, but she'll be even prouder if I stop worrying about her and go back to school.

One afternoon, my grandfather calls. I recognize the Northern dialect immediately, even though my mother has lost most of hers. He asks me about school and I tell him that I'm taking a break. He sounds mildly disappointed, and I ask him if he's talked to my mother lately. Not since Christmas, he admits. That's a long time, I say. Only five months, he says. Then he asks if he can speak with her now, and I tell him that she's at the store buying cucumbers for a cucumber salad. I've already decided not to tell him about the cancer. I can't do that. I don't know them well enough to do that. I don't know who would know someone well enough to do that. My grandfather laughs and says it must be my grandmother's recipe and I assure him that of course it is and he laughs again. Then he asks if my mother could call him when she gets the chance, and reminds me that their door is always open. I reply that I want nothing more than to visit them, and regret saying it as soon as we hang up.

There is green grass and flowers outside when the physician's assistant calls to remind my mother to come in early the following morning for her second surgery. "What a cunt," my mother shouts from the bedroom. Her voice is thin. With her still in bed, I begin packing the big brown leather bag.

"What do you want to bring?" I ask her.

"How about my yellow pantsuit?" she says, and I laugh. "I'm not joking."

"I know you're not," I say and put this ochre-colored creation into the bag. "Anything else?"

"How about that KitchenAid?" she asks. "Sure would be nice to have something to remind me of home while I'm there."

"I'll be there, you know."

"I know, but the KitchenAid can stay in the room. During."

"I'll see what I can do," I say and add underwear and socks, clean pajamas, toiletries, and a book."

When I zip the bag shut, my mother is already asleep.

In the morning, a navy Mercedes pulls up onto the sidewalk outside our building. "The cab's here," I call to her, and she says she's just going to throw up one last time before we go. It's July and it's hot. Cafés are crowded and people are strolling lazily along the sticky pavement dressed in shorts and skirts. Tanned arms and legs compared to our pale skin measure time and define life in a way words simply cannot. I recall my mother and me playing Yahtzee in the big park across the street. The folds of her tan stomach left white stripes whenever she stood back up and I would laugh at her. And she would laugh along with me. Seated next to me in the back of the cab, my mother rests her head on my shoulder. The leather seats whimper like rubbery soles on linoleum. I make sure we're both buckled up and the cab takes us to the hospital via the 12 tram and 20 bus route.

"You have what you need?" she asks just as we arrive outside of the hospital main doors.

"Sure," I answer automatically, but realize I'm not quite sure what I need. Was I supposed to bring something? What if I've forgotten what I'm supposed to bring? I don't want to ask my mother; she doesn't need the added stress. But what if I've forgotten something she needs?

"It's OK," she whispers. "It's OK to cry. Just don't cry yourself to death."

I wipe my face, but the tears won't stop. Even though no one is watching me, I want to hide the taut grimace that comes with the sudden swelling of sadness, but I fail and place the tip of my thumbnail between my teeth instead.

I learned that from her. Shortly after telling me that Ane had been wrong, calling her "the beard of a loveless marriage," I caught her masking her own tears in the bathroom. Seeing me see her, she instantly put her thumb to her lips, mumbling something about dinner while fiercely biting her nail.

"I'm sorry we weren't able to bring the KitchenAid," I tell her as I close the cab door behind us.

"Next time," she says.

The hospital greets us with its familiar quietness. The physician's assistant leads us into a private room and places my mother in a bed with crisp white sheets. "How are we feeling?" she asks my mother. "*We're feeling peachy*," my mother replies and asks if *we* could trouble her for a glass of water to which the physician's assistant replies "yes" with angelic resonance and disappears down the hall. I want to say something, but I'm not sure what and the assistant reappears in the blink of an eye holding one of those little plastic cups filled ⅔ with water. She hands it to my mother who takes one small sip and passes it along to me. "Here," she says. "Could you hold this for me until I get back?" And before I know it, they've rolled her out of the room and through swinging doors where I can't follow.

I'm escorted into a seating lounge for family members. I set the plastic cup down on a little table with a lamp next to a wooden chair with multicolored tweed upholstery. I reach for the bottle of water in my handbag, but instead pull out a blue bottle of iron supplements that I forgot to take while I was still in there with her. I glance towards the minimalist IKEA clock on the wall in front of me: six minutes in and an unknown amount to go. I'm the only person in the lounge. A large table stands in the middle of the room and on top of it are neatly stacked magazines that I could read if I wanted to. A book. That's what I forgot. I brought a book for my mother, but didn't think of bringing one for myself. Lucky me then, having a total of eight stacks of magazines to plow through. They want to keep us occupied, badly.

I find a magazine from the previous decade, forgotten in the stacks. I can tell by its outdated cell phone ads. I am temporarily amused by the lavish presentations of already replaced gadgets, but it doesn't take long before my mother's face floats before my eyes. Only, I can't see it properly. It is distorted somehow. In fact, no matter how hard I try, I can't seem to recall the details of her face. All I see is that sickly mask she's worn for the past months, the papery skin and the misty eyes. Will I ever see my mother again? I rip out an ad for a dark blue flip-phone I used to own, fold it, and slip it into my bag.

"How much longer, do you think?" I ask a young nurse who pokes his head into the room. He shakes his head and says he doesn't know because he is looking for someone else. And then he disappears back into the hallway. I carefully select another magazine.

My water bottle is empty and the stacks are no longer neat when a surgeon in scrubs I don't recognize comes into the lounge and looks directly at me. "You've waited a long time," the surgeon says, and then tells me that my mother is in recovery and that I can see her shortly. But she might be sleeping. She had to be conscious during surgery. I'm aware of that, I say. She didn't feel any of it, the surgeon wants to ensure me. That's good, I say. She is most likely a little disoriented, the surgeon continues. I might have noticed some changes in her personality in the past months, and there is a chance I might notice some changes in her personality in the months to come. These could be temporary and these could be permanent. Physical therapy will be beneficial to her recovery as well as follow-up exams. While they believe they were able to remove everything this time, continued chemotherapy may be necessary. "Also, she shouldn't drive for some time."

"She's never had her license," I say.

"Then forget that last part."

The surgeon signals for me to follow and we leave the lounge so I can see her. I've my handbag in one hand and her cup of water in the other.

The door to her room is white and closed shut. The surgeon tells me I can go in, and I nod "thank you," but don't go in. Not right away. For the first time in a long while I know what to do. I wait for the surgeon to leave, then I close my eyes and recall a photograph of my mother taken years ago. She doesn't know she's being photographed as she watches me blow out the four candles. In more ways than one, she's a giant next to me, but under those heavy lids, her eyes shine with anticipation. This is my mother.

The Widow's Daughter

Scott Sikes

On a grass covered hill in the very center of an unused pasture that slopes down to the spot where Coal Creek mixes into Chestnut Creek stands a house, or what remains of a house. It is a shell of emptiness shut up from the world, containing only breathed air that never had chance to escape. It was built in 1919, and it stands to this day as solid as the sky that surrounds it. If it moans in the wind or cracks and pops as it settles, no one is close enough to hear. It stands as it did on the day that George Williams, the man who built it, last turned the heavy lock on the front door and slipped the key into the pocket of his pants and walked through that field and up Coal Creek to his sister's house. He did not look back.

George Williams and his twin sister, Pearl, had been lonely children, born to a mother and father who had prayed long and hard for a child and who had grown tired and bitter with disappointment. Their parents had been childless so long that if we hadn't watched Mrs. Williams' growing belly for those months, we might have believed their birth to be in the same order as a miracle. For them, it was a sign. It was proof enough in the end that their faith had been steadfast and strong. Still, they had many fears of the world that made them skittish and afraid for their children. They kept them close to the house and they kept them busy. There were no friendships with the neighbors and when the time came for them to start school, George and Pearl stayed home. Such a thing was not uncommon then and, if we thought of it at all, we thought it no one's business but their own.

Brother and sister were like mirrors of one another and they only looked more alike the older they got. They were both ribby and lean and stunted and they walked around with hunched up shoulders that made their heads ride out in front of their bodies like turtles. Pearl's hair was cut just as a boy's would be and she wore faded jeans and flannel work shirts, tucked in and cinched tight about her scrawny waist, same as George. They came and went always together, looking down at their shuffling feet and paying no mind at all to the wide world. We watched out for them, but kept our distance. If they wanted anything at the store, it was handed over without a word. George's lower lip pouted out from his face as he simply pointed at the wares they needed, offering only a soft grunt. For a world as small as ours that kept no secrets, the space we offered them was generous and protective. We hardly knew what to make of them anyhow.

When they were fourteen years old, their mother died, their father hardly a year later. It was arranged then for George and Pearl to stay in the little house that had always been their home. It alone was the sum birthright their old mother and father could leave behind when they departed this world. Brother and sister made do with their garden and George gave his labor to small jobs while Pearl took in wash and mending. What bills they had were paid on time. The two of them slipped slowly into the background of our everyday, their oddness mostly ignored or only whispered about from time to time. Politely and with gracious good manners, of course.

George, inching through the world with a humming, deliberate patience, came in his adulthood to be skilled as a carpenter. In those days, we called people like him touched or simple-minded, but George turned that opinion on its head in due course. He may have had no formal schooling in such things as arithmetic and geometry, but his swollen-lipped and empty-eyed smile hid from us a kind of thinking that served a man well. He learned, maybe not quickly, but soon enough, to measure and to cut, to join and to plane, to hammer and to screw with neatness and precision. His hands were steady and stout. He could cipher the roof of a barn to the inch. He could square the frame of a shed true as the Word of God. And the chairs and cabinets he made are today heirlooms passed through families and bid up at auctions even still. The opinions about the quality of his craftsmanship began first as rumors until by years they unwound themselves through and around the community and became a part of what we told about ourselves with pride. His work was sought after and demanded.

George always was a smallish man, a bit bowed even, but the work he did pulled him a fair bit further upright. He came to have a stoutness to him. Firm muscles bulged against his shirt. Pearl, though, grew more frail and brittle, like she was shrinking into herself. She left their place only on Sundays for church, escorted to the front door up one plodding step at a time on the arm of her more solid sibling and then sat weaving as if in a breeze in the corner of their pew in the third row from the back. Communion was served to her there and not at the chancel rail. What sort of existence the two of them cultivated together in their peculiar partnership, we could only guess at. Questions may have been raised in more salacious minds about the possibility of certain irregular intimacies in their household, but by the most of us such things were never spoken of. We are a Christian people after all.

~

The widow Jackson had come raging into our county and bearing down like mad fury, every curve and hole in the road loosening the nails of the wagon she drove. It bore the weight of a sparse life lately ripped asunder by the untimely death of her husband who had been a foreman in the mines over at Austinville and whose demise may or may not have been an accident. Her six young boys ran barefoot alongside, doing their best to keep up, while her only daughter, Isabelle, held tight to the bench beside her. The widow's jaw even then was fixed as hard against her face as it was for as long as we knew her. There was a look of madness drilling out from that woman's eyes. Wispy flames of hair white as the moon flailed away from the bun on her head, trailing a face older than its time and spotted by dark flecks of the snuff she kept packed in her upper lip throughout the day.

Her husband's life had been worth enough money to buy her three hundred acres on Meadow Creek and there she set to work building her own kingdom in that corner of the county. It happened before anyone noticed that hers had become one of the largest dairy outfits around and, while propriety and custom kept her officially out of the seats of local government and law-making, her hand wanted not for power and influence over those who cast about for the support of the electorate. She single-handedly financed the building of the Meadow Creek Methodist Church and her tithe went far in supporting the preacher who circuited through each month. No one ever called her a godly woman, but she kept the Sabbath and expected the same of all others. She could be fearsome and she had no patience for her children. They shuddered in her shadow and dreaded the anger that would cut loose her tongue and set it to lashing about with such wrath that it sometimes sent her dentures flying forth amongst a blast of curses and condemnation. She damned them each to hell on a regular basis.

They could follow their daddy there for all she cared. It was her practice to always keep a good willow switch in one hand or at least near enough to reach, lest they forget for even a moment who was in charge. They were not the only ones to live in fear of her.

The widow's daughter, Isabelle, was never a beauty, but there was a grace to her. She had the same way of carrying herself like a good horse does. She was a plain girl from the beginning and she wasn't an especially joyful kind. In a world where few of us smiled besides, she stood apart for the abundant concentration she wore as countenance most all the time. But you couldn't find a more sensible type, even in the face of her mother's wild rages and plain meanness. If the widow plowed that household forward to prominence and prosperity, her daughter kept it steady and straight down the row. It was Isabelle who watched over her brothers and gave them their daily care, while the widow fumed and fussed about. It seems that in full spite of their mother, those children all turned out to be wholly good and decent people, the kind you hope to walk among all your days. Maybe it is suffering that begets such uprightness, because if anyone had to stand solid in the blazes of that woman's expectations, it was Isabelle Jackson.

~

It came to be a few years later that the widow hired George Williams out for a good amount of regular work. She was a woman who could not offer a compliment, but she respected good hard labor and she let it be known. For the widow, work was a noble thing. It was really all she ever knew. And, in George she found a man keen on taking orders. It steadied his soul to have a plan laid out for him, a thing to set his mind upon and to get done. Tell him what was needed doing and he got about it with hardly a question and without a grievance uttered. He was dependable that way, as sure as the sun in the morning. Their two minds fit together, the one wild and unbitted, the other dull and ponderous. It was a match of industry each had not known it wanted for.

By now, the widow's daughter, in the opinions of some among us, was far beyond the time when she should have left her mother's house and assumed charge of her own. The oldest boy, Joshua, was now married himself and part of the work George had been hired to do was spurred by the need to make the Jackson place accommodating enough for a larger family. Imagine being a daughter-in-law in the widow's house. There was hardly room to make your own way; you had to elbow yourself into your daily living. Isabelle, though, was resigned to her place in that world. What might have stirred inside her, the kinds of things a young woman might think about, we can only suppose she kept tamped down inside somehow. Besides, her mother had hold of that girl like a sprung trap. There was not a choice for Isabelle to be anything other than chaste, and no man with any bit of sense about him notioned to call upon that house. She found herself in a lonely fix.

The particulars of how the widow's daughter and George Williams first came to take notice of one another is known only to them, of course. Can we ever really know how two people come to see in each other the scattered pieces of their lives that they have yet to find elsewhere along the way? Some of us like to imagine it was a thing that startled them both. Maybe the widow's daughter, rushing about her chores, turned a corner of the house and ran smack into George Williams as he came from the other direction. Maybe George, slipping around back of the barn to relieve himself, was surprised to look up and find Isabelle headed just then up the path from the potato patch. There might have been a hot summer day when she thought to offer George a dipper full of spring water and their eyes had chance to meet, a thing passing between them that each understood clearly and right away. It is hard to say. Between those two, conversation would have been lacking. But some of the things we feel the most are never said out loud. Think, too, of the way George could smile. It had its charm. As has been told, George Williams, innocent as he was in most of the goings-on of the world, in a lot of ways showed as all man to a body cued to notice. A young woman stifling a certain yearning might have found that hard to ignore, even allowing for her otherwise sensible head.

Lust, though, was but one piece of the ties that bound these two together. The threads were knotted tighter between them because of a thing more considerable than mere physical need. That is for certain. We know this because of what George Williams did when he came to understand that he loved Isabelle Jackson and wanted her for his wife.

He started slow. Time was not a thing he paid much attention to. He knew it to be a force outside himself that could not be stopped anyhow, which is not to say that he tarried about this particular business. George

Williams rushed no job. And this one, he knew from the beginning, would be his masterwork, like a monument to all his years of gathering skill.

He had been hoarding away cash in a crock in the corner of the springhouse for years. He hardly thought of it. With that money he soon got hold of a piece of land just down the creek from the home he had known his entire life. He had been laboring for years by then with nary a debt to anyone and money ignored has a way of piling up over such a time. The man he bought it off of, Charlie McKnight, was as about as neighborly as a nest of hornets and the pasture itself was stuck well back on the far side of Colby Knob. The only way anybody got to it then was by the way George went. He walked in along the creek.

Because of where it was, George was able to go about his work in the way he liked best, without notice or bother. By the time word got around that he was building a house, he had it already under roof. It was not a grand thing. It was not meant to be. It was square, four rooms on either side of a wide hallway that led to the kitchen on the back, a loft above. But the seams were tight, the corners joined perfectly, the nails driven straight and true, all the things put just as they should be that you don't notice right away but that make a house sturdy and strong.

Looking up at it now, you can see, too, that it was not only what he put there that George was thinking of, but where he put it. If you know what you're seeing, you can't help but understand the care he took. The house is within easy walking of what we call lasting water. It stands on a westward slope, catching the most of the sun during the day. Below it runs those two creeks, clear and cold, through bottomland black with rich, loamy dirt. George chose a place to make a life, one that would take hold.

It is astounding how long a secret can be known only by two people if it is powerful enough to the both of them. George's true reason for building that house never crossed our minds. We puzzled over it, sure, but in the end it seemed he had finally found the gumption to strike off from his sister, weary of hearing her snores every night perhaps or just now figuring the strangeness of their situation and eager to amend it. We were glad for him.

The widow could not have suspected anything at play against her while George was building his house. She didn't take to thinking over such things. Like anything else with George, she paid it no mind as long as he did what she asked. She was a serious woman who acted on instinct and without mercy. Running up against her was like hearing a rattler buzzing at your feet. By then, it's probably too late. Anger was just not a thing she kept hidden. If she had had one whiff in all that time that there was anything between George and Isabelle, it would have ended then and there.

When she found out that her daughter was expecting a child, though, the gnashing rage that overtook her was not a thing to be contained. It was fed not only by the shame that Isabelle had brought upon that fair and upstanding household, but by the sudden realization of what had been going on right under her very nose. She thought her own mind cleverer than most others, and here's this slow-witted man of such low stock spreading his seed among her own. For she needed but a trifling moment to figure out who the father of that child had to be. She added up quick the things she had missed; mostly that George was the only man about the place that was not a brother to Isabelle. She knew then what had been pulled on her and that abrupt understanding was enough to make her seethe with a hot, hating anger. She brought down a kind of wrath born of the Devil, and Isabelle bore every bit of it in blood. The widow must have thought she could beat the child out of the poor girl's womb. The brothers only brought themselves to intervene when their mother was soaked in sweat and exhausted, nearly to the point of stopping herself. Even then, only Joshua, the oldest, had the gall to step between them. Before the next noon, before the lashed wounds all over Isabelle's body had chance to scab, the widow's plans had been settled to ship her daughter off to a place where, if the shame could not be drawn out, it could at least be hidden.

Joshua walked for the rest of his life as if he carried a heaving burden of regret upon his shoulders. He was a prosperous man, with plenty of land and children, and we always thought of him as the kind of upright person his mother could only suppose she was. She may have been infamous, but he was beloved and respected. He lived to be an old age, a passel of grandchildren crawling about his feet. But it was not a regret for having stood by while his mother beat his sister so savagely that lay upon him all his days. It was instead a sadness attached at a deep within place. It was a kind of evil that latched itself upon him the minute he walked into the barn just at first light on the morning Isabelle was to be sent off. He was the one to find her hanging there, the noosed rope creaking against the rafter as the weight of her body pulled so lightly down, swaying its cold stiffness in the early breeze coming in from the drive.

For the rest of his days, George Williams was like a ghost in his own memory. He became even more of a stranger to us. After shutting up the house he had built, he visited it no more. He left it to watch over the remains of all he had lost. To think that such a place, so finely made, never saw life inside itself, never held within it echoes of human voices, never bore scuffmarks on its floors or marks along its walls, never sweat with the breathed hopes of the living. It is haunted only by silences. The house stands there now to remember a lifetime that was stolen before it was hardly imagined. It stands in memory of the widow's daughter.

Ambushed

Kathryn Brown

Slipping out of the bright sun my patrol car creeps slowly towards the end of the alley, where I see the faces of three scruffy looking people seeking refuge on a filthy mattress against the far wall. A sliver of open air running between two tall buildings, the alley is steeped in shadow and a patternless collection of garbage. Radio signals are blocked by the height of the buildings in alleys like this. If I need help I'll be on my own.

What am I doing? Rolling down this alley filled with a simmering desperation to prove myself.

I am not who I was. A strange fear and shame sit high on my shoulders waiting to strangle any thoughts of value or bravery. It has been so easy to lose myself that I have begun to wonder what there was of me to lose.

A few months ago I had responded to a simple complaint about a car blocking someone's driveway. It was a bogus complaint so that when I drove up to the address I found no car anywhere near the driveway. That's when a sixteen-year-old with a .45 caliber revolver walked up behind my patrol car and blasted through my rear windshield. For many moments it was all thunderous sound and vibration and the smell of burning fabric as the explosions kept coming and the headrest next to my ear tore open. He was determined, this young gangster who wanted to be a big shot by killing a cop, and the explosive reverberations continued as nickel-sized holes opened up on the dashboard in front of me and a chunk of my steering wheel blew off. Bent over for cover amid the smell of gunpowder and flying glass, I pressed hard on the gas pedal and wondered if I might die. I sped down the street, the gunman running after me, shooting round after round, the roar of the blasts swirling around my ears and pinging off of car parts, until finally I was out of range and he was out of bullets.

Afterward I thought my blood would boil over I was so charged with anger and confusion. Wildness filled me so that when I stumbled out of my car fellow cops who ran to me in concern found me shouting at them to search the shadows for the gunman rather than pick shards of glass from my hair.

I went home and poured myself a shot of icy vodka to roll over the grit at the back of my throat. Sitting at the kitchen table I closed my eyes, my head dropping from exhaustion. Minutes later I found myself waking violently, my heart and lungs drumming as I imagined the gunman's bullet entering my back, breaking me into pieces. I held my face in my hands and felt a deep shudder rumble through my body.

I have come to know an intimate, brutal fear and it has caused me to be solitary and lost. Now I find myself suddenly slow to respond to calls, hesitant to work alone, shy with hardened criminals. Repulsed by my timidity, this weakness, I have developed deep roots of darkness and shame that cause me to believe that it would have been better if I had been killed that night.

For weeks I have hung motionless over the pieces that used to be me, wanting to put myself back together the way I once was, when I saw everything as possible. I find myself approaching every danger as an opportunity to prove myself, every peril as a duel between my soul and the fear that causes my hands to tremble. But nothing fits as it had before and as I drive down the alley I know that I am raw and lost and falling apart all over again, looking to be saved in the faces of those whose suffering might outweigh my own.

At the end of the alley Sammy is lying on his side across the lap of a woman I know as Pearl. She sits on a blue plastic milk crate and concentrates on the flesh of his neck, her long full hair falling over his pale face as if she were Mary tending to the suffering Jesus. She holds a loaded needle of heroin and searches the side of his neck for a cooperative vein. Through my eyes I see the intimacy of their movements. I drive up and she drops the needle, pushing him off of her and scrambling backwards onto the mattress where the others sit with indifferent eyes. Sammy sits on the ground, looking as if his heart has just been broken.

The sight of me causes them to hide whatever they're doing and toss their dope. An old guy in a poncho puts his paper bag covered beer behind him. He's crouched down and looks up at me, his rheumy eyes watery and unfocused. I walk to where he's sitting.

"Pour out your beer, pal." I order, hating the tone of my voice.

"Ah come on man, I only got this one. I ain't hurtin' no one."

"Pour it out."

There is an intolerable ugliness in my bullying so that I look down and let the shame wash over me unseen. The old guy tilts the can and watches the liquid gold of his Colt 45 foam up on the street and soak into the side of the stained mattress. Sammy sits up, his hungry eyes racing to the full needle thrown to the ground.

Why am I here? What good can possibly come of this?

Sammy is skinny and sick.

"Sammy, you've got a warrant."

The warrant is for a small, meaningless transgression.

"Shit, please don't take me in." His eyes flick back to the full needle.

I have rules.

"Come on, stand up."

Maybe he senses that the ground is no longer solid under my feet. Maybe he senses that the good in me is trying to find a way out.

"I gotta fix, you can see that," he pleads.

My purpose is fluid and lost, flowing out of my body so that I stand unsure.

"Stand up, goddamn it."

He stands. We stare at each other, the despair in our eyes reaching out and swirling together so that it is the same.

I reach for him and feel his muscles tighten. I push him and he pushes me back and we struggle in a slow motion dance of demons and despair. I can hardly hold on, my strength leaving me, replaced by the fear of knowing that I have to let go of the old. Not much of a fight, just my pushing him against my patrol car and him resisting my effort to get his hands behind his back and me trying to believe that this is worthwhile and him just trying to get his next fix and me knowing this isn't necessary but fighting anyway because I have to feel strong and tough again and he needs his fix and our desperation comes together and wraps itself around this sad mix of human despair. Here in this alley, this pathetic push and pull.

He has broken the rules, he has a warrant, but the rules have lost their meaning, and he asks to fix before I bring him in and that is against the rules too. The rules that no longer mean anything because the only thing that matters is that we are here together working through this human experience, both of us filled with a despair that has led us to each other. Here, together, wrestling through the dark haunts of our lives, both trying to survive in a place that makes no sense.

What am I doing? What have I done?

Now he is bent over the hood of my car, face down while I put handcuffs on him and he is crying with the agony of knowing he will be locked away from his bliss and I want to scream and beg him to forgive me.

They all stand now. Angry and resentful, they despise me.

Pearl comes closer when I ask, looking around and tucking her hair behind one ear. Her eyes are dark, accusing. She looks down at the loaded needle at her feet unable to grasp what I have just asked.

She is so tender with him and I watch in a trance as she runs her fingers over his arms and hands looking for the vein that will help end his anguish.

And then it is done.

Nothing makes sense anymore. I put Sammy into the backseat of my patrol car and suddenly I feel like I want to cry because I have lost myself in his pleading eyes.

Pearl rests her hand on my shoulder and I flinch but don't pull away. I feel myself no longer brave but somehow forgiven.

Nervous Systems

Heidi Czerwiec

> *I sing the body electric.*
>
> —Whitman

While you religiously schedule regular checkups—medical, dental, car, etc.—you're awful about going to the doctor for unscheduled breakdowns. You tend to save up lots of little problems and take the whole rag-and-bone shop in at the same time. Last May, right after classes ended, it was a wart on your finger, worsening plantar fasciitis, and an odd numb sensation you'd developed on the left side of your face.

Your doctor handily freezes the wart with a magical hiss of liquid nitrogen and arranges a shot of cortisone for your foot. But she says, "I don't like the facial numbness. I want you to see a neurologist." You don't think too much about it because you're freaking out about a needle being inserted in your heel, but it ends up being not that bad. You walk tenderly to the front desk and make another appointment. You go home, where your son pats you on the face and you barely feel it.

A neurological assessment is a bit like a DUI checkpoint—lights shining in your eyes while you touch your nose and balance and walk imaginary tightropes—except you also get poked with pins. Except the pins you're poked with feel dull, like ballpoint pens. In your Southern accent, "pins" and "pens" sound the same. In the southern part of your face, pins and pens feel the same. He also asks about your migraines, your mother's neuropathies, your grandfather's Lewy-Body. He says, "I don't like the facial numbness. I want you to get some tests."

You have some blood drawn, a chest x-ray and, a week later, go for an MRI. You haven't worn any metal—even your sports bra is underwireless. But you notice on the release form that they ask about tattoos. You don't want the magnets to make your cool new black-inked Bettie Page bubble and burst. The tech says they'll only be scanning your head, so your tattoos will be fine. He asks if you're claustrophobic, if you need a Valium. You say no, you've had an MRI before, after a car accident. It's loud but boring, and your legs are cold. Then, the tech injects you with radioactive ink, which is a little less boring until it's boring again. Then you go home and wait. You're sure it's a tumor.

A couple weeks later, the neurologist tells you that it's not a brain tumor. He says there were some small spots on the brain MRI—inconclusive— and mixed results on the blood tests—also inconclusive. He wants to do a spinal tap to check for a viral or bacterial attack, but can't schedule it until after the Fourth of July, so you spend the long holiday weekend unable to enjoy the lake or the fireworks or your son dancing along the edge of the small-town parade that has more participants than audience because you're freaking out about a needle being inserted in your spine. It ends up being not that bad. The neurologist tells you the fluid appears clear, but he'll have the results in a few days—try to stay horizontal for the rest of the day. And you do, though your son keeps pulling up at the side of your bed where you're supposed to remain horizontal, and wonders why you can't pick him up for a week.

A week later, on the anniversary of your son's adoption, you text his birth mother, with whom you try to maintain communication:

One year since our adoption became official.

Thank you for making that possible.

> My pleasure ☺

> I wanted to let you guys know that my doctor thinks I have multiple sclerosis. I'm going in for an MRI sometime next week so they can see if I have lesions on my brain.

Thanks for telling us. Keep us posted. I'll let our doctor know.

I'm going through something like that too. Kinda scary.

I sure will.

It is very scary. For 3 weeks now I feel almost retarded.

Really? Mine's a partially numb face.

My MRI wasn't very helpful, so more tests.

Here's hoping for answers, and for treatment, for both of us.

No doubt!

At the follow-up, the neurologist says that, having ruled out all the common mimics—sarcoidosis, Lyme disease, Vitamin B deficiency—he thinks it may be multiple sclerosis. He lays out the options: a wait-and-see approach with repeated MRIs each year, begin a lifetime of self-administered expensive shots to delay progression and deterioration, or get a second opinion at the MS Clinic in Fargo. You get the sense that he wants you to ask for a second opinion, but you can't tell for sure, and he won't tell you what you should do. You want to defer to the doctor; he wants to defer to you. Clearly, you aren't communicating clearly. You say you want to think about it, discuss it with your family.

Your perception of MS is limited to Annette Funicello, who just died of the disease, and President Jeb Bartlett on *The West Wing*, whose symptoms make for dramatic plot points in his fictional second campaign, second term. Ever the academic, you turn to online research, which is always the best way to calm your fears.

You find that MS is an inflammatory disease in which the immune system attacks myelin—the insulating sheath of nerve fibers in the brain and spinal cord—damaging it and causing scar tissue (sclerosis) to form. This damage disrupts the ability of parts of the nervous system to communicate—nerve impulses traveling to and from the brain and spinal cord are distorted or interrupted, producing a wide variety of symptoms: blurred vision, loss of balance, poor coordination, slurred speech, tremors, numbness, extreme fatigue, problems with memory and concentration, paralysis, blindness, and more. MS takes several forms, with new symptoms either occurring in isolated attacks (relapsing forms) or building up over time (progressive forms). Between attacks, symptoms may disappear completely; however, permanent neurological problems often occur, especially as the disease advances. With treatment, most patients experience mild attacks and are relatively unaffected except for minor adaptations, with the average time to disease progression being twenty years from diagnosis. (Annette Funicello died almost twenty years to the day from her diagnosis.)

It's been a couple of months since the start of this trail of tests, and the insurance statements and bills have started to appear in the mail. You spend hours on the phone with the university's HR department, with the North Dakota Public Employees' benefits program, and with Blue Cross/Blue Shield, trying to figure out coverage, options, and what your future needs and expenses might be if you do have MS and need injections. You've blown through your individual deductible quickly, which is kinda cool, but you still have to pay copayments for each appointment, and a coinsurance percentage of all procedures. And you can't get a definitive answer on how much of the shots would be covered, which is a major concern: depending on how often you inject they can cost up to $65,000 per year, and for now the major pharmaceutical producer has staved off the release of a generic drug, which drives up the price.

It's expensive, and it's making you worry, which for you is a constant state that just attaches itself to different things. You call yourself a realist. Not a pessimist. Just planning for the worst-case scenario. Already established as a professor when you married Evan, you've always been the family's main earner, but now as Evan prepares to enter law school, you will be the sole breadwinner for at least the next three years. You talk about this with him often, the stress makes you melodramatic, you make him promise to finish law school no matter what, in case he needs to be the sole income. You plan for the ugly stuff.

Though your son, Wyatt, is growing heavy and can walk on his own, you pick up and carry him around whenever he asks, even when he doesn't ask, because how long will you be able to?

And for now, you're able to carry him, able to carry your family, able to pay. Easily. But it makes you fantasize about Medicaid paying for everything. Until in your online research you find FAQs about Medicaid's handling of MS treatment and realize that paying is a privilege, that scheduling Medicaid appointments and submitting for coverage is a full-time job in itself, one that many patients who are hourly employees can ill afford, either in time or money. Minimum-wage employees like Wyatt's birth mother Kinzey, whom you need to call:

How is your testing going? Have your doctors given you any answers?

I'm trying to decide whether to do the MS shots.

A couple weeks go by—communication with Kinzey is often spotty. Then, your phone sparks:

> Hey it's Kinzey. I just got a new number! The doctors think I have primary progressive.... Not sure how I'm supposed to take it because it's really confusing to me. I can't take care of Elly [her daughter], so she's with my sister in Arizona. I used to call Elly every day and now it slips my mind until late at night most days. I even forgot for a week I had a daughter until someone asked me how's Elly and I said who's Elly?

I'm so sorry. For all of it—the MS, Elly. Keep us posted.
We love you. Wyatt is doing so great—he loves his preschool
& is such a lovey little guy. Right now, his favorite things
are tacos, the garden sprinkler, & singing Itsy Bitsy Spider.

> That is soooo awesome to hear!

Terrified by the thought of forgetting about Wyatt, you decide to discuss your case with the MS specialist in Fargo. Also, you want to know as much about the disease as possible so you can forge the way—in your online reading, you find it might be hereditary, though less so for sons. Kinzey has it. You may have it. Does our son have it? He's had early issues with eczema and bad allergies, which can be indicators of a sensitive immune system. You suddenly realize that you would have to worry about this regardless of who his mother is.

Ever the writer, the poet, the trivialist, you find yourself drawn to the less-useful information about MS. For instance, a young woman called Halldora who lived in Iceland around 1200 suddenly lost her vision and mobility but, after praying to the saints, recovered them seven days later. Saint Lidwina of Schiedam (1380-1433), a Dutch nun, may be one of the first clearly identifiable people with MS. From the age of 16 until her death at 53, she had intermittent pain, weakness of the legs, and vision loss—symptoms typical of MS. Both cases have led to the proposal of a "Viking gene" hypothesis for the dissemination of the disease, linked to vitamin D deficiency—a lack of sunlight in climes like Northern Europe, or here in the Upper Midwest with its Scandinavian settler roots and Vikings football fans.

Fears of forgetting and of heritage drive you to drive across the north of the north to Fargo for a second opinion. The woman who runs the MS clinic is a great listener, reviews your tests in depth, and does her own neurological exam, which includes extensive measuring of how signals are communicated, firing along the thin tinder of your limbs. Some of these include sticking electrodes to your skin and jolting you with a needle or taser-like tool which, while not painful, is unpleasant. But your favorite is her testing of your extremities, where she strikes a tuning fork, sets it to your foot or hand, and you're supposed to tell her when the vibrations stop. You're so charmed by the concept—the body electric actually singing!—that you forget to note its ceasing. She expresses concern that you exhibit some damage or deadened nerve communication, but also is perplexed that while you exhibit a range of diffuse deteriorations, none are significant, and while your brain contains lesions, they are minor, likely from migraines, and are not clustered like MS's constellation. She wants you to see the head of Neurology.

November ends.

Happy Thanksgiving, Kinzey! We are so grateful for you,
& for Wyatt. He was ok with turkey, no potatoes,
but he kept eating gravy with a spoon
& stealing pickles & olives off Evan's plate.

> Elly loves pickles and olives too!! Happy Thanksgiving to you
> guys!

He also sucks on lemons! How are you?

> Crazy! She does too!
> I'm doing ok.
> My MS has been messing with me really bad. I had to stop
> working.

That's awful. Are you on disability?

> Not yet, but hopefully soon. Mostly just scared about the future.

I'm sure. My symptoms are really mild,
but I worry about the future too. It's like a time bomb.
Thinking about you a lot. Much love.

> Much love to you guys!!

Over the next few weeks, you meet with the Chief of Neurology, a small
Chinese man who wears flamboyant ties. Communication is sometimes
difficult because he speaks quickly in accented English, but you like him.
He reviews your tests, repeats some of them, and orders a few new ones.
During one—which involves jolting you with a pronged instrument and
measuring the response through electrodes—his neurology technician
obviously gets an odd reading, because she frowns at the computer
screen. She jolts your left eyebrow a couple more times, making it leap
and sear repeatedly, but gets the same result. When the neurologist
comes in, the technician points at the screen. The neurologist gets very
excited, actually claps his hands. "Textbook!" he exclaims. It appears he
means this literally—he pulls a textbook from the shelf and flips through
it, finding a page whose illustration matches your brain's electrical

response. They talk animatedly for a few moments, and then he shows you the book. "You have a lesion on your brainstem. This is the textbook response," he points. "Are you sure?" you ask. He nods. "We could do more MRIs, but they will show this. I am sure." You think a minute. "That sounds awful." He shrugs. "Not really—nothing to worry about unless it changes or gets worse. Call if it gets worse. But it's not MS." As you leave, the desk asks if you need to make a follow-up appointment, and you say, "I guess not."

And that's it.

They had been searching for a Grand Unified Theory that could incorporate all your symptoms into one syndrome, but there was none. What you are left with is a collection of individual irritations, none insidious. Some numbness at your nerves' peripheries. Carpal tunnel. A tendency to migraine, which resulted in some minor brain lesions, but which don't form microclusters in the manner of MS. One terrifying-sounding-but-boringly-mundane lesion causing the dull facial sensation in your cheek that, in the following years, does not deteriorate further.

And yet, in the following years, signals between you and Kinzey deteriorate. She stops returning texts; messages bounce back; mail is undeliverable. A lesion, a blockage in communication. You find her on Facebook—because the two of you are not friends, you cannot read all her information, but she posts various MS awareness links before her account goes inactive. Wyatt lost his birth mother once; he may lose her again. But, for now, he won't lose you.

The truth is, for all the parallels between you and Kinzey, your situations couldn't be more different. The very system that kept Kinzey in poverty, left without a safety network and unable to take care of the children she gives birth to, is the very system that allows you to be the one who can afford to adopt and raise him. Who, even in the throes of considering what a diagnosis of MS might mean, knows that your son would still have Evan to care for him, and behind him, a whole body of family and friends.

And yet she remains there, a persistent blank at the bottom of your brain.

"Health" Theme Contest Winner – 1st Place

Art of the Body

Christine Stewart-Nuñez

—After *Aquaform* by Pauline Aitken

I see art in the body and the body in art
no matter where I look on this wall:
in canvases, in my son's darting shadow.

Aquaform, with its nucleus at the heart,
membranes and organelles I'll call
these shapes, and I'll make this a window

to consider seizures, how they part
neurons and words, how they stall
my son's learning. Mine feels shallow:

on a gallery walk, thoughts start.
I focus first, then fall
into paint, into cells, into sorrow.

*

Into paint, into cells, into sorrow
I focus first, then fall.
On a gallery walk, my thoughts start—

my son's learning. Mine feels shallow.
Neurons and words—how they stall
to consider seizures, how they part

these images and make this a window
Membranes and organelles I'll call
Aquaform, with its nucleus at the heart.

In canvases, in my son's darting shadow,
no matter where I look on this wall,
I see art in the body and the body in art.

"Health" Theme Contest Winner – 2nd Place

Souvenir from Where You've Been

Raquel Fontanilla

Numbness, as if someone crept in and anaesthetized the left side of my head, wakes me in the dead of a sticky July night, just outside a U.S. Army base in South Korea. I knead my skin and pinch my earlobe: still nothing. I attribute this phantom sensation to sleeping too long in one position and nod off again. An hour later, my eyes fly open as the bed plummets to the ground, spinning me around like an off-balance load of laundry, only to throw me up toward the ceiling again. My eyes roll in their sockets; moving my head even a fraction makes me vomit. My husband of five months fumbles in his wallet to find the emergency contact card handed out during in-processing, the kind of card you think you'll never need. There is only a small troop clinic on post, so the operator has to hunt down an interpreter, who in turn calls a Korean ambulance, and a three-way call ensues. We're the first and only residents in a newly-built duplex community; the road leading to Eastern Village is unpaved, unnamed, and unlit. In the hour it takes for the ambulance to find our house, I throw up, collapse face first onto the bed exhausted, and repeat the process over again, all the while aware of the terror on my husband's face as language fails him.

We moved to Korea from Japan two months ago, but it's been twelve years since I left my native New Zealand to study at graduate school in Tokyo. I have an ear for languages: I wrote my PhD dissertation in Japanese and I'm already picking up Korean, but language is inaccessible to me in this moment, my body pinning me to the bed, vomit blooming on the pillow like yellow algae.

What I don't know is that a catastrophic event is unfolding in my inner ear: a tsunami of infected fluid is washing over the tiny hair cells that stimulate nerves to change sound waves into impulses which the brain then interprets as understandable sound. It turns out that the inner ear also regulates balance, and the severity of my vertigo correlates directly to the degree of my hearing loss.

Dawn is breaking as I'm trundled into the optimistically named Good Morning Hospital. In snippets of lucidness, I learn from the ER doctor that something has happened inside my ear, but for a day I drift on morphine and don't completely understand the situation until I awaken to see a moon-faced young doctor standing over me. This is a provincial hospital and his English is marginally better than my Korean. Dr. Moon leans toward me, holding a metal Y-shaped fork that I associate with divining water. Like a magician, he holds it to the bone behind my right ear and a few seconds later moves it around to the front of the same ear. I hear a ringing noise and smile at his trick. He goes through the same motions with my left ear, but this time I look up at him with a soft dumb expression. Cocking his head to one side, he sucks in wet air through the side of his mouth, and in that instant no translation is needed. I know this language from Japan. *Not good.*

In the dim sealed space of the audiology booth, the beeps and buzzes of the audiogram reveal profound hearing loss, which means that a jet plane would have to roar directly overhead for me to hear anything in my left ear. Three days later, I leave the hospital with a new vocabulary—Sudden Sensorineural Hearing Loss, Single-Sided Deafness, acoustic neuroma—but without an answer to what I most want to know: *naze, wei,* why? This turns out to be a question that baffles even the most experienced medical professionals, including Dr. Google, who reports that 90% of cases of sudden deafness are idiopathic, meaning a myriad of possible causes, including viral or bacterial infection, head trauma, autoimmune diseases, tumors, neurological disorders, blood flow abnormalities, and genetics. What I am left with is the fact that the nerves in my inner ear are shot, rendering traditional hearing aids useless. I totter out the doors of Good Morning Hospital like a listing ship, clutching a prescription for ten days of Prednisone, and a skipping rope, because in Korea, as in Japan, you always get a souvenir from where you've been.

~

At home, woozy and disorientated, I lurk on Internet support forums for sudden hearing loss, devouring stories of spontaneous recovery: up to two-thirds of those afflicted regain all or some of their hearing, usually within a week or two of initial onset. As the weeks go by, I accept that I am not in this category and that the damage is permanent. I marvel at how "f" and "d" are so close on the keyboard, how easy it is to slip from "deaf" to "dead," like the tiny hairs inside my inner ear. I obsessively search the Internet for people deaf in one ear: Rob Lowe, Holly Hunter, Stephen Colbert! I take heart from the fact that their disability isn't visible, but as I discover, this is not always a good thing: people think I'm aloof, not realizing that they're talking to my deaf side.

Coincidences well up from deep in my memory: the constant string of ear infections I had as a child; the story of my grandmother's brother, who had been born in an age when he was called "deaf and dumb" and died of a kick to the head during a rugby game as a boy. When I ask my mother about him, she reveals a hitherto unspoken-of slew of deaf cousins and second cousins, which makes me wonder if there is a familial gene and I toy with the idea of DNA testing. In the dead of the night, when I lie awake pondering if I am destined to lose all my hearing, I press my deaf ear into my husband's chest, his steady heartbeat gone, and imagine what it would be like to inhabit total silence.

I recall the handful of times I saw deaf people on the train in Tokyo, how I stole glances at their animated facial expressions and deft finger work, unaware at the time that Japanese had its own sign language, separate from that of American or British Sign Language. Then there was my classmate in graduate school who was translating an English book into Japanese about hearing children born to deaf parents. I spent a few afternoons helping her with some of the more difficult English expressions; I asked why deaf was sometimes capitalized, to which she replied that deaf refers to the medical condition, while Deaf refers to the culture. But that was the extent of my interest. When I was packing up to leave Japan, I remember weighing the smooth cover of *Mother Father Deaf* in my hands, trying to decide whether to add it to my already overstuffed boxes of books. Reasoning that the topic had nothing to do with me, I tossed it onto the recycle pile.

~

The psychological impact of my single-sided deafness hits me hard a month later, when I'm at a restaurant having dinner with a dozen or so of my husband's American and Korean colleagues. K-Pop is pounding in the background, the room is dim, and multiple conversations are flying back and forth. One of the men punches the air every few minutes with an outburst of laughter that ricochets off my empty left ear and explodes into my hearing ear with all the force of a grenade. I am trapped in a grotesque carnival of noise, and when someone suggests karaoke, I rush out of the restaurant in tears, gasping for air. The irony is that while I have lost sound, the world is noisier, since all the aural information—horns honking, stereos blaring, dogs barking, coffee machines grinding—now pours in unfiltered through one ear.

I apply the same research skills I used in the writing of my dissertation to try to understand why I am more irritable than before, why I want to be alone more often. I discover that you need two functioning ears to triangulate sound, to filter out and make sense of what is coming in and to tune into conversations in the face of background chatter. The loss of one of those input channels throws nature's precise system off kilter, making sound one giant messy alphabet soup, a clamoring cacophony of foreign languages beyond my reach. I can no longer eavesdrop in cafes; I have to make a mad dash for the chair that will position me at just the right angle in relation to the speaker. In time, I learn to avoid crowded rooms, to choose quiet restaurants to meet friends, and good light by which to read their lips. I become an observer of mouths, noticing how lipstick bleeds into the vertical lines on a top lip, catching the flash of a silver filling in a molar.

I look to other people's faces to clue me in on who is speaking, trying to avoid those moments of dumb wonder when it appears as if a woman's voice is streaming out of the mouth of the man sitting beside me. I must constantly decide if it's worth investing my attention in conversations between people on my "bad side"; I find myself more often than not tuning out if I don't get the first few minutes. This reminds me of my first classes in Japan, when there was so much new vocabulary that my brain switched off and I sat there with a blank smile. It's been a long time since I've felt that kind of helplessness; this distance from my native tongue sends small aftershocks that displace what I thought I knew. People nod without understanding when I tell them I have single-sided deafness—at least you still have one good ear, they say, at least you can't tell from looking at you—and so I am marginalized further, not allowed to mourn my loss, the fact that my old friend language has turned on me. I catch myself giving that vague awkward smile the hearing impaired use when they don't want to rock the boat and stem the flow of conversation by asking the speaker to repeat themselves.

Noise is not only painful but terrifying. Binaural hearing lets you know where sound is coming from, so people with unilateral hearing loss are unable to localize sound. Walking across a parking lot with a supermarket cart clattering over the asphalt, my eyes dart from side to side as if I'm anticipating sniper fire while crossing no-man's land. I hear cars idling, reverse signals beeping, but I can't tell where these sounds come from, nor how near or far away they may be. At home in separate rooms, I call out to my husband, *Where are you? Here*, he says. *But where?* I sing back. *In the bedroom, by the window*, he replies, a ship's captain giving me coordinates in the darkness. My ears have become traitorous translators: I struggle with higher frequency sounds, consonants and in particular voiceless consonants, which happen to contain much of the meaning of English speech. "National" becomes "Nashville," "new leadership" becomes "nuclear ship," and hilarity, or frustration, follows.

My body learns a new physicality too, beginning with the act of regaining my balance as my brain adjusts to having only one working channel of equilibrium. And then there is the elaborate dance I do when walking beside someone, in which I make what I hope is an imperceptible swing behind them and pop up on their left, so they are talking into my "good ear." In Japanese, someone who is hard of hearing is *mimi ga tooi*— literally, their ears are far away. I imagine my ears galloping away from my body, further and further into the impenetrable distance.

And always in the background of my deaf/d, full, left ear, a symphony of taps, swooshes, a roaring that intensifies the more tired I am. There is an empty orchestra—the literal meaning of karaoke—playing pings, clangs, and ghost beeps in my head, the result of my brain scrambling to compensate for lost data. Other times it's as if I'm holding a seashell to my ear, except that my ear is the sea.

As I try to find my footing on this shifting aural landscape, I lose my desire to learn Korean, and ditch plans to teach English, doubting my ability to cope with the demands of a packed classroom. The narrow scope of life on a small army post is suffocating, and yet I cling to it because it means I don't have to go out and face the wider world. I am linguistically untethered not only from Japanese, but from my native tongue as well. I take my frustrations out on Korea, berating the noisiness, the dirtiness, the lack of refinement compared to Japan, and although my husband and I had

230

planned to stay for a few years, he starts looking for jobs back in the States, somewhere I have never lived before

And so less than two years after arriving in Korea, I find myself on a plane descending over the bleached Arizona desert, a raw sweep of landscape so foreign that I don't even have words for it. The first week in our new house we're infested with scorpions: they emerge from the pantry, the fireplace, the light fixtures, the bathroom sink. Shining a black light on the cinder block wall at night, they glow like green constellations and I wonder who really belongs in this land. But the change of continent is a passport that allows me to form a new identity, free from the taint of Korea, a place I will forever associate with loss. I make friends that don't live and breathe army life, and I learn how to drive again: the last car I drove was a manual transmission nearly 15 years before in New Zealand. After riding the trains in Asia for so long, I thought I would never have to drive again, but I embrace this newfound freedom. We adopt a Golden Retriever, an impossible dream in my Tokyo apartment the size of six *tatami* mats, and in an event almost as unforeseen as my hearing loss, I convert to Catholicism, wondering how I had never before noticed all the Bible passages about Jesus healing the deaf.

I take an American Sign Language class and, since I am a translator by trade, Japanese to English, I imagine that I can do the same with ASL, carrying meaning across from one cultural and linguistic space to another. My eyes follow the instructor carving words out of the air: "pain" is two index fingers jabbing towards each other like dueling knives; "die" is both hands turning over like someone rolling in their grave. But I'm a perfectionist when it comes to language: I must inhabit it body, mind, and soul. After one semester, I realize that although I am (partially) deaf, I am not Deaf. My ASL teacher favors me because I'm the only one in class who is Hard of Hearing, but I feel like a fraud. I live in a liminal world, neither here nor there, neither completely deaf nor completely hearing. I must negotiate the space in between. The irony does not escape me that this "third space" was the very topic I explored in my dissertation. And so I have come full circle.

People always told me I had a good ear: I learned the violin when I was younger and could play by ear; I sang in school choirs and choral festivals; I could mimic the Japanese accent so authentically that people often asked me if I had been born in Japan. The Japanese word for darkness, *yami* 闇, is written using the character for sound 音 enclosed in a gate 門. Shutting out sound can leave you in darkness. But not always. I'm can still discern the flat vowels of my mother's Kiwi accent; I can still be lulled by the soft monotones of my second language. I am charting a course through a new language, one of loss and adjustment, adaption and reinvention, one without textbooks and dictionaries.

Three weeks before I lost my hearing, Gary Sinise and the Lt. Dan Band came on a USO tour to our garrison. In the darkened rec center, my husband and I rocked out with a packed wave of soldiers and civilians, singing Journey's "Don't Stop Believing" at the top of our lungs. I remember the gleaming dog tags swinging in the close air, the sweat pouring down Lieutenant Dan's forehead, the music pulsing and vibrating through every cell in my body. Three weeks later, I left Good Morning Hospital with strict instructions to do everything possible to protect my remaining hearing, so I bought high-fidelity earplugs, let the battery on my iPod run down, and avoided karaoke. Since then I have learned to navigate a two-dimensional aural landscape, and I no longer glance back on what it was like to hear in surround sound. And sometimes, when I'm driving along a vast stretch of desert road, I lean forward to turn up the volume on the car stereo and revel in singing really loudly, the saguaro like guideposts as I continue on my way.

"Health" Theme Contest Winner – 3rd Place

Spring 2016

Nocturne without Counterexample

Jessica Goodfellow

The mechanical oracle of moon
spools its rumors of change
that is not
ruinous.

The chronically unchronicled
wait patiently
as smog rusts the stars
that staple up the night.

Each heart beats:
                        bamboo /
                                    bamboo—
sealing one emptiness
after another
into manageable chambers.

All Gratitude Being Mine

Chris Souza

July will have us roasted by noon. I'll work
the dewy light: water verbena, fill the baths

and offer seed, open-palmed, to chickadees
who sort for peanut hearts with abandon,

all gratitude being mine and misspent.
They weigh nothing with a firm grip and eye me

like round inscrutable mirrors or God at the Arnolfini
wedding, enough foreknowledge to choke anything.

I tell my students circles are signs of security,
the feminine, a general application of interpretation,

but don't be surprised when the artist reverses
your expectations, when it's what you trusted

that devoured you like a body gone rag with heat.
And the daughter you were has faded, and the daughter

you have acquires the usefulness of unlearning you,
and you still baffle over your mother,

who is your grandmother's ghost here to remind
you, all palms end in supplication.

Summer, in My Early Twenties

Merrill Oliver Douglas

Those weeks when the fan on the windowsill
mumbled apologies hour after hour,
I would wake up three or four times a night

and stand at the refrigerator
gulping cold water. Nobody told me
the taste on the mouth of the jar was just

rust from the lid: I was so sure
it was the kiss of disappointment.
Often, it was hard to tell the clutter

in my bedroom from the clutter in my brain,
loose stacks of magazines and notebooks,
postcards, paperbacks, all mixed up

with the name of some man who might
fly back from Costa Rica
or Nepal and hold still long enough to love me.

Nights when the t-shirt stuck to my back,
and I could feel the hairs sprout on my legs,
why didn't some grayer, fatter woman

sit me down and say, "Sweetie, this isn't your life.
This is weather." Maybe I did see the Empire
State Building's head on fire in a fog,

but wait a few hours and I would find it had cooled
to a blue coal, the streets all healed. Down the block,
the Italian ice guys would be lifting their garage door,

leading their carts out like ponies,
hosing them down, suds sliding in sheets
across the sidewalk and over the curb's lip.

There Are More Storm Clouds than What You See Outside Your Window

Lisa Grove

The census taker counts the empty shirts on clotheslines,
the shoes hanging from power lines, and a man
made of matchsticks, catching fire as he runs home.

A green bicycle crouches in the grass—
the yard floods with rust.
Anything created by a human has teeth.

Grandmother covers her heart with a linen tablecloth
and calls the family in. Slices of ham
glisten with rainbows: her covenant.

I watch from a window. My sister is a small god,
but still, she's bigger than me.
My trophy jar of fireflies settles in darkness.

Jerusalem is just another city, like all cities.
It fills with dust, and every few millennia a wind picks up,
and green weeds annex the cracks in the sidewalk.

Night files away the census taker, the bicycle, and my sister
in its repository of shadows. A few of the fireflies insist
on flashing their existence to the world.

Grandmother folds me into her arms with a kiss:
The darkness will keep its covenant with them.

What Barren Means

Robyn Anspach

The way fields look when we walk past them,
dried tangles of hair. We leave our heads
bare and wind comes in like breath
off the desiccated fields. The husks
of cornstalks grasp pointlessly at sky.
We do not stop to touch them. We are going
somewhere, which is to say elsewhere,
because we are just walking the way
we do when the gray sets in, walking
down any of the roads that lead from town
to empty fields, with heads bare and heat
twining like cigarette smoke around us. Another
neighbor is pregnant. We saw her laying her right
hand on her belly the way pregnant women do.
Outside cornstalks bob their heads like bodies
propped up on stakes. Another harvest is over.

Narcissus Brings Me Flowers

Leila Chatti

On principle I reject
their company, mute
satin mouths gawping, an insult.

I have had enough of beauty.

Look how selfish they are,
sapping water through slender stems
though they are dead. The impulse remains:

to drain as preservation.
I know you

bring me flowers not of kindness
but of need, to keep me
indebted to pretty things.

I place the vase by the window
of the room I seldom enter.
They bob and shudder against
each other like the drowned.

At every end, a wound.
The wound is what drinks.

Providence

Chris Harding Thornton

Bud, Dad, Bud:
Popper of Bennies.
Snorter of Crank.
Pincher of Barmaid Flanks.
Highway Hauler of
Sheet Metal Scraps,
Tar Covered Buckets,
Tarps and Carpet and
The Stink of Beer and Tacos.
Bud: The Provider.
Drunken and Jittery
Incidental Hunter of
Broke-Necked Pheasants,
Deer Limp With Head Trauma,
Rabbits Crushed Just Above
The Collar Lines of Kittens.

Granny dressed game
clobbered by
steel-belted radials,
the bug riddled grill,
the chrome bumper of
Bud's Ford Econoline.
She never blinked, only
slit, gutted,
boiled, plucked,
skinned, gnawed off
heads with hacksaws.
Then she said grace.

On mismatched plates:
the sweet steam of grease
and rosemary.
On Bud's beard and moustache:
a slick glisten.
In my mouth:
meat melted loose from the bone.

Dead Letter Drop

JJ Mitchell

St. Mary—newly recruited patron saint
to dead letter drops—inherits an assembly
of agents and spies. Sundays bring reports
of spycraft and foreign men—bearded,
barely shadows. Some feign muteness,
others inexplicable gestures, a cleverly-
disguised brush-pass, or speak in strange tongues,
stamping the church grounds in a Cold War cadence
where they buried hollow spikes filled
with the cigarette-thin papers of state secrets.

Still, She blesses these missals of espionage,
granting them their confessions as double agents,
forgiving them their doublespeak.
For the others, the regularly devout,
there must have been moments
of near miracles: the disappearance
of coins—some microfilm-loaded—offered
at the feet of St. Francis of Assisi,
the fragments of chalked Cyrillic notation
and the ever-expanding assembly of pious men.

Smoking Magnum, 1991

Peter LaBerge

for Stacy Dillon

Cleveland, Tennessee: unmoving boy
      and unrecovered gun. The silver

mouth of the .44, the chrome-plated
      lip, the handle stained the color

of churchwood. 1991, down history's throat
      like a pill he might swallow to see

the beauty in girls. He fired
      his lover's name into the sky, stars

knocked out and strewn like teeth: one
      beneath an end table, one behind

the bloodied couch. The unholy bullet
      left his lover's gun, knowing

it was to enter through the softness
      of his cheek. Cleveland: no more

than a faceless boy and a body full of bone.

We Are V

_____

Christopher Green

On the day that Emily Warren killed herself she changed her profile picture to a stock photo of a bird. It was the photo that we discovered first, in fact, hours before her parents and her older brother began to make phone calls, before the fog of our unease coalesced into news. We crowded around cell phone screens, lined the rows of the computer lab. That picture suddenly everywhere, like a conveyor belt full of milk cartons. We stared at it, knowing but not knowing how. Premonition churned inside us, made our breath catch and our vision sway.

The bird that Emily chose was a great blue heron. Pencil-beaked and alert, in a pool of shallow water, her long neck contorted into the twin hooks of an S. Sunlight marbled over the waves around her feet; shadows crept along the belly like charcoal shading. There was something in that posture, in the taut angles of her body, that struck us as unmistakably human. She looked contemplative, even resigned. Perhaps, we would later reason, this was how we intuited the depth of the photo's significance. That, and the fact that for three years Emily's profile had remained the same: herself at fourteen, standing in the doorway of a shop that sold band instruments, a lollipop stick protruding from her lips at a jaunty angle meant to suggest a cigarette.

All through the evening confirmation began to leap from bedrooms to backseats to restaurant booths. Sparking along network wires like the fuse on a stick of dynamite, carried over the air like a chill wind. The adults, for their part, seemed to have no idea why Emily had done this, what message she might have wished to convey. All they had—and this much we got only from her brother Caleb, who told a friend who told a friend and so on, as these things go, even when these things are tragedies—was that her estimated time of death was 1 PM. Within half an hour of the photo's timestamp.

"Look at its wings," said Denise Burroughs, a freshman. In the few weeks since school started she had cut in and out of Emily's periphery a number of times, passed within inches of her in halls and stairwells, but never known her as more than a hazy figure in a collage of uniforms. "Look how they fold back like that." She pointed. "See? Tucked together. They're like an angel's." And this was instantly what the picture came to signify to all of us—a concise, soothing analogy drawn by a stranger Emily had never exchanged one word with. That this was unlikely to have motivated her (she was an outspoken skeptic, a bitter opponent of sentimentality) was beside the point. From the moment she died, she suffused herself among the rest of us. Self-cremation, a spreading of her own ashes. She belonged to everyone now; she had become mutable.

~

Our grieving, at least in the beginning, was quiet. We tended inward. At our epicenter was Emily's best friend, Katie Grine, the one who first uncovered the new photo in her feed. This was in second-period AP Calc, amidst lecture on tangent lines, average rates of change. Her shoulders succumbed first, then her head. Her whole body slipping down, like a coat falling off its hanger, collapsing against her desk. The line of her torso full of tremors.

Ms. Lorre stopped, swiveled her head. Her chalk stick still raised against the board. We would all remember this moment later.

Katie went first, led from the classroom by a doting elderly administrator. After that was Tim Gunsher, first-chair clarinet, who we all kind of assumed was Emily's boyfriend even if they never said so. He had to be let out of second period, too, during History of Eastern Religion. After that it was a trio of girls in third-period Health. Then half of Mr. Langhani's Analysis and Composition class—and those were juniors, not even the same grade. Our belated affliction spread exponentially. It was a virus, a natural disaster. By 1:45 that afternoon it came down through the PA system that classes were canceled for the remainder of the day. Students flowed out through the school building's door in unprecedentedly orderly lines, hushed and staring. The whole afternoon felt drained through a sieve.

Miss Shain, the art teacher, watched for the next week as her classroom walls crowded with sketches of angels and birds. (There was another, smaller batch of sketches in Room 305, beneath the window next to Emily's empty homeroom desk.) The adjoining of the wings was an obvious common point of difficulty, and most of them ended up looking like a single clumsy, heart-shaped appendage, with scales like the belly of a fish. This, she informed us with bittersweet satisfaction, was the clear focal metaphor to aid us in what was likely our first act of public mourning. We were learning to put our goodbyes before our hellos, and it was hardly surprising if that process proved difficult to watch. She was wrong, of course, but we didn't fault her for that.

Mr. Fawkes, who taught gym, reacted more or less as you might have expected him to: with volume. He addressed us as though we were simply coming in from a heavy lunch, lounging about with half-closed eyes, like cats. He talked a lot about "overcoming adversity," as though what Emily had done had been some schoolwide shot across the bow—which, perhaps, it may have been. But we were unmoved, and we furthermore objected to demands for dodgeball and archery and flag football. We objected to all acts of violence. Instead, we filed out to the campus and made slow, winding circuits around the main building for forty minutes. Every period, one class after another, in groups of threes and fours. We didn't even bother to change out of our regular uniforms in favor of shorts and tee shirts.

At home, our parents were baffled. "Tell us," they coaxed, "what it is we should be doing." But we said nothing, just folded our legs up on the sofa, turned our noses into the creases of the pillow. Our long, clumsy bodies sprawling out over all the old places, eight hundred filled-in chalk outlines.

~

As the weeks crushed themselves into the past, though, our tenor changed. The grief began to reorient itself.

Jessica Frankl downloaded the bird photo and set it on her own profile. On the post that revealed this move she wrote the caption, "Because I miss you, Em. Because sometimes it's me, too." The rest of us, when we found it, were stunned. Someone went to check on Jess right away, but she was only practicing trumpet in the band room. It wasn't a cry for help; it wasn't a parting missive. It was just a picture. A choice that for all its simplicity was invisible to us until she did it. Something so tiny, but with so much disruptive power, like a pebble in the barrel of a gun. A few other seniors, in the second-floor study hall room, downloaded the photo from her profile and set it themselves. By third period, all the seniors had done it. By lunch, the upperclassmen. By sixth period, everyone. *Everyone.* The freshman boys, second-string varsity with empty letter jackets. The junior class academic team. The sophomore scenesters, cutting class in the shadow of the fire escape. And Katie Grine, who had returned to school after two days but spoken to no one except to thank them for their condolences.

Someone, it was never determined who, eventually discovered the photo's source, three pages deep in a website for a South Florida estuary. Whoever it was managed to secure the original image file from the website's host, and to have it printed at full size, 24" by 36", at a nearby shop. And on a Wednesday morning we filed in to find more than twenty copies taped up around the hallways and classrooms.

This was only the first in a string of anonymous acts of vandalism. Another kid, maybe even several kids, began to graffiti on that first series of prints. WE ARE V, one read. NO MORE FEATHERS, read another. And many more prints followed, too, some in black and white, and some in strange, unsettling palettes that resembled photo negatives. The following week, someone brought in a dozen copper heron statues from a home decorating store. The statues began to crop up everywhere: in boys' room stalls, behind the curtain in the auditorium. It was only when the principal, Mrs. McDaniel, found one in her big leather desk chair that the installations were deemed problematic.

An emergency assembly was called. Classrooms were emptied; folding chairs were unfolded and settled into long grids. The auditorium filled up with silence. From the stage it must have looked as though eight hundred heads were bowed in prayer, but really, we were all looking at our phones. "Will the students who are perpetuating this misbehavior please step forward!" Mrs. McDaniel bellowed into the mic. "Your disrespect is preventing this school's deep wounds from healing. You have no idea how your actions profoundly affect your fellow students. We ask that you come up here and speak with us, so that we can all learn from this terrible instance and start to heal."

We didn't rise to meet her. We kept our heads down. Mrs. McDaniel, we knew, was a smart woman. In the end, she wouldn't need our help to determine which of her words were true and which weren't. Chances were good she knew already. The point of calling us together was not to uncover something, but to turn away from it.

Class attendance grew increasingly erratic. Some days a mere half of the desks would be occupied; other days, almost none. Once or twice, teachers lectured for fifty minutes to an empty room. We weren't sure whether they hadn't noticed, or whether they had resolved to just do their jobs, one way or another. In the cafeteria, the din of conversation had been scrubbed from the walls and ceiling. Servers stood idle at their stations; trays of corn pudding and refried beans remained full. Meanwhile, the heron photo spread across school property, whole flocks assembling around trophy cases and bulletin boards and oil paintings of administrators from the 1960s. The hallways started to look like channels carved through great bodies of water. And everywhere, that same beady pupil staring out, ellipses spanning hundreds of feet at a time. Questioning, or accusing, or lamenting. Teachers started to come in through side entrances in the mornings. Mrs. McDaniel patrolled the building with her eyeglasses resting from their chain, half-blind, navigating by memory.

Jonah Park was the first of what we eventually came to call *sleepers*. One morning he was found in the center of the gym, just shy of the three-point line, curled up on his side. Down the lengths of his forearms were streaks of red magic marker, still thick and wet and pungent from recent application. Several teachers were called in to remove him; Mr. Fawkes had to be led back out to the hallway after he started to scream. But Jonah could not be made to move, would not, in fact, even respond to pleas or threats or negotiation. And it was illegal to force him. So there he lay, stilled, with only the rhythm of his breathing to separate him from the dead.

When a group of students appeared in the gym's open doorway, ready to lie down beside him, faculty members grew desperate. Punishments of mounting severity were heaped upon the newcomers, who shook their heads—maybe disappointed, maybe simply uncomprehending—and piled themselves atop Jonah, adding the shape of their bodies to his. That same red marker had stained all of them. Down a neck below the ear, or in the center of a white tee shirt. Each of them a monument, though to what the school staff could only guess.

Slowly, the sleepers began to outnumber the regular students. Faces that on one day had been seen dutifully taking their seats for Integrated Math or Environmental Studies were the next day meshed into a pyramid of cotton and skin. Eyes open, rarely blinking, settled on some distant point.

The smell of magic marker replaced those of paper or floor wax or cafeteria beef. Piles of children were discovered in locker rooms, supply closets, in front of chalkboards and in the middle of the desk ring in Miss Shain's art room. (Miss Shain resigned that same week. We all felt bad about that, but it was her decision.) None of them could be removed. They were as implacable as the tiles or the paint. What few students remained made no sign that they noticed, but like the teachers, their paths altered to accommodate it.

Courses were consolidated, or canceled. Gym was the first to go, then Chemistry and Econ. Mr. Langhani's Analysis and Composition was the last to be pared down—Mr. Langhani, fifty-eight and tenured, had long since altered the curriculum to focus exclusively on personal essays. For weeks he collected the work done in class to be graded, but offered neither the scores nor the work itself to the administration for review. When at last their requests grew terse and threatening, he revealed that he had taken the essays home, sheaf by sheaf, and burned them in his fireplace. He had taken the ashes and delivered them, in secret, to the senior class president, who in turn gave them to Caleb Warren.

We loved Mr. Langhani, in our way. We were sad to see him go.

~

In November there was a second emergency assembly. This one was held on a Saturday; what few practices and events had remained on the schedule were swept away to make room for it. We trickled into the auditorium as we had before, speaking only in the rustle of our sleeves and the brush of our soles on the carpet. Sometimes, in that sea of heads, the mewling chime of a phone, but we didn't bother to silence them.

Seats had been carefully arranged such that each child was paired with a parent or guardian. Chairs for the adults had square leather cushions, but they sat uncomfortably anyway, never touching the backs. They rummaged through their purses, the pockets of their coats, as though whatever they were looking for was trying to elude them. On stage, the entirety of the school staff, missing only Miss Shain and Mr. Langhani. They formed a semicircle around a large wooden podium, the glaring chrome head of a microphone. Outside, a low sky and the spindly tops of trees. Snow had been predicted and then refused to arrive.

When Mrs. McDaniel began her address this time, she had sanded down its edges until it was soft and plaintive. She sounded the way adults do when they try to get sick kids to eat. "Obviously," she told us, "the way things are going now is unsustainable. All of us, your teachers, we know that. What we can't understand is what started it. Why Emily? What was it about her loss that inspired all of you to behave this way?"

We were confused. We didn't understand the question.

"What I mean is," Mrs. McDaniel tried again, "For three years Emily was all but unknown to you. You were indifferent to her, maybe even neglectful. And we've lost other students before. So what made this time different?"

It wasn't a matter of *difference*, we tried to explain. Emily's death was no more or less a burden than any of the ones that had preceded it.

"Then why have you been doing all of this for the last two months?" she asked, and we could see that she was beginning to lose her composure again.

This, we said, had not begun in September. We had been like this for a very long time. Before Brian Taylor was shot to death when his four-year-old brother discovered their father's rifle, before Lucy Rosalin was crushed against a wall by a drunk driver, before Miri Lam was strangled by her stepmother. For nearly as long as we could remember. And with Katie gone now, too, we had no choice but to continue.

"But it wasn't Katie who died," Mrs. McDaniel said. "It was Emily."

No. That was before. Katie Grine had passed four days earlier. She was the first in a pile of sleepers one morning, in the foyer, between sets of doubles door. When the rest of us stood to leave she was the only one who didn't get up. She just kept lying there, staring. We had taken her body home to her family in the back of Tim Gunsher's pickup. There was a small memorial to her at her desk, and in the landing of the back stairwell, where she had often waited for her little brother to get out of class at the middle school. We couldn't tell Mrs. McDaniel how it was that she didn't know these things. That wasn't any of our business.

The teachers cast uneasy glances from one side of the semicircle to the other. In the seats, parents pressed their thumbs inside of closed fists, pressed the fists to their lips, and made small sounds of desperation.

"I'm sorry," Mrs. McDaniel said, and it was clear to us that she meant this. Her eyes were glossy with the threat of tears. Her long fingers clutched the edges of the podium. "I'm sorry, but I don't know what to do. I don't know how to make things better. Can you tell me?"

Again, we didn't understand the question.

"How do I make this stop? How do I make you all happy again?"

Why, we wondered, would she believe she could do that? Was *she* happy? Was that a part of adulthood we needed to be trained for? We were skeptical.

"You're still children," she said. "For a little longer, at least. And you deserve whatever happiness we can give you."

What you can give, we told her, has run out. And we haven't been children for a long time.

Out in the halls they had set up tables with glossy tablecloths and plastic cups for lemonade and Coke. There were dishes of cheap sugar cookies bought from the grocery store down the road, emptied in rings around the circumference of plates so that their pastel grains made them look like flowers or exploding fireworks. Parents mingled with one another, commiserating, while we drifted to our homerooms and waited to be told we could go home. We didn't speak, just sat at our desks, looking at each other, or else checking our phones.

Mrs. Warren eventually found her way to Room 305. By this point the space around Emily's desk had mostly cleared; only a handful of sketches remained in the basket beneath her seat, tucked away by the janitor. The new focal point was two rows up, at Katie's spot, where kids had started leaving a stack of Rita Dove poems.

Emily's mother crossed the room at the back, past posters shouting READ, past a long wooden table full of models of cell structure. For a few seconds she stood behind Emily's desk, hands on the back, and we watched her, all eyes set. Then she took in a small breath, held it, and sat in the desk. Reached down and retrieved the first of the sketches, smoothed it flat in front of her. It was a bird, but not recognizably a heron. Probably one of the freshmen had drawn it, someone who wanted to be a part of things without quite knowing what they were about.

We're sorry, we told her. Mrs. Warren. It's true what the principal said: we didn't love Emily. And we're sorry. And we're trying.

Mrs. Warren said nothing, but she didn't look angry either. None of us moved, or even breathed; out in the hallway, the faces of classmates from other homerooms crowded the boxy windows of the two doors. Questioning, waiting. Finally, she took in another breath, and her face crumpled, like the last moment before crying. But she only let the air out through her nose, and pulled out the rest of the pile of sketches. Then she stood, went to the nearest wall, and took down a copy of the heron photo, carefully, pulling each corner from its loop of Scotch tape. These she tucked under her arm, careful not to crease them.

She turned back to us. "No more feathers," she said.

No, we promised. No more feathers. But we were nearly adults now, and we understood already that promises were meant to be made more than they were meant to be kept.

Holy Water

_____

Fredric Sinclair

My father took me to the barn and showed me the bit brace. He removed it from its rugged case and handed it over. It was one of the oldest things I'd ever held. It had a smooth wooden knob you put your weight on when you cranked the u-curve handle, sheathed with a rotating cylinder of the same smooth wood, darkened with use and sweat. My father spun the chuck and eased in one of the larger bits and closed the jaws. The bit was thick, the grooves sharp and gleaming. You wanted to run your finger on it, tempt a nick.

We had buckets and metal spiles and hooks for the buckets. We selected the trees. My father did the first one. He set the drill head on the bark, leaned on the knob and cranked, dispensing ribbons of pulp. He leaned in more, churning more guts out as he bore the hole. I was ready with the spile and hook. I bungled the first one, denting it. They had to be tapped in the direction the hole was drilled. When I got it in, it had a satisfying feeling when something sits just right.

We waited. When nothing came, he handed me the brace. "Your turn."

I placed the tip on the bark, bore down, cranked the shaft. The head bumped on the bark. I leaned in, got a bite, cranked faster. Out came the pulp. My arm got shaky.

"Good enough."

I removed the drill and tapped and we waited for that gleaming drop.

Sometimes nothing came. It took a few holes to get the sap. Just the way it was. We could remove a few of the spiles that didn't work and re-use them, but most couldn't be pried from the tree or had gotten too banged up in the process to be of any use. Years later, on summer days running around the yard with friends, I saw them there, rusting in the bark, slowly being consumed.

~

Andy lived with his mother and stepfather through the woods in a tall, modern house with a Cape Cod wash and a couple of small barns. They kept two goats in a pen in one of the barns. I never knew why, what they were for, but it was always something of a thrill to see them. Sometimes they would be in the outside pen. Sometimes they would be inside, sleeping I guess. If they were outside, I would feed them straw through the fence and those mechanical lips would pull it in. Mostly they'd dither about, bleating, pooping, with those slit eyes like a dash that made me think of something alien. Robotic.

I'd go to Andy's after school. We'd watch cartoons. Voltron. He-Man. The Smurfs. Shows on Nickelodeon, like *Double Dare* and *Where in the World is Carmen Sandiego?* Andy had a younger brother, Mike, who was quiet and had a huge mop of brown hair and seemed to always be in the shadows. His mother was usually there too. She never seemed to do much. Her hair was big, black, and frizzy. She was in the shadows, too. I'd be having a great time with Andy, watching cartoons, drawing, playing GI Joe, eating Combos and drinking Capri Sun. Eventually his mother would call up. Hal's coming home. An hour. Half an hour. Too soon, anyway.

"Hal's coming," Andy would say, as if I hadn't just heard his mother. It wasn't the first time he would tell me what I could plainly hear, with that fatalistic shrug, like he was apologizing for it.

Hal. His mother's boyfriend. Or his stepfather. I honestly never knew which.

They would start their chores, Andy and Mike. Stacking hay and wood, hauling leaves, feeding the goats, shoveling manure. It was some kind of farm they lived on. Not even. The barns were like those classic red and white ones in children's books, Old MacDonald barns, not much larger than oversized sheds, one for the goats, another for god knows what. That was it. Goats and hay and barns and shit.

I never met Hal. I was always home when Hal was home.

~

The earth cracked overnight exposing its insides, needles of ice like miniature Fortresses of Solitude in the dirt. Its crunch underfoot was a singular sound. Ice and earth shattering under the weight of a giant.

I could tell before lifting the lid the sap was running. Plastic buckets sagged under the weight. I ferried them to the shed that had been used as an icehouse in the olden days. Now it kept lawn equipment—rakes, shovels, spades, bags of potting soil. I dumped the buckets into a plastic garbage can my father had lined with an oversized trash bag. He'd explained just how many gallons of sap it took to boil down one gallon of syrup. There was a formula for it. I emptied buckets full of the silvery stuff, two by two, every morning for a month. It was a stretch to believe so much would boil down to so little. A day's worth. Two day's worth. A week. Going to school. Coming home. Roughhousing with my older brother. Playing tea party with my younger sister, stuffed animals dementedly drooling old sugar crust. Time had an uncanny quality then, measurable by the light of day, subtle changes in the position of the sun. Sometimes I would go to the shed in the evening and take the top off the can and inhale. Barely a scent. It tugged at me, wouldn't let me go. There was portent in it. A downdraft gust on summer afternoons, divining storms.

~

Church didn't go with much of anything I knew. The fonts at the entrance. What made the water so special? My mother tried to explain it to me once. A priest's blessing. I'm pretty sure I feigned understanding just to get her to stop. No matter how deep the explanation, or simple, my young mind refused it, made holy water a literal thing. I eyed those fonts suspiciously, the men and women who casually dipped their fingers in them, dabbed themselves with it. What did they know that I did not? They seemed different, then. They walked into church like they belonged. That must have been some pretty powerful stuff, that holy water. They must have kept it locked up pretty tight.

My brother spoke of the Corinthians and Romans and Galatians earnestly and forcefully from the pulpit. That he was up there at all was not unusual and yet I didn't understand it. He wasn't part of the clergy, barely twenty-years old, yet so devoted, so close they let him read scripture. I wondered if I would be a part of the Christian youth ministry some day too, go on trips to build houses in Appalachia. After mass as they processed down the aisle I'd try to get his eye. Maybe he would see me and smile, and when he did it was like I was in on something, like I had a connection to the top. Whatever was at the top. Those men in robes and the secrets of their spooky water.

Outside the priest did his rounds, his arms upraised in his great, multicolored robes. He swooped around like some lost, flightless bird. The wings enveloped me as he talked with my parents. I felt his great palm like a leather mitt on my head, his ring knocking my skull. It was both a sound and a feeling, in the middle of my head. It made me dizzy, lost in a confusion of color and fabric, blotted sunlight, muffled voices. This was a strange and bewildering place. It smelled musty in there. Despite the thrill, I'd get a little short of breath and would want to get out of those folds. Sunlight. Voices. He'd ruffle my hair. The cloak would pass over.

I'd feel oddly abandoned when he'd move on. I wondered what else I could do to get his attention. If anything was the right thing. Somehow, already, I felt nothing was the right thing, that I wasn't quite right in his eyes. That was a strange thing to feel, having done nothing wrong.

~

A single bead growing into a drop. Once touched, it transfers, like it can't escape fast enough, like it's terrified to be in the open and has to spread itself as thin as possible. Sap has the quality of something that exists on the periphery. The flash of fish under water. I put my finger in my mouth. There it was. That non-existent something. That riverbed flash.

~

Swirls of frost on storm windows like an artist spent countless hours etching a design. The lawn brushed thick with it. I went out before anyone was up and began my collection. We had tapped four trees, each tree with two, maybe three buckets. I lifted a cover. A thin layer of ice bobbed down, then back. Andy was standing at the edge of our property where a dirt path entered from the street. He was dressed for school in his signature tweed pea coat and newsboy cap with his backpack on. We waited for the bus together, but he was early.

"Hey."

"Hey."

"You're early."

"Thought you might need some help."

I had a full bucket in my hand and held it there for a moment, then lifted it towards him. He walked over and took it and we walked together and dumped them in the can. He peered over the top, then looked at me and grinned. "Sappy," he said.

From that morning on he showed up and helped. Part of me was a little sore about it, like he was intruding on my thing. But another part looked forward to seeing him there in the morning, kicking around the corner of our property. First thing I saw in the morning, those little white puffs of breath.

~

I approached the shed with a saucepan, slipped inside, uncovered the can. Sap moved differently than water. It wanted to slip away, over the sides of the pan when I brought it up, carried it out. It had the quality of the little ball of mercury dashing about inside a clear plastic case my brother had shown me once. Frantic, like it didn't want to be in this world, madly repelled, trying to slip back into the unseen place it belonged.

There was already a fire going in the wood burning stove in my father's workshop, extending off the main house. There was a hotplate for heating a kettle under an arch through the center of the stove. I put the saucepan there. Within seconds the sap was churning away, as if it knew this was its big chance, its great escape. I had to take the pan off with an oven mitt, it was so hot. I don't know what I expected, but certainly not this. A blackened film, barely worth noting, on the bottom and sides of the pan. A faint whiff of burnt marshmallow. I knew it was a failure, a stupid one at that, and was about to take the pan away and hide the evidence when the door connecting the workshop to the house opened.

My father scanned the scene. He seemed perplexed, like he didn't know what to do or say.

"I just wanted to try a little," I said.

His hand went up to ruffle the hair at the back of his head, a sure sign of frustration. He wanted me to toss the pan, not do it again. I went to the shed and stuck it on a shelf and sat there next to the can of sap, my head in my hands. I felt very childish, then. Why did I do it? Excitement. Impatience. I felt I'd failed some test. Man enough to empty the buckets every morning, but still scurrying around doing childish things behind his back. He'd explained the impossible equation. I hadn't listened.

Years later when the house went up for sale I was clearing everything out of the shed with my brother. Under a ruined deck chair I found the pan half buried in the dirt and rusted through, its distinct curved handle arching out at me.

~

The woods behind our house. There was a steep hill and a marsh at the base that was once watery enough we'd skate on it, dodging the marsh tufts. Andy's house was visible through the trees from the marsh, but there was enough cover we felt like we were miles away. The remnants of an old stone wall and a shorter stand of trees marked where there used to be a path in the olden days. Down from the path at the western edge of the marsh there was a spring with an old stone casement. It puzzles me still, the things that fascinated us as kids, but for some reason we always had to check out the spring. There was something satisfying about how the water materialized out of nowhere and trickled over the dark jumble of mossy rocks. It was one of the main attractions in those woods, like that giant, rotting oak, the whole top of it shorn clear off by lightning leaving its massive, blackened trunk rising dozens of feet in the air.

We were playing down there, jumping over the thin ice from tuft to tuft when we arrived at the spring. In summer one could walk by and not notice it, but in winter its gray stones were plainly visible and the trickle of water over rock made its own ancient sound.

"Ever drink from it?"

The question surprised me because I hadn't, and there had to be a good reason but I couldn't think of it. I shrugged. "Nah. It was used for cattle or horses, I think."

"So what? It's spring water. It's clean."

"I guess."

"You wanna do it?"

"You brought it up. You do it."

"You do it."

"No, you."

Andy shrugged.

It was tricky getting to it. The casement was tight, four by five or so and crumbling. He tried a few approaches and couldn't reach far enough from a crouching position.

"Gonna have to get in there," he said.

He took off his coat, rolled up his pants, and gingerly lowered himself into the casement. He began to clear away some rocks in the small pool of icy water below. I kneeled by him to observe.

"What's that?"

He looked over his shoulder and saw where I was looking. A mottle of bruises on his calf, deep and shiny like rotten leaves under snow. "Oh. It's a condition. A blood condition. I bruise easily." And that was that. A rapid-fire response. He kept working at the rocks and freed one and a little spout of water gurgled out. "Got it." He cupped his hands, the water splashed in, he gulped it down.

"How is it?"

He drank and drank like he'd been thirsty all his life and didn't know it.

Eventually he got up out of the spring. His face was wet, his cheeks bright red from the cold. He quietly rolled his pants back down and put on his coat. He didn't offer for me to try and neither did I and we walked silently out of the forest.

~

It wasn't hard to do, becoming an altar boy. Just asked and got that white robe. At least that's how I remember it. There was the little room off the antechamber where the other boys and clergy changed. It was a tense little room. The other boys didn't speak much. They barely acknowledged me. We changed into our white frocks silently. We all had our duties. Some held candles, one led the procession with the gigantic, clothed Bible almost half the size of us, another held the incense chalice, whatever it was called, I forget the name. I held candles and the Bible once. There was the bell ringer. He rang the little set of bells at specific times after the priest spoke certain words. I suppose it was to signify the purity of the angels or something, although at the time it was the only thing I looked forward to in mass because it was bright and cheery.

I was about to graduate to ringing the bells when an older boy told me as we disrobed, "Better get it right." I asked him what he meant. Something about if I didn't ring them at the right time, the priest would be angry. What did this mean? Angry how? "Just be sure you do it at the right time," he said. "He'll let you know."

At home after mass, I was walking to my bedroom, my tunic tucked under my arm. My brother stood in his door with an odd smirk.

"Do you know what he calls you?"

"Who?"

"Little Willy. He calls you little Willy. Do you know why?"

I stood mute.

"Because he knows you'll grow into big Willy some day."

I started laughing because it sounded funny. Little Willy. Big Willy. My brother's smirk vanished and his face darkened and I stopped laughing.

"That's not true," he said. "I'm just fucking around with you."

But I understood. I understood in the same way I understood sap coming out of a tree or water from a spring. Partly in the light, partly hidden in places unseen.

The day of the bells, I accompanied my parents and sister to the pews and sat with them. There were some uncomfortable looks from my parents, a few guarded questions. I greeted them with a demure complaint about not feeling well and sat dejected and miserable, unable to escape the horror of not being in the right place, of nowhere being the right place. I tried to hide, make myself small. The priest rushed up in those black slacks and shirt with the tiny white square at his Adam's apple and leaned in, his face inches from mine – *You better get yourself back there and get changed. Right now. Do you understand?* That enormous face. Lined and folded and stark as those bored, well-fed faces trapped in portraits in museums they took us to as children, gazing out with those dull, rheumy eyes. He had such eyes, weary of a past. It happened so quickly, this outburst, this near infantile rage. A few seconds and he stormed off. I stayed where I was and slumped in the pew.

Church was awful after that. One day I curled up under the pews and held my stomach in my hands it ached so badly. My father had to remove me and take me home. I was never wrapped up in that cloak again, never felt the knock of that ring, never greeted mass with any sense of curiosity or wonder. He barely noticed me then. Dead to him. Little Willy.

~

There was a sense that nothing was going to happen at all, that we'd collect forever, get more and more garbage cans, fill those too, till we had a whole barn full of sap. I lay in bed at night and tried to imagine what was happening, sap rising up through roots, through hidden cracks and crevices, though I knew these things didn't exist, cracks or crevices in trees. I did know that I could never see it, this deeply internal process. I could never know what it meant, what it signified, how the tree existed and why, in what manner it related to me.

The can was getting full. When I opened the door to the ice shed to empty the pails, I was greeted with a heavier scent. Not only sap, but the plastic of the garbage bags that surrounded the sap. They have a sweet smell too. But heavier. Overwrought. The sweet smell of plastic and the sweet smell of sap. Alien worlds commingling, untouching.

There's no way to move a garbage can full of sap. The momentum of the stuff is too great. So my father and I offloaded most of it using the same buckets that collected it. Andy was supposed to be there to help on boiling day. He had been so excited about it. But he didn't show. I ran in and called him but got no answer. I did this a few times before giving up.

The boiling pan was propped up by four cinderblocks with a wood fire in a pit beneath it. My father fashioned a smokestack of tubular metal with an elbow joint to funnel the smoke away. We boiled the sap in stages, adding more buckets as it boiled down. When the can got low enough, we were at last able to carry the sloshing dregs over and empty it.

It was one of those mild, milky days of early spring, the air light and translucent with moisture rising up from the thawing ground. The moldering leaves of autumn, crushed and blackened by the compression of snow, peeled back a little. The buds at the tips of branches made a green fuzz in the sky like an algae bloom in a pond. We sat out in plastic lawn chairs most of the day. My mother and sister drifted by at various times. I remember my brother looking on, mildly interested in the process, more as a curiosity, something he didn't quite get, why we were doing it, what for. The sap boiled in giant plumes of swirling white steam, returning to the air, to the rainwater that eventually burned rust holes in the pan itself as it sat in the barn for many years after, gradually released of its bonds of form and function, dissolving back into the earth, its various compounds, metals, minerals.

We poured the syrup through several filters of cheesecloth, catching bits of bark, twig, ash, and all the little winged insects that had managed to infiltrate the can as it sat in the shed. There was only so much that could be filtered out. This residue gave the syrup a distinct flavor. It was smoky, one might even say a bit ashy, but it was maple syrup all right. We jugged a pint and it went to the refrigerator for weeks of pancake, waffle, and French toast breakfasts.

Later that evening, I stood at the edge of our property by the woods where there was an electric fence. Why there was an electric fence I cannot recall. An extra perimeter for those goats, perhaps. Smoke was rising from the chimney of Andy's house. I stood there and kicked around and it didn't really matter what I'd done, what I'd accomplished. The sap collection. The syruping. My father's trust. Nothing really mattered when there was still so much I didn't understand, the ache growing deep inside me that sat there and pulsed, a blind and anxious fury.

~

For weeks after boiling day I'd wake up at the same time. Emptying those buckets had programmed me. One morning I awoke and sat on the side of my bed and looked out my window. Distinct against the gray, those little white puffs. I got dressed and went downstairs and put on my coat and boots and went out.

He was sitting by the maple tree.

"Andy?"

I knelt down.

He had a black eye. His bottom lip was cracked and bleeding. He was shivering, wearing nothing but his pajamas, looking at me but not at me. I was terrified. "C'mon." I took his hand and he flinched a little. "C'mon." I gave his hand a little tug and he stood up with me and we walked back to the house together.

Inside, I sat him down on top of the closed toilet and ran some hot water over a washcloth. I dabbed his lip with it. He barely flinched. I only noticed now how filthy his face was. Tears had cleared away great circles and rivulets of white down his soiled cheeks. I dabbed his face with the washcloth till he was as clean as I could get him. Then I led him upstairs to my room. I closed the door and took off my coat and boots. I took his hand and led him to my bed and he lay down and I with him and I pulled the covers over us and he curled up next to me and fell asleep.

~

In memory it was nighttime, or at least dark. I have no recollection if I changed out of my pajamas after everyone had gone to sleep, or woke up early and snuck out before they awoke. I did sneak, though. I ended up exactly where I intended.

They stood silently in the dark. I scaled the fence and cornered one and straddled it easily. It didn't buck or give much resistance. They were such small, wobbly creatures, their legs like twigs ready to snap, always about to give way. I put my right arm under its throat and pulled up and held it there. After a few seconds it made a grotesque rattling sound in its throat. Its robot eyes stared out at nothing, comprehended nothing. The rattling continued. It made a few jerky motions. I let go. The animal gave a little heave, dazed for a moment, then trotted away as if nothing had happened, as if distancing itself from a momentary nuisance. I circled round to the other and cornered it. It gave an anxious bleat. I held my arm under its throat, pulled up, trying to cut off its esophagus. Again, that rattling sound, those robot eyes. I tried again, and again, holding longer each time, and each time the animals just stared with those glassy eyes and rattled and wheezed. No bucking or biting. No fighting back. Why didn't they? Why didn't they fight back? What purpose did they serve? They didn't feel a thing. And I saw nothing in their eyes that I hadn't seen every time I'd fed them straw. That same dumb, alien stare. "Fight back," I yelled. "Fight back you little shits!" I made to kick one, aimed right for its fleshy gut to inflict the most pain but missed my mark and only caught its flank. The animal scuttled off. I chased it and caught it by its nubby horns and mashed its head into the wooden railings of the pen. "Fight back!" I mashed it again, hard. "Fight back!" Again. And again. Its head kept bouncing off. Exhausted, I let go, the animal darted away, and I lost my balance and fell into the railing where my arm scraped against the rough wood. Slouched over in the dust and dirt and shit, my arm mottled with blood, the goats bleated frantically now. This was a dark, terrible place, cold and smelling of urine and must. It was a hopeless place and I hated it. I hated it for being there. For my being there. I wanted to get away from it, as far away as I possibly could and never come back. So I scrambled and fled and ran through the woods back home, the whole time thinking someone, something was behind me, watching, knowing.

This is how I want it to end. I want to make it a clear spring morning with a cooling fog hovering over the earth. I want to say I approached the house at the first light of day, that I fell to the ground, my knees digging into the soft earth, and bawled my eyes out, mourning everything that was and was yet to come, what I knew and what I did not, the wonders and horrors that were at work underground. Surging. Cinematic. Soaring.

But it was nothing like that. When I got home I crawled into bed. And once a reasonable amount of time had passed and no grim faces came to report that someone had witnessed it all, I got on with life. And I imagine in time I felt I had gotten away with something secret and dastardly and it made me feel big.

Not too long after that, Andy moved away. I never knew what happened to him. Never saw or heard from him again. I'd visit the spring in the forest all through my childhood, and those maple trees grew up side-by-side with me, the bark swallowing up those busted old spiles. And countless times I'd take the trash out to the garbage can in the shed where we'd kept the sap. And every now and then I'd step over the rusting boiling pan in the barn as I'd play with friends. And many times I'd think about that morning I found a boy crumpled up under a maple tree. And how I loved him. And how I never needed anyone to explain to me what is holy and what is not again.

Ice Fishing

Caitlin Mullen

Declan's hands shake as he lifts Meghan's green plastic tackle box and stacks it on top of his own. It rattles with hooks, bucktail jigs made of deer hair that expand into white puffs in the water, the steel leaders, the bright metal jigs that shimmer their way down to the bottom of the lake, and splitshot sinkers that she sometimes holds in her mouth, even though at eleven she is too old for this, to taste the cool tang of the metal on her tongue. He senses her in the doorway, watching.

"You can take it with you," he says, nodding to the tackle box. "There's that little pond at back of your grandmother's development."

"I think I remember," she says. Neither of them mentions the way the brown water hummed with dragonflies, the green cigars of goose shit everywhere they stepped. She tilts her head up to him. Milk white skin like her mother's, winter-pale freckles that will brighten to the color of cinnamon in the sun. He points to the end of her braid, smiles at a fleck of blue paint in her red hair.

She gets that from you, Denise had said, when Meghan began spending hours in her bedroom with her pencils and paint. He knows what she meant. He also takes refuge in precision, steeps himself in quiet. Likes the concentration of building a mount, stitching the skin, determining the shape of the teeth, the angle of the jaw, the texture of the scales or skin. Fixing a thing in time.

"Are you bringing your skates today?" he asks. "Not much snow last night."

She nods, reaches her figure skates down from the nail where they are hung by their laces, tucks them under the passenger seat of the station wagon.

Meghan will join Denise at her mother's in Fort Lauderdale at the end of the school year. He would have fought harder if he had been convinced that the separation would last. If he had really thought Denise wasn't coming back from her mother's, that she wouldn't show up just as suddenly as she had left. All those nights staying up, waiting to see headlights sweep across the living room, hear her suitcase roll up the drive, the rattle of her keys in the door. His shoulders tighten. His fists clench at his sides. He wants to say the selfish thing but the phrase stays stuck in his throat. *You'll always be mine too.*

~

The bumper rattles and the brakes squeak in the silence as they drive. They clear the clutter of their street, which is less of a neighborhood and more of a residential strip of Route 20 in Canandaigua. Fences lean in the snow, aluminum siding has faded into weatherworn grays, rusted swing sets creak in the wind. Some of the front porches of their neighbors' houses are packed with trash—broken baby toys, flattened aluminum cans, dead car batteries. Things change when they turn down Main Street. Landmark homes are marked with brass plaques—three-story Victorians with turrets, fireplaces in every room, stables and carriage houses preserved around back. The people on Main Street are celebrating. Shamrocks cut from green construction paper are taped to the windows of all the shops. *The Saint Patrick's Day Snap*, they called it in the paper. He doesn't care what the weather is named, only that it means they'll get to try again.

They pass a telephone pole, looped with green tinsel, one of his flyers stapled to the south-facing side. *McGovern Taxidermy Call Declan for a Quote.* He gets a few leads now and then, but not enough to make up for a slow winter. Things are hard all around, no one's shelling out for a mount. There were a few beautiful pike in January and December but not much since. It's mostly drunk kids who call anymore, on their way home from the pub down the street. The first few times he groped for the phone in the night he still thought *Her.* Then the joke, or some riff on it.

Hey McGovern, I've got something you can stuff.

He pulls the car to the side of the road, sinks into a snow bank as he steps out. The paper comes away in three soft, soggy peals. He stuffs the balled-up wad of it in a metal trashcan at the end of the block, empty save a few ice-crusted cans of Keystone Light. He's reaching for the door handle when he thinks of her pen and ink drawings. A different one for every poster. A smallmouth bass. A black bear. A fox.

The car rocks with his weight as he climbs inside again.

"Crank calls," he says. She stares out the window. "I'm sorry," more quietly. She gives him a small nod, but he's still talking to the back of her head.

After another mile or two the town reverts to roughed up farmhouses, squat split-levels with old boats set up on sawhorses in the front yards. They sit at the intersection leading towards the lake. It's a long light. He drums the pads of his fingers against the wheel. His knuckles are rubbed raw by the cold, the skin hardened into white scales. His hands get stiff when the wind chill dips into single digits, the aftershocks of a childhood frostbite. Every now and then he still dreams about it, after a drink—the cooing voices of the nurses as they dipped his fingers into metal pans of warm water, the smeared glow of the florescent lights above his head.

The exhaust from the car puffs around them as they wait at the light. The phone lines are coated with ice; road signs shine with frost.

"Did you ever go?" she asks. "When it's red and no one is around?"

"No," he says. Then, "Yeah. Once or twice."

"Did it feel different than going on a green?"

He turns to look at her, the corners of her mouth turned up in a sly smile. Her mother's smile. Denise at eighteen in the passenger seat of his first truck, reaching for the six-pack at her feet. The click and hiss of the beer bottle she opened with her teeth. How it made the hair on the back of his neck stand up.

He creeps up to the intersection, glances long down the road, hits the gas.

She laughs as they cross, complicit. He's pleased to offer her this small satisfaction. Maybe a chip of forgiveness in it. They have to stretch the groceries and he'll be a few days late with the rent, but he doesn't have to deny her this. He thinks about running the next light too but it changes to green before he has a chance.

~

The lot where they park is edged with blackened snow. Icy asphalt is crossed with tire treads. On the march across the lake other anglers ride past them on snow mobiles, leaving behind the parallel prints of runners and spirals of exhaust, but they always walk the two miles to the center. He pulls most of their supplies behind them, bungeed to a sled and carries the

269

rest on a woven basket strapped to his back. His papoose, Meghan calls it. Halfway there she sits to lace up her skates. He picks her boots up from the ground and carries them too, the rest of the way.

She's a bright blur of movement in the still world of the lake. It's the opposite of her painstaking painting when she's on the ice: force over discipline, velocity over grace. She works her way into a backwards crossover, the sun flashing off of the blades. They cut south on a diagonal. She uses the landmarks along the shore to guide her way to their place— the three snow-covered picnic tables in the clearing, the cabin built from yellow pine. Meghan has looked up a rink twenty minutes from her grandmothers' house. He makes a note to put away a little money when he can, in case she wants lessons someday.

The augur grows heavy in his hands as they walk; sweat dampens his temples underneath his hat. He feels the heat trapped close to his skin underneath his shirt. The game warden cuts towards them, the ice too thin after February to bear the weight of his truck. Declan recognizes his walk, the same since they were in high school together. In those days he was always wearing a sports jersey, earned something like eleven varsity letters. He always struck Declan as a man who wouldn't know what to do with himself if he didn't have a uniform to put on. But he likes him enough. J.R. in high school, Jason Roberts now, according to the brass-plated nametag he pins to his uniform. He only learned Declan's name after graduation, when they met again as adults on the lake. Until then he was the just the quiet kid who sometimes showed up to class wearing the occasional bruise. Now both have earned the same lines around their eyes, the creases in the forehead. But there is something light and easy about Jason that still clings to him from the early days. A little bit of that quarterback swagger, while Declan knows he's more weathered. More gray under his hat. That map of broken capillaries in his cheeks.

"Declan," Jason says. "Little lady," tipping the brim of his hat in Meghan's direction. "About five inches thick today. This nice little cold snap firmed things up a bit. On Monday we were starting to get slush on the surface." He knows that Meghan is trying her best not to roll her eyes at the salutation.

"You can hear as much," Declan says, and it's true. The ice lets out a low groan around them, the sound of it thickening, struggling against the changes in pressure.

"Good luck," Jason says as they walk on. Meghan leans into Declan.

"Like we need luck," she says, under her breath, her face bright with the pleasure of her newfound sarcasm.

Luck, he thinks, as she skates ahead. Like a word in another language. He thinks of the last fish he worked on. Great Northern Pike. 36 inches. The other before it, 34. Back then he thought it was only a matter of a weekend or two before he and Meghan had their turn. Denise was still here. From the basement he could hear her humming, talking to herself, through the kitchen floor as he worked.

It doesn't take long for Meghan to get far ahead, slicing into the distance. There was a time when she would double back, flushed and cheerful, but now she's only interested in speed. The surface is bumpy from the lake cycling through another thaw and freeze. He sucks in his breath when he sees her jerk forward like she's caught the toe of her skate, windmills her arms back for a last grab at balance. He stiffens where he stands, as if he could lend her some of his steadiness, absorb some of the shock when she falls. He closes his eyes and his guts twist; he swears he hears kneecaps smash against ice.

When he opens his eyes again she's righted herself, waves to him. No snow on her knees, no sign of a fall. He tries to unclench his jaw as she starts up again, a little cautious at first but too soon she's off, just as fast as before.

~

He takes his jacket off to drill, spreads the dark cloth on the ground. The ice screeches in resistance when he makes the first few turns then yields to the augur's slow grind. She watches him. Maybe not scorn yet, but she's questioning, he thinks. The way Denise did. His snow pants, dirty with rock salt up to the ankle, his oatmeal-colored flannel, the songs he plays on the radio. Why he has to be what he is. Always, only, what he is. He feels his face grows ruddy with cold air and work, and for the first time, with her attention. He hasn't felt anything like this since she was a baby. The way he felt humbled by all that need and love directed at him. Made him want to look over his shoulder as he reached to pick her up. Like there was another father just behind him, one who might sing to her as he told her not to cry.

The augur breaks through the ice and the water rises with a glug, pale green. Meghan kneels to strain out the slush that falls into the hole. The men closest to them are still nothing but small dots on the horizon. Meghan holds up her hand, closes one eye, pretends she can swat them off the lake with the back of her mitten. They interfere with her running daydream that the ice is theirs alone. He feels it too, this desire for austerity, for all things human to be hushed to a whisper. The ends of her hair are already crisped into icicles of auburn, her eyes pale; the very color of the cold.

He looks across the ice at a few of the slower, more hunched forms moving between their lines. The old men, the lifers. Solid, deliberate, patient. He thinks of old Jack Robinson, the neighbor who first took him out as a kid, distracted him from what might have been an adolescence of smoking Marlboros and hot-wiring cars in Quik Mart parking lots. More fathering in those few afternoons with Jack than a lifetime with his own father. Dead for eleven years, estranged for longer, and still Declan remembers the way his father looked at him, a part of the room only as much as the furniture.

It was Jack who first noticed the way he rubbed his fingers together when they started to tingle and numb, Jack the first person to tell him *boy, that ain't right.* His hand on Declan's arm as he said it. He could have stood it, but for that. The solid weight of that touch, the simple consolation of it even through the thick of Jack's mitten, Declan's coat. He broke down and cried like a baby, head in his hands while Jack watched, patient and knowing while Declan, old enough to shave every morning, sniveled and snotted into his gloves.

He still remembers all of it, the night in the parking lot. Six years old. Sour smell of the truck, its stained upholstery. Shells of sunflower seeds, bottle caps, cigarette ash all over the floor. The crunch and squeak of snow under the tires of the car as they pulled up to the bar. The one other car a lone Rambler with six inches of powder on the hood. Looking through the window at the oval of his father's belt buckle, the play of the neon window signs on the brass before he zipped up his coat, the way his father held up his index finger through the glass before he disappeared into the dim rectangle of the tavern door. The man was a great liar in gesture—firm handshake, confident walk, earnest hands held out to receive communion, the finger that said *just one drink.*

~

After they drill their holes he sets up the shanty, although neither of them uses it much unless the wind really starts to pick up. Still, the small rectangle of the hut breaks up the white stretch of lake and horizon in a way he finds reassuring. When he's checking one of the further tip ups he likes having something to look at, to orbit, somewhere to return. He snaps the legs in place, raises the frame, fits the aluminum braces to support the roof, places the joist between them. The tarp swishes in the wind as he zips the door shut behind him, steps back onto the ice. Meghan steps into the other side, tears away the window flaps from their Velcro fasteners, stares through the pane. The plastic windows have gotten scratched over the years and the effect is like one of her paintings; her face put together in brush strokes. He does the rest of the drilling and she follows him, slower now that she's traded her skates for her boots, to rig the tip ups at each hole. Regulation allows five lines in the ice per angler. He does his best not to picture his camp next year, halved.

They catch a half dozen perch in the first few hours, the little red flares of their bottom fins bright against the white and gray landscape. Meghan holds them up, spins them slowly on the line like Christmas ornaments held to the light. He has the sense that there is something bigger waiting for them, that the lake has more of itself to yield. He pats the front pocket of his jacket, feels the cigar he's hung on to since the beginning of the season, the box of sparklers for her.

"Think we'll get a big one today?" she asks. They've had a few good-sized pike this season, but all just an inch or two above the limits set by the state. Nothing like those mounts he worked on back in November.

"It's about time, huh?" he says.

She turns over an empty bucket, sits on it and surveys their camp, the ten holes they've rigged up, as if she's trying to decide which line their big catch will bite. He turns away from her to take a pull from the flask inside his jacket. She's interested in all this now, but maybe in a year or two she'll turn a corner. She'll visit on her Christmas vacation clutching a new cell phone. Twice this month he's seen her turn her head to look at a boy passing by on the street. Last week she came home from school with a smear of silver eye shadow on her eyelids. He didn't know if he was supposed to discipline or encourage her. *Wash that off,* or *You look nice.*

"Cheers," she says, raising the thermos of hot chocolate to him. He thought he'd been discreet. Not that it matters, really. Sometimes he wonders if he's making secrets out of nothing just to feel like he's got something to keep.

She takes a few sips, holds the heat of it in her mouth and watches the Saint Bernard trot out towards them. The dog makes its rounds from camp to camp all winter, fat on scraps. It's not the dog she first saw on the ice when she was young--a different arrangement of brown on its coat—but they all eventually walk back in the same direction to a gray house on the North shore. Bernie, she calls it, although they've long since realized it was a girl. The dog pushes twin puffs of hot air through its nostrils, noses behind them for a little while as they move around their camp. Underneath the woolly wet smell of its coat are hints chimney smoke and a man's aftershave.

"Sit," she says. "Shake." The dog lays a giant paw in her mitten. "I'll have to say bye to Bernie for a little while," she says, working her fingers behind the dog's ears, its tail thumping the ice.

Out of the corner of his eye he sees the orange flag of a tip up signaling a bite and walks away to check their bait.

He pulls the tip up out of a hole, knows at the first tug on the line that it's another perch. He brings the fish in quickly, pulls the hook from its mouth, tosses it back into the hole with a plop. He hasn't worn his watch but guesses it must be close to three, and all they've had so far are throwbacks. The temperature is hovering around twenty; he's grateful there's no wind. The ice is still responding to the cold, and every now and then the groaning gives way to something sharper, more like a sudden boom of thunder without the rain.

"I bet that's what God sounds like," Meghan says, as he works a can opener around the tops of their chicken noodle soup, sets it on the burner. She cuts the flame when it starts to simmer, turns for their plastic cups and spoons that they keep inside the pack.

He knows what she means. To him the sound has always seemed even bigger than the ice, an echo of some kind of origin. The lakes being carved, the ancient glaciers cutting though rock. But he is surprised to hear her talk about God. He consented to a baptism at his wife's insistence, but otherwise has made a point of bringing her up outside the church. All he remembers from his early days at Saint Thomas is the creak of the pews as the congregation sat and stood, sat and stood at mass, the rustle of fabric as everyone crossed themselves at once. And the Sunday his mother propped the hymnal open for him when both his hands were bandaged, how she frowned at him when she realized he was only mouthing the words. He wonders if his daughter really believes in God. He wants to tell her that there are so many better words for awe. That for him, one of them is her name.

They are still staring off in the direction of the sound when the small orange flag on one of their lines starts to quiver in the latch, snaps straight up in the air. Fish on.

"Why don't you pull this one in, Meg?" He sends her off and she runs to the hole, slipping a bit in her boots. The sun is falling behind the dark bars of tree trunks along the shore. She pulls off her mittens, holding them between her teeth while she takes the line in her hands and sets the hook hard. His love for her is a vise around his ribs.

He knows by the way she braces at the knees that they've hooked something big.

"That's it," he says as the fish pulls line off the reel, yard after yard unspooling. "That's it. Let it take what it needs. We'll fight soon enough."

Usually she teases him about his tendency to coach, as if she's never caught a fish, but this time she's quiet.

"It seems angry," she says, as more filament slides off the reel.

"They don't' have feelings, just instincts," but he's not sure that this is any consolation. She is still letting it take out line, until it starts to peel out more slowly. She reaches down to pull some back. They both like to bring in big fish hand over hand instead of using the reel, to feel every bump and tug. She gets a foot or two before there is another series of jerks on the other end and she needs to ease up. There is a moment when she holds on a second too long and the line goes too taut.

"That's it," he says. "Let it have room. Just fight it when you can. Don't rush, even if we're here all night."

"We'd have to eat it," she says. "We're out of soup."

She watches more and more line slide out. "Don't worry," he says. "We only need to keep it on." He was like this too at her age. So many times when he first took himself out he finally managed to hook something, only to try to wrestle it in and break the line and was left with that sudden, terrible lightness when it got away.

The fish finally seems to go still and he nods to her to start bringing it in, as if it might hear them talking from under the water, through the ice. She's taking it back inch by inch. This is the part he likes the most. The tip of the scale. When the uncertainty shifts to assurance. Her bare hands are marbled red and white with cold. She shrugs at him, offering him the chance to finish the job, but he only smiles and shakes his head. She's pulling the line in a little faster and it curls into a coil on the ground, glistens in the last of the day's light.

He looks down at the dark outline of the fish's body just below the water's surface. He reaches in, hauls it up with a finger through the gills, props the tail up with his other hand. The light glazes the waterslick scales, silver-green, and the heft of its middle sags between his hands. The pike must be at least 35 inches. Big enough to keep. His laugh rings out and echoes back from the shore.

"You did it, Meg," he says, holding out the fish. "Good fight, huh?" He lays the catch on the ice and first it flexes and flops before slowly going still. The soft slap of the tail on the ice, the heave of its red, woundlike gills. She crouches low and stares into the pink vaulted ceiling of the its mouth, runs her finger along it's side fin, still so delicate on such a large fish. There is a scar on the other side of its lip; a time when the luck tipped in its direction and it slipped itself off of a lure.

"Look," she says, running a finger along the puckered flesh.

"Don't worry," he says, still giddy with victory. "I'll fix it when I do the mold."

He'll be grateful to have it, a landmark back to the past. She'll be able to come back and point to it. *It was a really cold March. We caught that pike and you ran the red light on the drive over. All the Saint Patrick's Day decorations on Main Street were covered in ice.* He takes a celebratory swig, not bothering to turn his back to her when he slides the flask from inside his jacket.

He steps away to grab the tape measure from the tackle box. Back at the hut he cuts his cigar, turns the end in the flare of his lighter. He likes the play between sticky thickness of the smoke and the clean feeling of the night air. His body feels loose with relief. Meghan breaks down the rest of the tip ups. It's dark enough that he can only make out her movement, a sense of her in the distance, the slight scuff and shuffle of her boots.

"Thirty seven," he shouts, after he lays the tape measure alongside the pike. She raises an arm in what he guesses is a thumbs up, lets out a muffled cheer.

He stares down at the fish at his feet, the dead eyes already taking on their flat, cartoon look. Small black circle inside a bigger white one. He studies the barb of the old rusted hook worked through the side of its mouth. He's surprised it lived through that. Usually it would injure a thing into starvation. He could repair it when he does the mold, but he realizes that he likes it better this way, how the scar was built, cell by cell, to accommodate the wound. Its colors have already started to change. The white of its underside goes slightly yellow, as if jaundiced by the air. He'll lay it flat on their sled for the walk in, try not to jostle it too much.

He whistles to Meghan to come back to the shanty. The tip ups are bundled in her arms, all of the flags hooked back in their latches, the lines wrapped tight into the reel. She drops them into the basket. She frowns when he holds the flask out to her, studying him before she takes it from his hand. She sips like it's something hot. A dribble of whiskey slips down her chin and she drags her coat sleeve across her mouth with a flourish.

"Not bad," she says. And when he raises his eyebrows, "just kidding." He laughs, but seems to feel the joke in the backs of his knees. He knows it's cheating. Breaking off pieces of the future and tucking them in places where they don't belong.

He stuffs the tape measure deep into his pocket, rustles among the car keys and scraps of gum wrappers, shakes a sparkler loose from the box. At first she only squints at the stiff, slim object he is holding out to her, until it snaps into meaning and she smiles as she takes it from his hand.

He tries to light a match but it breaks off at the head. He breaks another, drops the third to the ground. The air is tinged with sulfur, the matches lie stern as tallies at his feet. The temperature has fallen as the day faded; the old numbness comes back into his hands. She trades him, lights the match in a single strike. He should be unnerved by her deftness but has nothing but admiration as the sparkler bursts to life. He pulls another from his pocket, holds it to the first until it also hisses. They watch the sparks fly in the black of one another's pupils. They light two more and watch them sizzle down to embers, two more after that, until the box is empty and already too light in his hands.

Asleep

Nathan Alling Long

Growing up, I loved watching people sleep: my sister, my brother, my parents—even our dog. Asleep, their faces lay blank, still, without a twitch of direction or emotion, as if revealing some hidden self. They resembled trees, or stones, something neither good nor bad, but purely themselves.

Seeing them as they slept made me feel a calm lightness inside—the way I felt when my sister Ellie wrapped her hands in old socks, making two puppets, Oscar and Brown, who talked to each other in high, barky voices:

"Hey Oscar, would you fly to the moon with me?"

"The moon? Sure. But what's there?"

"Cheese. Lots of lovely cheese. And not the stinky kind, either."

"How do you know?"

"There's no atmosphere there, so it can't stink."

I don't know why I laughed so hard at those puppets, but they always transformed me. We fell into a different world, Oscar, Brown, Ellie, and me.

Other times, Ellie made me feel small, too young. "Mom, I don't think Alex changed his clothes since three days ago." Or, "You don't know where babies come from? Come on, you're almost seven!"

Awake, anyone could make me feel that way. Mom, who complained of being too tired to make our school lunch or help me tie my shoe, Brandon who'd slap me on nights he babysat, if I didn't go to bed fast enough. And Dad, who always loomed, ready to strike.

My dad was not a bad father. He could make me smile just like Ellie— or Mom, or Brandon. But that was the thing: anyone in my family could move me, one way or the other. That's why I didn't trust them. At least not awake.

I figured when someone made you smile, they were usually hiding some part of themselves, temporarily, to give you what you wanted. I'd seen Mom do it all the time. And when people are angry, they let some bad part of themselves take over, an exaggeration of themselves. Dad could be like that. "Don't hate him!" Mom would say about him, after he would yell at me. "That's not who he really is." I believed her, but wondered, *How can I know when anyone is ever acting as they really are?*

I'm not sure how old I was when I started to watch people as they slept; I must have been around seven or eight. I remember once when Mom and Dad were fighting, I slipped into the living room and saw our dog, Omar, asleep on the rug. I sat on the sofa and watched his body lift and sink with his breath, his feet twitching as if touched by electrical pulse, his face relaxed and content. Except for his feet, there wasn't much difference in how Omar looked from when he was awake. Still, I couldn't help feel that I was witnessing something private, getting closer to him than I ever had, closer than when we wrestled in the back yard or took walks in the woods behind our house and sat by the stream, watching crayfish dart from beneath the gray stones in the water.

I began hanging out in the living room, watching Omar rest whenever I could, though I wondered if somehow what I did was wrong. Once, when my grandmother was visiting, I was staring at Omar when she came in and sat on the comfy chair in the corner. She was silent and, as usual, let me do whatever I wanted. So I stared at Omar, and grandmother stared at me. After a few minutes, she said, "The way you look over the dog, Alex, I can tell you'll make a good father one day." She never remembered Omar's name.

I smiled, but I wondered if she was right. If I was a father, I would want to stay up all night watching my child sleep, so I could always picture it calm, without worry.

Grandma telling me that made me feel better. I looked up, to give a silent thanks to her, but she was already dozing in her chair. So then I stared at *her*: a tranquility slowly spread across her face like warm, fresh water. I saw then that her tolerance, which she offered all of us endlessly— even her son, my dad—took a great deal of effort. Only now did she seem to be completely free of worry, a person who seemed as happy to live a long time, or not at all.

For a while, I simply waited for a chance to watch someone sleep. Often, it would be while we were riding in the car during a long trip. Brandon was the oldest, then Ellie, then me—each of us separated by three years. Since I was the youngest, I had to sit in the middle of the back seat, which of course brought on many fights—until Dad, who always drove, threatened to kick us out of the car. Once we were silenced, there was nothing to do but stare out the window or take a nap

I would glance up at Brandon as soon as he nodded off, his hair falling over his eyes, the tough, deep-voiced certainty of his personality now drained from his face. Just looking at him made me forget whatever he'd done to make me mad. His skin seemed so soft then and his eyelashes curled in a way that made him almost look like a girl. He was so sweet looking that I wanted to touch that face.

The same was true with my sister's face when she slept. Her eyelids and freckled skin turned smooth, like they were made of clay. Often, her mouth opened and her two front teeth showed, a bit like a gopher. If she were awake, it would have made her look a little stupid I guess, but in sleep it seemed to make her open to the world, as if nothing could bother her.

I couldn't stare long at either of them, not in the car. Otherwise, the other would look over at me and ask what I was doing. They would say something like, "You perverted," and shake their head. And I would stiffen and stare straight ahead, afraid they were right.

To find people sleeping was difficult. I learned to sense when someone disappeared from the common spaces of the house. They took with them a certain sight and sound. To me, that absence was like an instrument suddenly disappearing from a band. While everyone else kept busy, listening blindly to the soundtrack of our life, I went off to explore the sudden silence. What I didn't think about was how I formed more silence when I left. I was making the silence louder.

Once when Dad was shouting for me, I hid in the laundry hamper at the top of the stairs. After a few minutes, Dad gave up, slamming the front door and starting up the mower. Before I could get out of the hamper, I heard someone climbing the steps. I knew it was Mom. She often slips away to nap, and often she and Dad try to stay in different parts of the house. She walked down the hall and closed a door behind her. I waited a long time, smelling dirty socks and the sweat of my family, then snuck into my parent's room.

I stood just inside the door, with it almost shut, so no one could see me, and I stared at her sleeping.

Often a sleeping face is not a pretty face, at least not by normal standards. The mouth is open wide, asymmetrically, and there's often drool involved. Their hair is disheveled. But they are also deeply relaxed. The body sinks into its most comfortable place, like it's wearing its favorite clothes, like it's going on a brief vacation somewhere warm and safe. Even if people have a hard time breathing in their sleep, like my dad—his snores half wake him with every breath—they struggle peacefully, the way a mountain climber might steadily climb a tall mountain, though he's wearing a heavy pack and the air is getting thin. Their bodies seem to simply know what to do. They seem to enjoy the work of breathing, of taking each difficult step.

What I loved about my mother's sleeping face was how it did not try to be anything at all. I was staring at it, feeling just as calm and still as she looked, when Mom woke and looked at me full on. "What's wrong?" she said. "What's wrong?"

"Nothing," I said, panicked. "You're just having a dream."

"Oh," she said. "Really?" And then she fell back asleep.

I stood there stiller than ever, but also shaking. I waited, watching the second hand crawl around the face of her bedside clock five painful minutes. Then I slipped out the door and closed it behind me.

Later that day, Mom said nothing; she didn't act distant toward me. In fact, she hugged me as I came up to slip a dirty plate into the kitchen sink, where she was washing the dishes. She had never before hugged me when her hands were wet or she was busy with a task. It was as though I had entered her dreams and some part of her recognized me as being a part of her quiet, private world.

I decided later that I could have asked her anything at that moment she awoke—*Did she really love me? Did she love each of us the same? Did she want to leave us all?*—and she would have told the simple truth. After that, whenever I watched her sleep, I imagined her opening her eyes again, and being able to ask her one question before she awoke fully, before she had time to think.

One afternoon, I noticed Brandon disappear while we kids were in the living room watching tv before dinner. He often had to be called to dinner several times, and I had begun to suspect that was when he took a nap. I slipped off the couch, told Ellie I was going to the bathroom, and crept upstairs.

The door to the bathroom was only a few feet from Brandon's room, and I stood in the hallway between the two doors, listening. I heard a short flickering sound from behind his door, then silence. I was wearing socks and slid down the hallway soundlessly. I turned my head a few inches from his door and listened hard. There was a sound, something faint and muffled, which sounded like a body rustling under covers.

I knelt down, with my hands over my knees so they wouldn't creak, and looked through the key hole. Brandon's bed was in the far corner, and I could see almost all of it. He was lying in bed, half under the covers. He was turned away from me, his head on the pillow, a magazine beside him. At first I thought he was reading, then I thought maybe he had fallen asleep, but his body was moving, more than the rustle of sleep. Whatever he was doing, he seemed completely lost in it.

My knees were bent awkwardly, my left eye was squeezed shut, and I leaned my right eye as close to the door as possible. I stared hard. I felt as though my eye were entering the room, as if, had he looked, Brandon would have seen my pupil coming through the hole.

I was concentrating so hard that I must not have heard Dad walking up the stairs. When he suddenly called, "Alex!" I jumped back.

Dad grabbed my arm and shook me. "What do you think you're doing?"

I could think of nothing to say. I let myself be shaken and didn't try to pull away. I had watched everyone in the family so many times, believing that what I was doing was not a bad thing, but I knew that this moment, this staring, was not right.

Dad yelled at me to never spy on others. I nodded, silent. He didn't hit me, only bruised my arm where his thumb had pressed down, but I felt I had deserved it this time. Once he left, I slipped into the bathroom, telling myself in the mirror that I would never look secretively upon anyone, ever again.

I stared at my reflection, wanting to believe my words, but a part of me knew it was a lie. I felt awful, but I could not give up looking any more than I could give up food or air.

I decided then to only look at others during the night, when everyone was in bed and not likely to be doing anything else, like reading magazines. If I got caught, I would say that I must have been sleep walking. I tried several times to stay awake, after my parents had showered and gone to bed, and the house was silent, but I always fell asleep and awoke in the morning disappointed.

Then, summer came. We lived in an old house that didn't have air conditioning, and I found on very hot nights, I sometimes woke covered in sweat. One of these night, I woke sweaty with the full moon glowing on my face. It was nearly two in the morning. I slipped out of bed and opened my door.

My parents' door was unlatched, in case any of us ever had an emergency, and I slipped into their room. My mother slept closer to the door, but was turned away from me, toward the window and my father. I came around to the foot of their bed and gazed up at her face, the moon light softly highlighting her forehead.

I looked at her, then my father, but something felt wrong. Their faces were not like I had seen them when they slept alone. At first I thought it was the moon, but that wasn't it. Although my mother's head was close to his, it seemed pulled back, as though they had been nearly touching, when a hair or a thought caused her to draw away. And the muscles in my father's face were tight and tense. Even in sleep, the two of them reacted to one another.

I would have to come back, when my father was out of town on a trip, or my mother was away with her sister for the weekend, to look upon their solitary faces. I slipped out of their room and went back to sleep.

The next morning, I had a hard time waking up and at breakfast, I didn't want to look at Mom or Dad. All day, as I biked around the neighborhood, the image of their faces from the night before filled my brain. What if they no longer became their quiet selves in sleep? What if that part of them had disappeared completely?

The next night when the moon and the heat woke me, I was tired, but I got up again. This time, I crept down the hall, past Brandon's door, to Ellie's room, which was at the opposite end of the hall from mine.

On the way, I passed the clothes hamper where I had hid that one afternoon. A pair of socks stuck out of the lid and looked like Oscar and Brown, the two sock puppets, their heads sleeping over the edge of the hamper. Ellie's door was closed, but I had opened it many times during the day and knew it opened silently. I turned the knob slowly, standing stiff in the doorway.

A streetlight shone into the room. In its light, I saw Ellie lying naked, a sheet tangled at the foot of her bed. Her body was relaxed, her arms and legs bent across the bed. When we were little kids, we used to bath together, but that was many years ago. The last few years she had kept to herself, and though she would play hand puppets with me, she would no longer wrestle or give me piggy back rides.

I told myself that this was just like back when we were little kids, but while my body had not really changed, hers had. There was a mound of hair at the bottom of her belly now, where her legs met. I knew she would not want me to see this. I knew I could not stay there, but I hesitated, to feel what I was feeling, and to take in whatever it was I was seeing.

I looked at Ellie's body, but I couldn't look at her face. I did not know if her mouth were closed or open, her two teeth exposed. I felt horrible things inside, like a hundred colored ropes and threads, all knotted together, some beautiful, some dangerous as live wires. I couldn't sort them out, except for one. It made me angry as I found it and pulled it loose from all the rest. What I wanted, what I had woken up for, was to look upon something safe and certain. What I saw now was that this was no longer possible. Sleep revealed too much.

Somehow, I was able to shut her door silently. I turned and started to run down the hall toward my room. As I passed the hamper, the speed of my body made the two socks lift up slightly. Oscar and Brown seemed for a split second to come to life, without anyone's hand inside. They appeared to be doubling over, laughing, like they were watching a play, relieved to finally be in the audience.

I could not get to my room fast enough. I held my breath and drew the curtains shut, but still the moonlight came in. I promised never to stare at the sleeping again. I wanted to lie down and quickly go to sleep, but I could not even sit on my bed. I stood there, outlined by moonlight, suddenly afraid of what the morning would bring, and of the night.

A Bolero in Havana

Stephen Benz

Havana was easily the most affable and unpredictable place I had ever been. As I walked around the city, it seemed I was constantly falling into conversations—chance encounters that inevitably altered my plans and led me in unexpected directions.

Case in point: I was walking along the Malecón, the photogenic seaside boulevard that gives Havana much of its visual identity, when a peanut vendor intercepted my path. He greeted me like an old friend, calling me compañero and asking about my activities for the day. Shortly into my Havana visit I had learned to welcome these encounters. No need for the usual tourist leeriness: Habaneros are innately curious and outgoing, an attitude worth emulating. So I stopped to chat with the peanut vendor.

I had just left my hotel, I told him, pointing to the Riviera a block away, and now I was on my way to the Cementerio Colón to see its famously ornate mausoleums and vaults. The peanut vendor approved of my intention to visit the cemetery (and advised me not to miss the firefighters' memorial therein), but he did not approve of the hotel. The Riviera was, in his view, much too expensive and not sufficiently Cuban. Before he continued on his way, the vendor gave me a packet of peanuts—a gift, he insisted, when I tried to pay. He also gave me a handwritten card bearing the address of a house with rooms to let—his parents' house. It was now legal, I had learned, for ordinary citizens to rent rooms to foreigners and to operate restaurants in their homes, an initiative the Cuban government had recently adopted to allow for modest private enterprise. The peanut vendor's parents were trying to make a little money by renting out a spare room. I would find it hospitable and comfortable, he said, and much cheaper than the Riviera.

It seemed like a pretty good idea—forgoing the tourist hotel for a private home. The peanut vendor was right about the Riviera: it was expensive, on par in fact with hotels in Miami Beach. I had wanted to stay there primarily because of the hotel's connection to pre-Revolutionary Havana—a period of glamor, intrigue, and vice, when mobsters ruled the city and Cuba advertised itself as "a tropical playground." Reading about the period in a couple of novels—Graham Greene's Our Man in Havana and Cabrera Infante's Tres Triste Tigres—had piqued my curiosity. All around the city you could find vestiges of this louche era—hotels, casinos, and nightclubs—some now shabby, some nearly pristine—that imbued Havana with retro allure. The Riviera was one of these vestiges. The mobster Meyer Lansky had built the swanky hotel in the late 1950s, just before the Revolution brought an end to the party. It had not been updated since then, and the musty but gleaming tropical moderne interior looked like a stage set for the Havana scenes in The Godfather II. Cool as this was, staying at the Riviera had its drawbacks, and the peanut vendor had pegged them exactly. Besides being expensive, the Riviera was also cut off from the city around it. Ordinary Cubans could not enter the hotel, and I was aware that staying there meant that I was getting a distorted picture of Cuba. So I decided to leave the Riviera in favor of rooming with the peanut vendor's parents. Better to stay with a family and learn more about daily life in Cuba.

The next morning, I gave the peanut vendor's card to one of the many taxi drivers waiting at the cabstand outside the hotel. The driver frowned at the address and called a second driver over for a look. This compañero also frowned at the address. Soon, six or seven drivers got in on the discussion—a typical Havana confab with everyone talking at once. Eventually, the drivers agreed upon a solution, and I was on my to visit the peanut vendor's parents at last. Or so I thought. Once we got underway, the driver asked me if I was already renting the room or just looking.

Just looking, I said. This revelation gave the driver his opening. He announced that he knew a better place—good family, nice house, great location, and (he added with an implied wink) a pretty daughter. Two daughters. By this point I had figured out that Havana was best experienced through a kind of acquiescence—just go along with whatever suggested itself and something unexpected and intriguing would soon manifest. In Cuba, it seemed, all my plans were fluid, changing moment to moment, such that I could not reliably predict where I would be in an hour's time or what I would be doing or with whom. I started to insist on the original address then thought, why bother? After all, I owed no allegiance to the peanut vendor and had no reason to believe that his parents' house would be any better than the one now on offer.

I agreed to check out the place that the driver recommended, and the old taxi lumbered toward this new destination. But the spirit of randomness that sometimes presides in Havana would not let things resolve so neatly. Although the place looked agreeable enough, no rooms were available. The landlady suggested another house—her cousin or somebody—and off we went, only to get lost. Meanwhile, along the way the driver stopped to pick up a few additional passengers, and the four people now in the back seat, strangers to one another only moments before, immediately and eagerly entered into an animated conversation about how best to arrive at the notional address. Sitting up front, I tried to follow along, my Spanish no match for a full-blown Cuban charrette.

The talk was fast-paced, but the denouement was slow in coming. Eventually, one of the passengers, a middle-aged woman clutching a live chicken, realized that the yanqui was looking for a room. She had a bedroom available in her house, she said, and the yanqui was welcome to stay there if he so desired. I gladly accepted the offer, and off we went to the señora's house, the yanqui paying enough at the end to cover everybody's fare (though it was never clear to me where the others in the car were headed; they seemed all too content just to ride around to find out what would happen).

I now found myself in Miramar, a formerly elegant section of Havana where the houses were larger and the streets more tranquil than elsewhere in the city. The señora lived in a spacious three-story house; but only the first story belonged to her family. After the Revolution, most of the larger houses (formerly belonging to families that had since fled to Miami) were divided into flats and assigned to multiple families. The señora's family—five people in all—shared the flat, a tight squeeze. Even with so little space, they had partitioned the largest room in two, creating an extra room that they hoped to rent to foreigners. They had not yet filed the appropriate papers or paid for the license, which meant that I was technically an illegal guest. There were government spies on the block, the señora said, so if the matter came up, I was to say that I was visiting the family. Under no circumstances should I disclose that I was paying the family twenty dollars a night.

Because I was their first American boarder, I was treated as a great curiosity and received plenty of attention from the family, which consisted of the señora—her name was Esmeralda—her husband, two sons, and the wife of the eldest son. For two days, I was their chief entertainment, and our conversations went long into the night. During these conversations, my Spanish—competent in most situations—was put to the test. I generally had a hard time understanding Cuban Spanish (not at all like the Mexican and South American Spanish that I was accustomed to) unless people spoke slowly and deliberately—which almost never happens in Havana, for Cubans do not like to speak slowly. I was forced to concentrate, trying to catch a few key words that would allow me to guess at the gist of the conversation.

Our discussions ranged over a variety of topics, with money and baseball being the recurring themes. The family questioned me about life in the United States, about salaries for different occupations, about fashions, about the cost of various consumer items, and about the political opinions of Americans. Struggling to keep up, searching for the right Spanish words for my answers, I fielded their many questions (often asked simultaneously) and tried to feed their apparently genuine enthusiasm for learning about my daily life back home.

When they asked about my reasons for visiting Cuba, I told them about my interest in the pre-Revolutionary period—especially the famous nightclubs and casinos that had once made Havana a glamorous (and lurid) tourist destination. Hearing this, they all agreed that I should meet Lety and Orlando, the señora's aunt and uncle. Before the Revolution, these two had worked at some of the biggest nightclubs, Lety as a cocktail waitress and Orlando as a musician. They could tell me all about it. So the next day, I went with Esmeralda on an excursion to another part of the city to visit with her relations.

To get there, we had to take a bus. I offered to pay for a taxi, but Esmeralda said that the bus was a true Havana experience, a good way for me to learn how Cubans live. She was right.

A group of people had clustered on the sidewalk at the bus stop. Upon reaching the cluster, Esmeralda called out, "Ultimo." A young man answered, "Yo." Moments later, a new arrival called out ultimo and Esmeralda responded by saying yo. This was how Cubans determined the order for boarding a bus, Esmeralda explained. Rather than actually queuing, the people waiting on the bus formed an imaginary line according to temporal precedence. Upon arriving at the bus stop, you have to ask who is last in line (ultimo). That person responds (yo) and you know that you are to board the bus after the respondent. The next person to arrive at the bus stop follows the same procedure, and it is incumbent upon you to respond yo to the newcomer, who will follow you aboard the bus. And so on.

We waited about ten minutes, during which time some ten or twelve people arrived to engage in this call-and-response exercise. Then the bus came, and the boarding went smoothly, although there were no available seats. Somehow, we squeezed in among the other passengers standing in the aisle. The buses in Havana were rather odd looking. Called camelos (camels) they were actually trailers attached to truck cabs. Despite the stuffy, crowded conditions and the heat inside the camel, the passengers seemed good-natured, even upbeat. They certainly kept up the chatter, which never really ceases in Havana. All around me, there were probably a good ten discussions—lively discussions—going on simultaneously. On a couple of occasions, participants in different conversations appealed to me, as if seeking my insight on some matter that remained inscrutable to me. Clueless, I offered my assent to whatever was said, much to the passengers' gratification.

When we left the bus at last, we were in an outlying part of the city, a street of concrete-block houses reminiscent of a Florida bedroom community, circa 1950. There were small, fenced-in yards and carports—though few cars were in evidence. For the most part, hammocks and bicycles occupied the carports, with one exception: a mammoth rusted Chrysler from the 1950s. Its wheels missing, the car was propped on concrete blocks. It sat like a stalwart old gentleman in the shade ready to collar a passerby with stories of the good old days.

Esmeralda led me to a pink house, wherein we found precisely such a gentleman seated in a wicker rocking chair, a cane by his side. He was wearing a dapper guayabera shirt. An elderly woman sat on a couch whose cushions were protected with clear vinyl covers. Esmeralda introduced me to Orlando and Lety. In their late seventies now, they belonged to the last generation still alive that had grown to adulthood before the Revolution, a generation that dwindled by the day. They were a living connection to a bygone era.

Hard of hearing and apparently senile, Uncle Orlando sat grinning and disconnected throughout the ensuing conversation. In contrast, Aunt Lety was animated, energetic, and sharp. She was pleased that an American had come to her house. She had always liked Americans, she declared, and she didn't believe that America was really an enemy. Lety had a very good memory, and when Esmeralda explained that I was interested in learning about Havana nightlife in the 1950s, Lety launched into an animated discourse about how wonderful Cuba had been in those days. I caught only a small portion of her exuberant monologue, but I readily understood Lety's main point: In those days, Cuba was a paradise. Food was abundant, movie stars came to visit, and everyone was happy.

Lety waxed nostalgic while I sipped homemade lemonade and listened. A warm flower-scented breeze blew through the open windows and door. Now and then the old man coughed, shifted his weight, and kept on grinning bemusedly at the people in his parlor. My attention drifted toward a tabletop clock. Like the other furnishings in the room, it was old and well worn. It kept ticking, its pendulum swinging back and forth, but the hour and minute hands never moved. Our visit lasted hours, but the clock stayed stuck on two twenty-five.

At one point, Lety took out some old photographs to show me, photos of places where she and Orlando had worked—the Tropicana, with its lovely glass arches; the Montemarte with its streamlined art deco bar and stage; the Capri, where movie star George Raft had greeted patrons at the entrance to the casino; the Sans Souci with its exotic garden setting. Each photograph, Lety seemed to think, provided further evidence of a lost paradise. Studying a picture of herself in cocktail waitress attire, she fell silent, the first pause in her steady discourse. Tears came to her eyes. During the momentary silence, I heard a distant grumble of thunder. It was getting on toward late afternoon, when the heat of the day would generate the inevitable daily rain shower.

The tabletop clock still marked two twenty-five.

Collecting herself, Lety flipped through some photos of a young Orlando dressed in Desi Arnaz type outfits, posing with his band mates. He had been a trumpet player in various groups, including the big band of the Sans Souci stage show. He had played with all the great ones, Lety said. Beny Moré. Nat King Cole, Pérez Prado.

At that moment, the old man cackled something and then started singing. Lety laughed with pleasure. "Ah, he heard me say Beny Moré, pobrecito. He loves Beny Moré. All right, papi, we will listen to Beny Moré."

"Do you know Beny Moré?" Esmeralda asked me.

"Yes, I know the name."

"Ah, well, Beny Moré is the greatest Cuban of all," Lety said. "Not only the greatest Cuban singer, I tell you, but the greatest of all Cubans."

And with that declaration, she took out a record album and placed it on a creaky Soviet turntable. There was a crackle through the old speakers, then big band music and the silky romantic tenor of Beny Moré. It was one of the old songs, a bolero. The three Cubans in the room were instantly transported. They sang along, but softly, as though chary of competing with the greatest of singing voices. I watched and listened. This was soul music, I thought, the music of the Cuban soul.

Halfway through the third song, the thunder intensified. The day darkened considerably, and a strong wind picked up. Thunder boomed and lightning crackled. Then came the first splatter of rain on the tile roof, prelude to a hard tropical downpour. The room's single low-watt bulb struggled against the gloom. Beny Moré sang on—the rain and thunder seemed to be nothing more than new backing instruments to the music.

At the height of the storm, the electricity failed. The room went dim. Beny Moré was silenced. But after the briefest of pauses, the senile old man—in a quaking, tremulous voice—picked up where the song had left off. And he sang the rest of the song straight through, a voice in the shadows, the words of the old song fixed in his mind no matter how much else had vanished. Lety and Esmeralda joined him. It was extraordinary to hear, sitting in twilight while lightning flashes illuminated the three ghostly Cubans singing a cappella over the grumbling thunder: *Cómo fue, no sé decirte cómo fue...*

More than anything else I experienced in Havana, this one tableau stands out as emblematic somehow: a nostalgic, bittersweet song of the old days interrupted by a power failure; an aging generation left to sing to themselves.

They sang and sang. Oh, how they sang—imperfectly, but with conviction, undeterred by whatever storms raged outside.

A Busload of Banjo Players

Jon Pearson

So Elya and I are sitting at a small patio table in a nice little breakfast place in Santa Barbara. It's our anniversary, not our wedding anniversary but the anniversary of the day we first got together at Starbucks five years earlier. It's a Sunday and the place is packed. We've ordered and I'm waiting for my great big cinnamon apple pancake and Elya (like all women) is waiting for something more sensible, a spinach omelet or something, and I say, "Okay, I want you to imagine something, and I mean *really* imagine it." And Elya, gorgeous as hell in her Jackie- Kennedy-looking sunglasses, is drinking in my every word. The smell of bacon and pancakes is in the air and roses and I am so happy I practically don't have a head. The summer sky is my head. "You're shooting a documentary," I say, "a nature film. And in the camera frame"—I frame my head and shoulders with my hands like I am *in* a camera frame—"you have just come across a tree frog, a rare, I don't know, Amazonian tree frog. And for the next thirty seconds I am going to *be* that rare, whatever-it-is frog," I say. "And your job is just to simply watch. But watch like it's a frippin' miracle cuz I'll be going to a place beyond all human understanding—doing funny, subtle little things with my face and hands. I just hope to *God* the waitress doesn't bring our food while I'm doing this. The people around us may think I'm having a seizure. But it'll be worth it. And then, afterwards, you can do your *own* nature scene."

Now, many women might say, "Cut it out," or "What the hell will people think?" or "Not another one of your crazy imagination games," or "You're gonna get us arrested?" But sweet Elya, removes her sunglasses and fixes me with her big, beautiful, brown eyes as if to say, "Go ahead, cowboy. Knock yourself out." And moments later (because along with being a former kick-ass corporate lawyer Elya was also a professional actress) she is doing a dead ringer of a glow fish from the Sargasso Sea, pinching her face into something scary and fishy and ugly and intense while looking gorgeouser and gorgeouser by the second and suddenly I just want to make some kind of primal, prehistoric love to her right there on the patio table as she proves once again that greatest of all secrets—that beauty, real beauty, is far bigger than mere pretty. Pretty paints its toes and hopes you like its purse. It primps. It dallies. It dolls itself up. It licks its lovely teeth and prays somebody's watching. Beauty, on the other hand, could give a shit. It breaks the rules. It goes for broke. It is an all-or-nothing, radioactive busload of banjo players flying off a cliff; because while pretty can be sweet or cute or nice, beauty is a raging fire. It doesn't wish or want or worry or wait or look back.

And that is why, Elya, my now wife, is to me the most beautiful woman alive. And it is my solemn, God-given, every-single-day job to keep it that way, to stoke the fires of her deep down beauty, to help her be exactly and fully her one-and-only self. And in fact, in my wedding vows I proclaim: *"I shall love her like no man has ever loved a woman."* A tall order. But when the vow first popped into my head, I got so happy I felt like I was riding a bicycle upside down on a cloud and everywhere I looked was Saturday and ice cream. I knew I could never live up to it. I knew I would fail on a daily basis, on a moment-to-moment basis.

Like, for example, there is this little yellow knife in the knife drawer in our kitchen that I am only supposed to use for cutting fruit or something. It's Elya's favorite knife or her childhood knife or a knife handed down from the gods. To *me* it looks like a regular old paring knife. Anyway, I always forget, because when I am looking for a knife I am just looking for a friggin' knife, let's say to cut open a box. *"Not the yellow knife!"* Elya yells. And a near panic seizes me. Damn it! Yes, the *yellow* knife. Why can't I ever remember?! Shit." I think to myself. "I am so sorry." I tell her. When privately I want to buy a hundred of the stupid things and retire *her* knife to the Knife Hall of Fame. So here's another secret: Marriage is about failure. I don't mean lying and cheating and stealing. I mean garden-variety screw-ups. And, of course, here, I am not referring to the *ladies* in the audience, only the guys. Every day with Elya I learn how to be a man. My simple new definition of manhood is: the capacity to love a woman without making her your mother. I aspire to be the man-space in which Elya can be all of herself, where she doesn't have to walk on egg shells or hold back or fit into some unconscious, idealized, self-serving movie in my head.

I met Elya after I had given up all hope. *All* hope. I was sixty. I had never been married. I figured women had too many working parts, any one of which could go wrong, and I knew that no woman *I* would want would ever want *me*. I knew that like I knew triangles had three sides. Then I met Elya, brilliant, beautiful, amazing Elya. And oddly, blessedly, I didn't feel an *ounce* of neediness. All I wanted to do was love her. As if I had been storing up love all my life, as if I were this great big circus wagon full of tricks and surprises and all I needed was the right woman, the one who could see past all my clever defenses, and see in me the man who wanted to love her with all his might in his own crazy-ass way. "Why me," I ask her, "when you could have anyone?" And always she says, "Cuz you bring out the *silly* in me." We run through the house like seagulls, we kick our legs in bed making up random poems, we switch childhood memories. I call her Bambina. She calls me Coconut Head. Every day I make her a birthday card and every time we come into the house we hug.

It's not easy to love. It's easy to get lazy or selfish or driven or lost in a hundred ways and when the going gets rough to want a fantasy. I always wanted a fantasy. Now I don't. I've had a miracle. And I've learned that just as beauty is bigger than mere pretty, intimacy is bigger than any dream. So I don't care anymore about looking good. I care about being seen. I want to stop running and come home. And I want Elya to feel seen and safe. I want her to feel loved and free. I want her to feel, every single day, like I am the answer to her prayers, because *she* is the answer to mine.

CONTRIBUTORS

Paul David Adkins grew up in Fort Lauderdale, Fla., and lives in New York, working as a counselor. He served in the US Army for 21 years, three months, and 18 days.

Nick Almeida is an MFA candidate at the Michener Center for Writers in Austin, Texas. He holds an MA from Penn State University, and edits fiction for *Bat City Review*.

Robyn Anspach has an MFA from University of Michigan. She currently works as a data analyst at Google.

Along with two books of travel essays—*Guatemalan Journey* (University of Texas Press) and *Green Dreams: Travels in Central America* (Lonely Planet)—**Stephen Benz** has published essays in *Creative Nonfiction, River Teeth, TriQuarterly,* and other journals. Two of his essays have been selected for *Best American Travel Writing* (2003, 2015). Formerly a writer for *Tropic*, the Sunday magazine of the *Miami Herald*, he now teaches professional writing at the University of New Mexico. He is also on the faculty of the Taos Summer Writers' Conference.

Destiny Birdsong is a Pushcart-prize nominated poet and essayist whose poems have either appeared or are forthcoming in *African American Review, At Length, Little Patuxent Review, Potomac Review,* and elsewhere. Her critical work recently appeared in *African American Review*, and a co-authored chapter on Black Atlantic and Diasporic Literature (with Ifeoma C. K. Nwankwo) is forthcoming in the *Cambridge Companion to Transnational American Literature*. She is a recipient of the Academy of American Poets Prize, and has received fellowships from Cave Canem and BinderCon. Destiny is a lecturer and academic adviser at Vanderbilt University, where she earned her MFA in 2009 and her PhD in 2012.

Venita Blackburn earned her MFA from Arizona State University in 2008. Her stories have appeared in *Pleiades, Madison Review, Bat City Review, Nashville Review, Smoke Long Quarterly, Café Irreal, Santa Monica Review, Faultline, American Short Fiction, Devil's Lake Review, Bellevue Literary Review,* audio download through Bound Off, and others. Her home town is Compton, California, but she now lives and teaches in Arizona. She was awarded a Bread Loaf Fellowship in 2014 and Pushcart prize nomination the same year among other accolades. In the near future, she hopes to complete two novels and a collection of stories all currently in progress and somehow about the misuse of super human abilities.

Therese Borkenhagen is a freelance writer and translator from Oslo, Norway. She completed her BA and MA in English Literature at the University of North

Dakota. She has been awarded the John Little Prize for fiction. This is her first publication. She currently lives in Oslo where she is juggling life as a freelance writer and an elementary school teacher.

Kathryn Brown is a retired captain with the San Francisco Police Department. She is currently working on a collection of short stories based on her experiences while working in high crime areas of the city, particularly the Tenderloin. Her intention is to take the reader beyond the surface experience of interactions between police and the public, to provide a deeper understanding of the psychological and perhaps spiritual impact of those encounters. Her short story "Misty" was published by *Two Hawks Quarterly*, whose editors described it as "both compelling and unique." This is her first appearance in *The Baltimore Review.*

Adam Carpenter loves writing like a fat kid loves cake. He teaches English, produces music, and is one-half of the band Yacht Party. Most of his work is sonic and has been featured on radio stations from Boston to the UK and in various venues in the Northeast United States. His writing can be found, well, here, at *The Baltimore Review* and in the margins of the papers of his patient AP Lit students.

Leila Chatti is a Tunisian-American poet and received her MFA in poetry from North Carolina State University. The recipient of fellowships from Dickinson House and Quest Writers Conference and awards from *Narrative Magazine*, *Nimrod Journal*, the Gregory O'Donoghue International Poetry Prize, and the Academy of American Poets, her work appears or is forthcoming in *Best New Poets 2015*, *Narrative*, *The Missouri Review*, *North American Review*, *Indiana Review*, and elsewhere. www.leilachatti.com

Adam Clay is the author of *A Hotel Lobby at the Edge of the World* (Milkweed Editions, 2012) and *The Wash* (Parlor Press, 2006). A third book of poems, *Stranger,* is forthcoming from Milkweed Editions. His poems have appeared in *Ploughshares, Crab Orchard Review, Boston Review, Iowa Review, The Pinch*, and elsewhere. A co-editor of TYPO Magazine, he serves as a Book Review Editor for *Kenyon Review* and teaches at the University of Illinois Springfield.

Heidi Czerwiec is a poet, essayist, translator, and critic who teaches at the University of North Dakota, where she is poetry editor of *North Dakota Quarterly*. She is the author of two recent poetry chapbooks—*Self-Portrait as Bettie Page* and *A Is For A-ké, The Chinese Monster*—and the forthcoming lyric essay sequence *Sweet/Crude: A Bakken Boom Cycle*, and the editor of *North Dakota Is Everywhere: An Anthology of Contemporary North Dakota Poets.*

Jen DeGregorio's poetry and prose has appeared in *Able Muse, The Collagist, PANK, The Rumpus, Salon.com* and other publications. She teaches writing in New York and New Jersey and runs the Cross Review and Reading Series, which seeks to bring New Jersey and New York poets together west of the Hudson River.

Stephanie Dickinson is an Iowa native who lives in New York City's East Village. Her novel *Half Girl* and novella *Lust Series* are published by Spuyten Duyvil, as is her just-released novel *Love Highway*, based on the 2006 Jennifer Moore murder. Her poetry and fiction appear in *Hotel Amerika, Mudfish, Weber Studies, Fjords, Water-Stone Review, Gargoyle, Rhino, Stone Canoe, Westerly*, and *New Stories from the South*, among others. *Heat: An Interview with Jean Seberg* is available from New Michigan Press. She has received multiple distinguished story citations in the *Pushcart Anthology, Best American Short Stories*, and *Best American Mysteries.*

Stevie Edwards is a poet, editor, and educator. She is Editor-in-Chief at *Muzzle Magazine* and Acquisitions Editor at YesYes Books. Her first book, *Good Grief* (Write Bloody, 2012), received two post-publication awards, the Independent Publisher Book Awards Bronze in Poetry and the Devil's Kitchen Reading Award from Southern Illinois University - Carbondale. Her second book, *Humanly*, was recently released by Small Doggies Press. Her poems have appeared in *Verse Daily, The Offing, PANK, Vinyl, Devil's Lake, The Journal, Indiana Review, Salt Hill*, and elsewhere. She holds an MFA from Cornell University and a BA from Albion College. She currently lives in Charleston, SC, where she works for a nonfiction publisher by day and is a poet by night. www.stevietheclumsy.com

Robert Evory is a poet and musician from Detroit, Michigan. With an MFA from Syracuse University he currently teaches creative writing as a Doctoral Assistant at Western Michigan University where he is the poetry editor for *Third Coast*. He is also the managing editor and co-founder of *The Poet's Billow*. In July of 2015 he was the artist in residence at Gettysburg National Military Park. His poetry is featured or is forthcoming in: *Spillway, Spoon River Review, Natural Bridge, The Fat City Review, Nashville Review, Wisconsin Review, Ghost Town, The Madison Review, Arroyo, Water~Stone Review*, and elsewhere. http://thepoetsbillow.org/

Lina Ferreira is the author of "Drown Sever Sing" and currently works as a visiting assistant professor in The Ohio State University. She is a graduate of The University of Iowa's Creative Nonfiction and Literary Translation programs, and her work has been featured in *Arts and Letters, The Chicago Review, Fourth Genre* and *Brevity*, among others.

Raquel Fontanilla is a freelance translator with a PhD in Comparative Literature from the University of Tokyo. A native of New Zealand, she lives, hikes, and writes in the American Southwest. Her work has appeared in *Paradise Review, Passages, Outside In Literary & Travel Magazine, Cecile's Writers Magazine, Unbroken,* and *Jabberwock Review,* where it was a finalist for the 2015 Nancy D. Hargrove Editors' Prize for Fiction.

Merrill Oliver Douglas lives in Vestal, NY, where she does freelance writing for trade magazines, university publications, businesses and nonprofits. She holds a BA from Sarah Lawrence College and an MA in English from Binghamton University. Her poems have appeared most recently in *A Narrow Fellow, Connotation Press: An Online Artifact, Barrow Street, San Pedro River Review,* and *Eunoia Review.*

Jehanne Dubrow is the author of five poetry collections, including most recently *The Arranged Marriage* (U of New Mexico P, 2015), *Red Army Red* (Northwestern UP, 2012), and *Stateside* (Northwestern UP, 2010). Her work has appeared in *Virginia Quarterly Review, The New England Review, Ploughshares,* and *The New York Times Magazine.* She is the Director of the Rose O'Neill Literary House and an Associate Professor of creative writing at Washington College, where she edits the national literary journal, *Cherry Tree.*

Jaclyn Dwyer has published poems in *Ploughshares, Prairie Schooner, Iron Horse Review, Rattle, Columbia Poetry Review, New Ohio Review, The Journal,* and *Witness,* among others. Her prose has appeared or is forthcoming from *Pleiades, Salon, Fairy Tale Review, Hayden's Ferry Review, The Pinch,* and *Brain, Child.* Jaclyn lives in Florida with her husband and daughter.

Kate Folk is from Iowa and now lives in San Francisco. Her stories have appeared in *Monkeybicycle, Word Riot, Colorado Review, Puerto del Sol, Tin House Flash Fridays,* and elsewhere. She was a 2014 fellow at the San Francisco Writers' Grotto and has attended residencies at the Virginia Center for the Creative Arts and the Vermont Studio Center. Find her at www.katefolk.com or on Twitter @katefolk.

Cal Freeman was born and raised in Detroit. His poems have appeared in many journals *including The Journal, Commonweal, Berfrois, Birmingham Poetry Review, RHINO,* and *The Drunken Boat.* His first collection of poems, *Brother of Leaving,* was recently published by Antonin Artaud Publications, an imprint of Marick Press. He lives in Dearborn, MI and teaches at Oakland University.

Sarah Giragosian's first book of poems *Queer Fish* won the 2014 American Poetry Journal Book Prize and will be published by Dream Horse Press in 2015. Her poems have been published in such journals as *Crazyhorse, The Missouri Review, The Baltimore Review,* and *Blackbird,* among others. She is a visiting lecturer in English at Bridgewater State University.

Jessica Goodfellow's books are *Mendeleev's Mandala* (Mayapple Press, 2015) and *The Insomniac's Weather Report* (Isobar Press, 2014). Recipient of the Chad Walsh Poetry Prize from the *Beloit Poetry Journal,* she's had work in *Best New Poets, The Writer's Almanac*, and *Verse Daily*. One of her poems was made into a short film at *Motionpoems*. Currently working on a manuscript about the death of her uncle on Denali, she'll be an artist-in-residence at Denali National Park and Preserve this summer. Jessica lives and works in Japan.

Christopher Green currently lives in Brooklyn, where he also hosts a monthly fiction reading series, The Prose Bowl, and its accompanying podcast. He holds an MA in English from the University of Toledo. His stories have previously appeared in journals and magazines such as *Burner, The MacGuffin*, and *The Ampersand Review*. He is currently working with his agent to publish two novels.

Lisa Grove's poems and translations have appeared in *Poetry, Beloit Poetry Journal, A cappella Zoo*, and elsewhere. She lives in Los Angeles, where she's a senior editor for the *California Journal of Poetics* and an interview host for Poetry.LA.

Megan Grumbling's Vassar Miller Prize-winning poetry collection, Booker's Point, is forthcoming from the University of Texas Press in spring of 2016. Her work has appeared in Poetry, The Iowa Review, Crazyhorse, Memorious, and other journals, and awarded the Ruth Lilly Fellowship, Robert Frost Award, and St. Boltoph Emerging Artist Award. She is the librettist and co-creator, with composer Denis Nye, of the Hinge/Works opera Persephone in the Late Anthropocene, which will premiere in the spring of 2016, in Portland, Maine.

Gary Hawkins is a poet, teacher, and scholar who grew up in the suburbs of the West. His debut collection of poetry, *Worker*, is forthcoming from Main Street Rag in 2016. His poetry, pedagogy, and criticism have appeared in *Virginia Quarterly Review, Third Mind: Creative Writing through Visual Art, Emily Dickinson Journal, Los Angeles Review of Books*, and other venues. He teaches creative writing and serves as associate dean at Warren Wilson College; he sets type in the letterpress studio; and he lives in Black Mountain, North Carolina. With his wife, the poet Landon Godfrey, he edits and produces *Croquet*, an occasional letterpress postcard broadside.

Gabe Herron lives outside a small town near Portland, Oregon with his wife, son, and daughter. He's had a winning story in *Glimmer Train's* Short Story Award for New Writers. His fiction has appeared in *Portland Review, [PANK]*, and *Prairie Schooner*. He has worked at Powell's Books for thirteen years.

Matthew Hobson's work has appeared in literary journals including *Hayden's Ferry Review, The Chattahoochee Review, River City, South Dakota Review, Gulf Stream Literary Magazine*, and *Driftless Review* where, in 2014, his story "Real Guts" won the annual flash fiction contest. Currently, he is completing a literary mystery novel set in Baltimore and a collection of flash prose pieces of which "Dream Car" is one. Another such piece, "The Audubon Guide to North American Suicide," was published last year in *The Baltimore Review*. He teaches at Loyola University and lives in Baltimore with his wife and two children.

Michael Johnson is from Bella Coola, British Columbia. His poetry and essays have appeared in *The Southern Review, The Fiddlehead, Weber, Shenandoah*, and *The Malahat Review*, among others, and been selected for the *Best American*, and *Best Canadian* poetry anthologies. His first collection, *How to Be Eaten by a Lion* is forthcoming from Nightwood Editions. He works at a vineyard in Okanagan Falls.

Leslie Anne Jones was born and raised in Anchorage, Alaska. Dark winters, big glaciers, neighborhood moose—all that stuff. She spent four years working in China and Taiwan, but presently lives in Brooklyn. Her fiction has appeared in *Day One* and *Necessary Fiction*. She is an MFA student at Rutgers University-Newark. On twitter: twitter.com/lesleslielie

Roisin Kelly is an Irish poet who was born in Belfast and raised in Co. Leitrim, and has since found her way to Cork City via a year on a remote island in the west of Ireland. Her poems have appeared in *The Stinging Fly, The Timberline Review, The Irish Literary Review, Synaesthesia, The Interpreter's House, Aesthetica, The Penny Dreadful, Bare Fiction* and *POETRY* magazine's Young Irish Poets issue. More work is forthcoming in *Banshee*.

David Kirby's collection *The House on Boulevard St.: New and Selected Poems* was a finalist for the National Book Award in 2007. Kirby is the author of *Little Richard: The Birth of Rock 'n' Roll*, which the *Times Literary Supplement* of London called "a hymn of praise to the emancipatory power of nonsense." His forthcoming poetry collection from LSU Press is *Get Up, Please.* See also www.davidkirby.com.

Katie Knoll is currently a MA student of fiction at the University of Cincinnati. Her work has appeared or is forthcoming in *Narrative, Nimrod,* and *Rattle,* among others. Her poetry and prose have been featured as one of *Narrative's* 2013 Top 5 Stories of the Year and awarded the George M. Harper prize for fiction and the Jean Chimsky Poetry Prize.

Elena Kua is a freelance editor-writer in Malaysia. Her work has appeared in *Newfound Journal*.

Peter LaBerge is the author of the chapbook *Hook* (Sibling Rivalry Press, 2015), recently included on the American Library Association's Over the Rainbow List. His work appears in *Beloit Poetry Journal, Best New Poets 2014, Colorado Review, Hayden's Ferry Review, Indiana Review, Iowa Review, Pleiades,* and *Washington Square Review,* among others. He is the recipient of a fellowship from the Bucknell University Stadler Center for Poetry, and the founder and editor-in-chief of *The Adroit Journal.* He lives in Philadelphia, where he is an undergraduate student at the University of Pennsylvania.

Matthew Landrum is poetry editor of *Structo Magazine.* His poems and translations have recently appeared in *PANK, The Michigan Quarterly Review,* and *The Notre Dame Review.* "Mortling" recently appeared as a 1x1 inch illustrated mini-book available at www.darkoakbindery.com. He lives in Detroit.

Nathan Alling Long lives in Philadelphia and teaches creative writing and literature at Stockton University. His work appears in over a hundred publications, include *Tin House, Glimmer Train, Story Quarterly,* and *Crab Orchard Review.* He is currently seeking publication for his story collection, *Everything Merges with the Night* (which "Asleep" is a part of), as well as a collection of flash fiction, *The Origin of Doubt.*

Dan Malakoff's short fiction has appeared or is forthcoming in *Pleiades, Prick of the Spindle, The Long Story, Ellipsis, River Styx,* and other journals, and he has a novella out from Comet Press. He's a graduate of University of Pittsburgh's MFA Program.

Kate McQuade's first novel, *Two Harbors,* was published by Harcourt under the name Kate Benson and released in the Netherlands as *De Vrouw Die Haar Leven Acteerde* in 2008. Her more recent fiction and poetry have been published or are forthcoming in *Black Warrior Review, Harvard Review,* and *Verse Daily,* among others. She is the recipient of fellowships and awards from the Ucross Foundation, the National Foundation for Advancement in the Arts, and the White House Commission on Presidential Scholars. A native Minnesotan, she holds degrees from the Bread Loaf School of English and Princeton University and teaches at Phillips Academy, Andover, where she holds the Harkness Instructorship in English.

JJ Mitchell is an essayist who writes widely on environmental and socio-political issues for the *Huffington Post* and other publications. His poems have either appeared or are forthcoming in *Tar River Poetry Review, Poetry East, Meridian, Ambit (UK), Carolina Quarterly,* and *Portland Review.* He lives in London, UK.

Caitlin Mullen is a first year student in the Stony Brook Southampton MFA program. She received an MA in English from NYU and a BA in English from Colgate University. She lives in Brooklyn, where she is at work on a novel and a collection of short stories. This is her first published work of fiction.

Patricia Colleen Murphy founded *Superstition Review* at Arizona State University, where she teaches creative writing and magazine production. Her work has appeared in many literary journals, including *The Iowa Review, Quarterly West*, and *American Poetry Review*, and most recently in *North American Review, Smartish Pace, Burnside Review, Poetry Northwest, Third Coast, Hobart, decomP, Midway Journal, Armchair/Shotgun*, and *Natural Bridge*. Her work has received awards from the Associated Writing Programs and the Academy of American Poets, *Gulf Coast, Bellevue Literary Review, The Madison Review, Glimmer Train Press*, and *The Southern California Review*. She reviews literary magazines at *Lit Mag Lunch* and books on *Goodreads*. A chapter of her memoir-in-progress was published as a chapbook by *New Orleans Review.*

Jon Pearson is a writer, speaker, and artist. He has been published in numerous publications and was nominated for a 2014 Pushcart Prize. He lives in Los Angeles with his beautiful wife and writes now for the same reason he played with his food as a kid: to make the world a better place. You can read more of Jon's work at www.jonpearsoncreative.com.

Jane Rose Porter is a writer and editor based in Brooklyn, New York. She was a 2013 Emerging Writer Fellow at the Center For Fiction and has been awarded residencies by the Jentel Artist Residency Program and the Kimmel Harding Nelson Center for the Arts. Her stories, essays, and articles have appeared in publications including *Real Simple Magazine, The Wall Street Journal, BusinessWeek, Fortune, Fast Company, Kenyon Review, Colorado Review, Fourteen Hills, The Chronicle of Higher Education*, and *Men's Health*. Jane has an MFA in Creative Writing from Warren Wilson College and a BA in English from Brown University. She is currently at work on her first novel. You can read more of her writing at janeroseporter.com.

Zana Previti was born and raised in New England. She earned her MFA in fiction from the University of California, Irvine and is currently pursuing her MFA in poetry from the University of Idaho. Her work has been published in *The New England Review, Hayden's Ferry Review, RHINO Poetry, Ninth Letter*, and she was recently named the recipient of *Poetry International's* 2014 C.P. Cavafy Prize for Poetry. She lives in Northern Idaho.

Eliana Ramage holds a BA and MA in creative writing from Dartmouth College and Bar-Ilan University, respectively. A proud Cherokee Nation citizen, she is at work on a collection of linked stories concerning indigenous girls and women. She recently won the Grazia Deledda International Literary Prize, and her stories have appeared or are forthcoming in the *Beloit Fiction Journal*, the *For Books' Sake* YA anthology, and *Four Chambers.*

Annie Reid is a double expat American currently residing in Sweden after a decade in Canada. She writes apocalyptic video games for a living and fiction for her sanity. She has stories published in *American Short Fiction, Alaska Quarterly Review, Nimrod, Another Chicago Magazine, Ergo!*, and on the CBC Canada Writes website as a finalist for the CBC Short Fiction Prize. She is currently completing a novel.

Virginia Smith Rice is the author of *When I Wake It Will Be Forever* (Sundress Publications, 2014.) Her poems appear in *Cincinnati Review, Denver Quarterly, Massachusetts Review, Meridian, Salamander*, and *Third Coast*, among other journals. She is co-editor of the poetry journal *Kettle Blue Review* and associate editor at Canopic Publishing.

Maxine Rosaler's fiction and nonfiction has appeared in or is scheduled to appear in *The Southern Review, Glimmer Train, Witness, Green Mountains Review, Fifth Wednesday*, and other literary quarterlies, and has been cited in *Best American Short Stories*. She lives in New York City and is currently at work on a novel.

Caitlin Scarano is a poet in the University of Wisconsin-Milwaukee PhD creative writing program. She was a finalist for the 2014 Best of the Net Anthology and the winner of the 2015 *Indiana Review* Poetry Prize, judged by Eduardo Corral. She has two poetry chapbooks: *The White Dog Year* (dancing girl press, 2015) and *The Salt and Shadow Coiled* (Zoo Cake Press, 2015).

Originally from Atlanta, Georgia, **Stephanie Ellis Schlaifer** is a poet and installation artist in St. Louis. She has an MFA in poetry from the Iowa Writers' Workshop, and her poems have appeared in *AGNI, Denver Quarterly, LIT, Colorado Review, Fence*, and elsewhere. Schlaifer was a semi-finalist for the 2015 Discovery/Boston Review Prize, and she was selected for Best New Poets 2015. Her first book, *Cleavemark*, is forthcoming from BOAAT Press in 2016. She frequently collaborates with other artists, most recently with Jeff Pike on the illustrated chapbook of poems, *Strangers with a Lifeboat*, and with Cheryl Wassenaar on the installation *Cleavemark Drive*. Schlaifer is a compulsive baker and is also very handy with a pitchfork.

This is **Scott Sikes'** first published work. He is thrilled and also keeping his day job, which he loves. He works for a publisher. He lives with his wife and daughter in the mountains of Virginia and has a garden that his neighbors admire, although they don't yet know about the chickens coming in the spring. He runs many miles most days and is hard at work on a collection of linked stories.

Fredric Sinclair grew up in Connecticut and currently lives in Brooklyn, NY. His work has appeared or is forthcoming in *Jersey Devil Press, Chelsea Station*, and *Long River Review*, among others. He also has written and produced plays in New York City, most recently at the Midtown International Theatre Festival. In 2015 he was awarded a spot at the Sewanee Writers' Conference for work in fiction, and this fall he will be pursuing his MFA in fiction at Boston University.

Chris Souza lives and works in Massachusetts. Previous publications include: *Gulf Coast, Bellingham Review, Connecticut Review, New Delta Review, West Branch*, and *Laurel Review,* among many others*.* Her work has been featured on "Verse Daily" and is forthcoming in *Natural Bridge* and *Cape Rock Review.*

Curtis Smith has published over one hundred stories and essays. His most recent books are *Beasts and Men* (stories, Press 53) and *Communion* (essays, Dock Street Press). Next spring, Ig Publishing will release his next book, a series of essays on *Slaughterhouse-Five.*

Poet and essayist **Christine Stewart-Nuñez** is the author of *Untrussed* (forthcoming 2016 from the University of New Mexico Press), *Snow, Salt, Honey* (Red Dragonfly Press 2012), *Keeping Them Alive* (WordTech Editions, 2011), and *Postcard on Parchment* (ABZ Press 2008). Her piece "An Archeology of Secrets" was a Notable Essay in *Best American Essays 2012*. She is an Associate Professor in the English Department at South Dakota State University.

Robert Edward Sullivan is from the Midwest (Iowa and Michigan) but now lives in Oregon. He holds an MFA from Portland State University. He has stories published by *The Southeast Review, McSweeney's Internet Tendency, A Capella Zoo, Fiction Fix, The Northville Review*, and others. He is currently working on a novel as well as a novel-in-stories.

Chris Harding Thornton is a seventh-generation Nebraskan who writes fiction, poetry, and creative nonfiction. She holds a BFA in creative writing from the University of Nebraska at Omaha, an MFA in fiction from the University of Washington, and a Ph.D. in English from the University of Nebraska—Lincoln, where she teaches literature and writing classes. She is currently drafting a book of poems, revising a creative nonfiction book titled *Road to Thacher*, and finishing her first novel, *Reclamation*.

Daniel Uncapher is a graduate of the University of Mississippi in Oxford, Mississippi, where he won multiple awards in the Southern Literary Festival for his poetry and nonfiction. In his spare time, he operates a Heidelberg letterpress from the restored antebellum home in Water Valley, where he lives with his dog. His short fiction has appeared and is forthcoming in *Neon Literary Magazine.*

John Walser, an associate professor of English at Marian University in Wisconsin and a founding member of the Foot of the Lake Poetry Collective, holds a doctorate in English and Creative Writing from the University of Wisconsin-Milwaukee. His poems have appeared or are forthcoming in numerous journals, including *Barrow Street, Nimrod, The Pinch, december magazine, Naugatuck River Review, Fourth River, the Hiram Poetry Review, Packingtown Review,* and *Bird's Thumb*. He was a featured poet in September 2014 at *Connotation Press: An Online Artifact*. A Pushcart nominee as well as a semi-finalist for the 2013 Pablo Neruda Prize for Poetry, John is currently submitting three manuscripts for publication.

Kate Washington is a freelance writer and essayist whose work has appeared in a wide range of publications, from *The Bellingham Review; Brain, Child; and Ninth Letter to Sunset, The Washington Post,* and *Yoga Journal*. She and her husband are the founders of a small not-for-profit literary publishing house, Roan Press. They live in Sacramento, California, with their two daughters.

Marlys West is an award-winning writer living in Los Angeles. She has been published in journals and anthologies including *American Poetry Review, Best American Poetry, Burnside Review, Duende, Fence, Ploughshares,* and more. She was a Hodder Fellow at Princeton University, an NEA grant recipient in poetry, and received her M.F.A. from the Michener Center for Writers. The University of Akron Press published her first book of poems in 1999. She is currently editing a new collection of poetry, writing a novel, working as a nurse, and raising children.

Amie Whittemore earned her MFA from Southern Illinois University Carbondale and her poems have appeared in *North American Review, Smartish Pace, Gettysburg Review, Cimarron Review, The Hollins Critic, Sycamore Review,* and elsewhere. She won a Dorothy Sargent Rosenberg 2013 Poetry Prize, the 2012 Tennessee Williams / New Orleans Literary Festival poetry prize, and a fellowship to the Vermont Studio Center in July 2011. She lives in Charlottesville, VA.

John Sibley Williams is the author of eight collections, most recently *Controlled Hallucinations*, and the editor of two Northwest poetry anthologies. A five-time Pushcart nominee, John serves as editor of *The Inflectionist Review* and Board Member of the Friends of William Stafford. A few previous publishing credits include: *American Literary Review, Third Coast, Nimrod International Journal, Hotel Amerika, Rio Grande Review, Inkwell, Cider Press Review, Bryant Literary Review, Cream City Review, RHINO,* and various anthologies. He lives in Portland, Oregon.

Gregory Wolos's short fiction has recently appeared or is forthcoming in *Post Road, Nashville Review, A-Minor Magazine, JMWW, Yemassee, The Baltimore Review, The Madison Review, T. J. Eckleburg Review, The Los Angeles Review, PANK, A cappella Zoo, Superstition Review,* and many other print and online journals and anthologies. His stories have earned five *Pushcart Prize* nominations, and story collections have been named as finalists for the 2010 and 2012 *Flannery O'Connor Short Fiction Award* and the 2015 *Serena McDonald Kennedy Award* (Snake Nation Press). Gregory's stories have won competitions sponsored by the *Rubery Book Awards, Gulf Stream,* and *New South.* He lives and writes in upstate New York on the bank of the Mohawk River. For full lists of his publications and commendations, visit www.gregorywolos.com.

Amy Wright is the author of *Everything in the Universe* and *Cracker Sonnets,* both forthcoming in 2016. She is also the Nonfiction Editor of Zone 3 Press, Coordinator of Creative Writing and Associate Professor at Austin Peay State University, and author of four poetry chapbooks. Her first prose chapbook, *Wherever the Land Is,* is scheduled for release next year. For more information, go to www.awrightawright.com.

Geoff Wyss's book of stories, *How,* won the Ohio State University Prize in Short Fiction and was published in 2012. His second novel is forthcoming from Brooklyn Arts Press. His fiction has appeared in *Glimmer Train, Image, Ecotone, Tin House,* and others and has been reprinted in *New Stories from the South* and the *Bedford Introduction to Literature.* He teaches and lives in New Orleans.

Made in the USA
Middletown, DE
17 October 2016